Theory, Culture & Society

Theory, Culture & Society caters for the resurgence of interest in culture within contemporary social science and the humanities. Building on the heritage of classical social theory, the book series examines ways in which this tradition has been reshaped by a new generation of theorists. It will also publish theoretically informed analyses of everyday life, popular culture, and new intellectual movements.

EDITOR: Mike Featherstone, *Teesside Polytechnic*

EDITORIAL BOARD
Roy Boyne, *Newcastle upon Tyne Polytechnic*
Mike Hepworth, *University of Aberdeen*
Scott Lash, *University of Lancaster*
Roland Robertson, *University of Pittsburgh*
Bryan S. Turner, *University of Essex*

Also in this series

The Body
Social Process and Cultural Theory
*edited by Mike Featherstone, Mike Hepworth
and Bryan S. Turner*

Consumer Culture and Postmodernism
Mike Featherstone

Talcott Parsons
Theorist of Modernity
edited by Roland Robertson and Bryan S. Turner

The Symbol Theory
Norbert Elias

Global Culture
Nationalism, Globalization and Modernity
edited by Mike Featherstone

Images of Postmodern Society
Social Theory and Contemporary Cinema
Norman K. Denzin

Promotional Culture
Advertising, Ideology and Symbolic Expression
Andrew Wernick

CHANGING CULTURES

Feminism, Youth and Consumerism

MICA NAVA

SAGE Publications
London • Newbury Park • New Delhi

SAGE Publications Ltd
6 Bonhill Street
London EC2A 4PU

SAGE Publications Inc
2455 Teller Road
Newbury Park, California 91320

SAGE Publications India Pvt Ltd
32, M-Block Market
Greater Kailash – I
New Delhi 110 048

British Library Cataloguing in Publication Data

Nava, Mica
 Changing Cultures: Feminism, Youth and Consumerism.
 – (Theory, Culture & Society Series)
 I. Title II. Series
 305.4

 ISBN 0-8039-8607-6
 ISBN 0-8039-8608-4   332426

Library of Congress catalog card number 92–053702

Typeset by Mayhew Typesetting, Rhayader, Powys
Printed in Great Britain by Biddles Ltd, Guildford, Surrey

305. 4 NAV
7Di

CONTENTS

ACKNOWLEDGEMENTS

Many people have contributed directly and indirectly to the ideas developed in this book. Among those whom I want to thank for their personal support and constructive criticism are my colleagues and students at the Polytechnic of East London; members of the *Feminist Review* editorial collective; my women's group, now in its fifteenth year; and Erica Carter, Peter Chalk, Diana Leonard, Angela McRobbie, Suzy Oboler, Mitra Tabrizian and Sarah Thornton who have generously given valuable time and detailed comments at various stages of the writing. The book is dedicated to the memory of my father, who died in 1965, and to my family and household whose dynamic existence over the years has nourished and challenged me, intellectually and emotionally.

The publication details of the original versions of the chapters in this book are as follows:

'From utopian to scientific feminism? Early feminist critiques of the family', in Lynne Segal (ed.), *What Is To Be Done About the Family?* Harmondsworth: Penguin, 1983.

'"Everybody's views were just broadened": a girls' project and some responses to lesbianism', *Feminist Review*, 10, 1982.

'Youth service provision, social order and the question of girls', in Angela McRobbie and Mica Nava (eds), *Gender and Generation*. London: Macmillan, 1984.

'The urban, the domestic and education for girls', in Gerald Grace (ed.), *Education and the City*. London: Routledge & Kegan Paul, 1984.

'Drawing the line: a feminist response to adult–child sexual relations', in Angela McRobbie and Mica Nava (eds), *Gender and Generation*. London: Macmillan, 1984.

'Cleveland and the press: outrage and anxiety in the reporting of child sexual abuse', *Feminist Review*, 28, 1988.

'Consumerism and its contradictions', *Cultural Studies*, 1(2), 1987.

'Discriminating or duped? Young people as consumers of advertising/art' (with Orson Nava), *Magazine of Cultural Studies (MOCS)*, 1, 1990.

'Consumerism reconsidered: buying and power', *Cultural Studies*, 5(2), 1991.

1

INTRODUCTION: INTELLECTUAL WORK IN CONTEXT AND PROCESS

The idea of a book presupposes a coherence and thematic continuity that occurs only rarely in the intellectual culture of today. During the 1980s we were confronted increasingly with the transitory nature of the phenomena that we observed around us, as well as with rapid transformations in the debates with which we engaged. The pieces of work included here were written not only in this changing political and conceptual climate, as comments on these changes as they occurred, they were also written in response to commissions and the exigencies of teaching, in time carved out between working and domestic life. Such, increasingly, has been the fragmented pattern of intellectual production in a world and a decade in which the grand narratives of an earlier moment, the certainties of socialism and feminism, have progressively dissolved.

This then is the context in which the chapters of this book were produced. They reflect the broader cultural changes of the time. They reveal also, as all writing does either less or more covertly, the influence of the cultural and psychic history of the author. My intention in this introduction and in the commentary which links the chapters to each other is to focus on this context, to delineate the intellectual moment in which the work was originally written and received, and provide a biographical narrative which places it in terms of the more personal features of my own history and development. These aspects of intellectual production are not normally made visible. The conventions of work of this kind, particularly of academic work, presume that books and published articles stand alone and should be evaluated as such. Yet their contextualization can enhance our understanding of the ways in which theoretical and political themes and positions are taken up and defended, and sensitize us to the complexity of the writing process itself.

The culture from which the work included here emerges, has its roots in the political upheavals of the late 1960s and early 1970s, in the student movement, the New Left, decolonization struggles and, not least, the (re)emergence of feminism.[1] A significant legacy of these new movements and of feminism in particular has been the challenge to the boundaries of formal academic disciplines and to what counts as knowledge, or indeed the 'truth'.[2] Knowledge, culture, identity and the complex structuring of power have been central theoretical preoccupations in this scenario. A few academic institutions have both contributed and responded to this intellectual flowering with the provision of innovative new degree courses at the intersection of the humanities and social sciences. Based on a recognition of the cultural coding of the social, these courses integrate spheres of study formerly kept separate – like philosophy, history, literary and media studies, sociology and psycho-analysis – through asking the political questions and applying the critical analyses generated in the first instance by the new movements (Mercer, 1990; Rutherford, 1990a). Although this is an account of certain general historical developments in Britain over the last decades, it is at the same time a snapshot of my own trajectory. My passage – from women's liberation and mature student of sociology at the London School of Economics in 1970, to postgraduate student and part-time temporary lecturer specializing in questions of gender within the sociology of educa-tion in 1980, to permanent lecturer in cultural studies at a London polytechnic and member of the editorial board of *Feminist Review* today – is both specific and typical of a generation. The chapters included here derive from the unstable conjuncture of feminism, sociology and cultural studies.

Another aspect of the intellectual climate of the last decade which is relevant to the production of this book has been the focus on the personal and the significance of experience. One of the most enduring and influen-tial contributions here has been made by feminism, which has had as a fundamental tenet since the late 1960s the politicization of the personal: the family, relationships, sexuality and the minutiae of everyday life. As Juliet Mitchell put it then: 'Women's Liberation is crucially concerned with that area of politics which is experienced as personal. Women . . . find that what they thought was an individual dilemma is a social predica-ment and hence a political problem' (Mitchell, 1971: 61; see also Coote and Campbell, 1982). A major project of feminism since that period has been to analyse personal experience, and to locate it in relation to more orthodox theoretical paradigms.

Michel Foucault is one of several postwar writers who have noted a parallel and not unrelated development in the practice of the intellectual over the last decades. He identifies the shift as one from 'spokesman of the universal' and 'master of truth and justice' (as it is put in translation) to a new mode in which:

> the connection between theory and practice has been established. Intellectuals have got used to working, not in the modality of the 'universal' but . . . at the precise points where their own conditions of life or work situate them (housing, the hospital, the asylum, the laboratory, the university, family and sexual rela-tions). This has undoubtedly given them a much more concrete awareness of struggles. (Foucault, 1980: 126)

These contemporary figures, referred to by Foucault as 'specific' or 'local' intellectuals, are contradictorily enmeshed in what he has persuasively defined as regimes of truth and the micro-politics of power. They also reflect feminist initiatives, though this influence on the historical movement that Foucault describes is not acknowledged by him.

His categorization is nevertheless pertinent here in that, combined with the feminist insistence on the personal as political, it illuminates the context of the production of this book.

The impact of feminism has been substantial not only in the sphere of ideas – on the content and methodology of formal disciplines[3] – but also on the academic lives of individual feminists. Feminism has provided the engagement and motivation since the 1970s for a generation of women (myself included) conscious of the marginalization of 'woman' both as object of study and as political agent. It was particularly in the context of, yet also against, the Left that feminists in this country, both individually and in groups, honed their initial critiques and developed their skills of argument (Rowbotham et al., 1979; Wilson, 1980). Subsequently, fired by absences in the academic canon, some went on to pursue intellectual work on questions of gender and then more generally within their fields, with a confidence, commitment and sense of entitlement that they might otherwise not have had.

These certainties and the sense of justice and unity about the feminist project were not however to remain unfractured. The commentary and several of the chapters in this book address in one way or another the political and academic fissures which developed over the course of the 1970s and 1980s and the way in which ethical and ideological imperatives were drawn on increasingly in the evaluation of intellectual work. Theoretical differences between feminists ranged themselves along a number of distinct continua. In the course of this book, divides between radical/separatist and socialist feminists, and between sexual libertarians and those who stress the dangers of sexuality, are among the most closely examined. There are others also of course. More recently divisions have opened up between those who prefer to hang on to more rigid explanatory schema, to binary and essentialist notions of masculinity and femininity, and those who want to explore ambiguity and problems in feminist arguments (Segal, 1987; Riley, 1988).

These are likely to have been influenced by a perceptible shift over the last decade in the assumptions underlying cultural analysis. In a very general way this movement can be referred to as postmodernism. The later chapters in this book both document and are at the same time evidence of the influence of this intellectual shift. Postmodernism is a contested term, frequently debated in the course of the 1980s, which refers to a number of levels, to cultural practice, to the impact of new visual and computational technologies and the 'hyperreal', and to what concerns us most in this context, the crisis of the intellectuals. This last phrase represents a growing sense of loss: of certainty and authority, and moral and cognitive absolutes. It refers also to the rejection of totalizing theory and metanarrative (and the generalizations of sociology) as well as the impossibility of the notions of truth and progress in the (post)modern world.[4]

It is interesting to observe that commentators on the postmodern have on the whole denied feminism any credit – or for that matter blame – for this 'loss of mastery' and renunciation of the 'master discourse'. Is not the crisis of the intellectual also about the decentring of masculinity and the chaos of not knowing – that is to say an effect, albeit at some distance, of the feminist challenge? It may well be. On the other hand, the development of the postmodernist critique in the course of the 1980s has also destabilized the earlier certainties of feminism. The simplicity of the emancipatory project and the utopian imaginings of the early 1970s no longer carry conviction. Metanarratives and totalizing explanations have on the whole been rejected by feminists also. The idea of the integrated and unified subject, and of the possibility of truth and moral justice find decreasing support, particularly within the academy. Feminists too are now much more inclined to acknowledge specificity, complexity, fragmentation, and not knowing, whether they adopt a position which more fully embraces postmodernism or not.[5] Ultimately, however, the pessimism of postmodernism is incompatible with the feminist sense of agency and commitment to progress. Nevertheless it too has been part of the intellectual climate which has influenced my work.

The question of the fragmented subject and the contradictions of identity have of course been raised outside the postmodernist dialogue as well. Psychoanalysis has been the most significant influence here, though the take-up within social and cultural theory has often been partial and contested. Nevertheless psychoanalysis has advanced the terms of the debate and has offered enormous insight into the contradictory ways we experience ourselves and negotiate the world we live in. The seminal theory of the unconscious has for example been drawn on heavily in the attempt to understand how masculinity and femininity are acquired and in the analysis of cultural texts. The work of Lacan and his stress on the inevitable incoherence of subjectivity has been particularly influential here and has operated across a range of fields. Exactly how this influence has been played out is of course difficult to assess. Sometimes it has merely tinted the premiss of debate; at others it has coloured much more vividly the entire critical framework.[6] The insights of psychoanalysis have permeated the full range of my work, and indeed my life. In the pieces included here they surface particularly in the interrogation of voluntarism and in the insistence that agency and contradiction can coexist.[7]

This emphasis from within psychoanalysis on the fragmented nature of identity has also proved fruitful as a way of understanding the contradictions embedded in the contemporary experiences of migration, racial otherness and sexual difference: that is to say of marginality, not belonging and the complex interaction of the different social positions that we occupy simultaneously. The insights and cultural practice of the analysts of race and the postcolonial diaspora have had a major impact on the intellectual climate of the metropolis, and the repercussions, like those of feminism, are likely to be extensive.[8] Racial difference is not centrally addressed in the chapters included here, yet as I shall spell out below, it has played a part in the construction of my own identity and political allegiances. Another significant contribution to this intellectual climate has been the work of gays and lesbians on sexual identity and orientation, on sexology and heterosexuality, and on culture and representation more generally.[9]

The more conventional political transformations of the last decade, the decline of the Left and of municipal socialism, have of course also played a part. During this period the question of class has become increasingly problematic and it has become common on the intellectual Left to express a loss of confidence in the primacy of the economic and the correspondence between class and class consciousness (Hindess, 1978; Hall, 1988b). In fact class and its ambiguous relation to feminism is addressed in several of the chapters included here. The hypothetical disjuncture between socialism and feminism has been a major item on the agenda since the latter part of the 1970s and it is ironic that this should have been borne out in the course of the 1980s partly as a consequence of the growing gap under Tory rule between women of different classes, between professional and high-earning women on the one hand and single unemployed mothers, whose material standard of living has declined, on the other. Yet paradoxically this feminization of poverty has been partly a result of the growing influence of feminism and the readiness of many women to exchange the vicissitudes of dependence on men for the greater autonomy of dependence on state benefit (Brannen and Wilson, 1987; McRobbie, 1991).

In fact the last decade has seen an astonishing popularization of feminist ideas. These now permeate all social strata and are regularly articulated at the cultural level, on television and most particularly in women's magazines (Moore, 1986; Stuart, 1990; Winship, 1985). Articles of this genre focus typically on relationships, (hetero)sexuality, child-care and domestic responsibility, though jobs, power and financial independence have not been neglected. Feminism has succeeded in turning outwards and appealing to a broader audience, even if at the cost of surrendering its brand name and quality control, to draw on the jargon of the 1980s. Some feminists insist nonetheless that changes over the last twenty years are no more than cosmetic (Cockburn, 1988; Wolf, 1990) though others have stressed the very substantial transformations in consciousness that have occurred particularly in the domain of the domestic (Segal, 1988). Thus we see an interesting new division opening up, registered not only in the literature but also in everyday engagements, between, loosely, optimists and pessimists. Whether the uptake of these polar positions is influenced by generation or disposition remains to be explored.

The 1980s have also seen the consolidation of 'Thatcherism'. This expression, developed in the course of a wider debate about the crisis of the Left (Hall, 1988b) refers in part to the ability of Margaret Thatcher

as leader of the Tory government to harness popular desires and discontents through a celebration of consumerism (see also Mort, 1988). At
the theoretical level this phenomenon has revived some of the concerns
about the effects of popular culture expressed by members of the
Frankfurt School over fifty years ago; it has slotted into preoccupations
of writers about the postmodern like Baudrillard (1988) and sharpened the
debate about pleasure and the complexity of agency and subjectivity.
This, the emergence of Green politics, and most recently though less
directly, the embracing of market economy principles by Eastern Europe,
provide the background for the discussions about consumerism in the
final three chapters of this book.

These are some of the political and theoretical components which make
up the changing intellectual context of my work. Taking them into
account in the analysis of the work itself will have its own contradictory
effects. On the one hand it can act as a kind of endless qualifier, always
softening the edges of the argument by seeing it as part of a wider
process. On the other, it can enhance understanding by making connections both across, to other issues and authors, and internally, between
chapters. One thing that this process of contextualizing will inevitably do
is undermine the idea that 'research' is the process of discovering and then
documenting what is already out there, waiting to be found in the archives
or people's thoughts. Because, of course, work of this kind is always
invented. It always emerges from the author's embeddedness in a specific
configuration of inextricably intertwined historical, cultural and psychic
narratives. Although at some level we all know this, the implications of
taking it on board are so complex that the issue is rarely addressed. Why
we think what we think is largely a suppressed question in intellectual
work.[10] This is despite the shift to the local and the personal referred to
earlier. The conventions of social science and other related disciplines
persist and continue to demand that we struggle over methods, interpretations, theories and histories – over what is written down – without reveal-
ing or investigating why we identify with a particular intellectual culture,
focus on a particular subject, adopt a particular position and refuse
others, or opt for indeterminacy and contradiction. What I am attempting
to do in this introduction and in the commentaries which follow the
chapters is to put on the agenda and begin to explore both the general and
the specific factors of this kind which have contributed to my own
intellectual formation and production.

How to disentangle the specific from the general is a problem to which
there is no solution. Specific factors do not exist in isolation from the
general, even though, as I pointed out earlier, the specific and the
personal have increasingly become objects of study in their own right.
Included in this category are questions ranging from those initially posed
within the discourse of psychoanalysis, to biography, the experience of
marginality, the politics of collectivity, the influence of family and friends
and the conditions of the workplace and the domestic. It verges on the

banal to point out that underlying the study of factors of this kind is the assumption that they affect our lives. Yet like the broader cultural factors, how they do this is really not established. Influences are incoherent, contradictory, uneven. It is impossible to anticipate the impact of any particular set of events and imaginings – because they will always be made sense of and transformed through the prism of other experiences and memories. Likewise with the relationship between biography and the production of a particular text: we can guess at determinations, and it can be significant as well as fun to do so, but we can never be sure.

This is also the dilemma of psychoanalysis. We judge the accuracy of an insight or connection by whether it *feels* right. So what I am going to go on to do – through a process of rational distillation as well as feeling – is to try to pull out some of the more specific features of my life which might have had an impact on the particularities of the construction of myself as author. How and what to select in cases like this is inevitably a problem and it must be remembered that the past is always inflected through the present, through the context of its telling (Middleton and Edwards, 1990). Stuart Hall has said that 'Identity is formed at the unstable point where the "unspeakable" stories of subjectivity meet the narratives of history, of a culture' (1987: 44). The story of my subjectivity, even a very short version, will not be easy to speak, since whatever the mode of its expression it will expose personal vulnerabilities to public scrutiny. Additionally I am conscious of the limitations of the confessional as discursive form, of the 'regulatory aspects of psychobiography' as Gayatri Spivak has put it,[11] following on from Foucault (1979). Yet, since I am arguing for its significance in the production of my work, I must address it, however difficult.

The elements which seem to me today, now, as I write, the most significant in my formation as an author and a feminist are as follows. I was born of migrant parents, one Jewish, the other not, refugees from the cities of central Europe, atheists, socialists. My first language was German. Through a series of fortuitous events I spent my childhood and adolescence – the 1950s – in the conservative climate of the English Home Counties where to others and myself I seemed uniquely foreign, dark-eyed and other. My parents were comfortably off but they, and in turn my brothers and I, seemed incapable of mastering the rules and skills of Englishness. To this day I feel that for me to 'pass' as English (as I sometimes do) is absurd, even in some way fraudulent; I find the 'we' of national inclusion impossible to utter. So perhaps it is not a coincidence that I have selected as my life work that which for me, with my European provenance, most epitomizes belonging to England: the speaking and writing of English. This then is part of the struggle of authorship. But my powerful sense of marginality did not operate in one direction only; it also placed me firmly against the xenophobic English middle classes and I went on to marry and have three (male) children with a working-class

Mexican of African-Native American descent (whence Nava), which achieved what I suppose was intended, that is to say it simultaneously confirmed my Englishness and my sense of difference. My children of mixed race, now adults, belong to the community of others in north London who are engaged currently in the project of 'the centering of marginality' as Stuart Hall has put it (1987: 44).

My own experience of cultural marginality and racial difference has been on the periphery of my conscious life and is surfacing only now, though sometimes with a force that startles me. But I have long been aware of its transposition on to other 'others'. Early on, before I was twenty, I became a supporter of a number of oppositional and ethical-political positions, among them racial integration (as it was then constructed), CND, free speech, the Cuban revolution, Reichianism and sexual liberation. At eighteen I escaped from Britain and spent five important and radicalizing years in New York City and Mexico. But it would be too simple to explain these developments only in terms of the incongruence of my dislocation in the English countryside. My three brothers experienced the same contradictions and are all middle-of-the-road conservative liberals. No, what I became was of course overdetermined, and the configuration of causal elements included also what it meant to be female in a family of brothers. As far as my parents were concerned it was quite acceptable for me to be rebellious and clever. And since I was more formally clever than were my brothers (I was the only one to get through the 11-plus) this, and defiance, seemed to compensate me for the lack of phallus. Since my mother thought that submissive women were stupid, being not stupid seemed one way out of the constraints of femininity. Besides, my father loved me to be smart. So to think in my family was to act out both my sibling and my Oedipal rivalry. But these pleasures were also full of guilt and shame. My older brother fought fiercely against my challenge and his own displacement. His tactic was not to acknowledge me, and it reverberates to this day. Meanwhile, in the outside world I was chastised for 'showing off' and forced to learn the painful English lessons of modesty and femininity. 'What you need is to eat humble pie', I remember a teacher telling me when I was ten. But I could not understand her.

I learned the lessons over time, however, even if improperly. I learned that to be questioning and imaginative was not always rewarded and that the symbolic possession of the phallus was a delusion. My punishment for being so bold as to think I could get away with my fantasy was to be humiliated and ostracized. An all-girls boarding-school I attended between the ages of ten and eleven was the most sadistic in this respect. I learned both there and later that my best defence against such abuse was to acquire the skills of femininity. Femininity became then a kind of masquerade (Rivière, 1986) – a way of being accepted in my English schools and at the same time an apology to my older brother for robbing him of his rightful place in the family. Both Englishness and femininity, which for me were intricately intertwined with each other and with learning, in the end took only partial root, and when I took off at eighteen for the New World, perhaps I hoped to be able to discard them altogether. Yet those complex lessons learned imperfectly and long ago surface still in my contradictory feelings about writing, which fluctuate to this day from the fearful and insecure to the bold and provocative. Perhaps even now I am unable to separate out the sense of fraudulence about my Englishness from the business of writing English.

It is feminism, aided by psychoanalysis, which has illuminated these contradictions and the injustice of these lessons. Yet for me, the logic of feminism, which came to me as an overwhelming and passionate surprise after the birth of my children, and which I took with me at thirty on my return to formal study, was prompted in the first instance by the inequities of domestic responsibility and the temptations of the public sphere, of political activism and sexual liberation, rather than the problem of identity. The psychic conflicts which I describe above have their own materiality, but during the early days of the women's liberation movement they seemed less urgent than the physical impossibility of reading and writing for concentrated blocks of time when there were children to be cared for. This is a consequence of the nature of parenting and housework, of the incessant and conflicting demands that are made, and of the sexual division of labour within the domestic sphere, of who does the work that has to be done. As is well known, it is women who usually do most of it. Raymond Williams in a fascinating account of his intellectual history in which he identifies the traditions of English scholarship that he has written 'against' in the course of his life – a useful way of thinking about how work gets produced – refers nowhere at all to who looked after his three children, whom we see from the chronology at the beginning of the book were born while he was a young man (Williams, 1979). His work routine at the time, he informs us, was one of 'extraordinary regularity', he wrote in the morning, read in the afternoon and taught in the evening (Williams, 1979: 82). Where were the children while he was doing this? Who did the cooking? There is not a mention of these things. Not only do his children disappear as labour, they also seem not to figure as agents of discovery or objects of love and despair. His is not only an ungendered subjectivity but one apparently untouched by parenthood. This is of course quite normal, particularly among men of his generation. It is also one of the things, perhaps the most important, that mobilized my feminism, that I wrote 'against', when I could find the time.

Across the years, struggles over time and recognition became less fierce. Children grow up, need a different quality of time and, with a bit of luck, nourish their parents in return. This happened to me and the evidence is here. Over half the pieces included in this book are rooted in one way or another in my relationship with my sons and their friends and contemporaries. There is a complex, unpredictable and not much explored psychic conjuncture where mothering – maternal responsibility and passion – combines with our sense of identification with young people, our conscious and unconscious memories of our own childhood and adolescence. For me this was (mostly) a powerful and enriching convergence, fruitfully balanced in terms of my relationship with my children and intellectually productive. I certainly take no credit for this. How our compulsions are acted out and mesh with each other in the context of parenting is a process propelled largely by forces beyond our control. In my case it seems to have worked quite well though, and in terms of the writing, must be responsible for the preponderance of 'youth' articles of one kind or another that I wrote in the course of the 1980s. Invariably the nature of my relationship with my sons, my protectiveness towards them as well as my identification with them, has also affected how my feminism has been lived out. It has contributed to making certain radical feminist absolutes about the nature of masculinity quite impossible to accept.

Heterosexuality, as an aspect of who I am and hence how I write, must be counted here too. But heterosexuality is no more likely to involve simple models of femininity and masculinity – to be coherent – than is homosexuality, and whom and which bits of whom we identify with and whom we desire are often contradictory, again the outcome of complex psychic processes over which we have little control. And again these processes undermine the earlier certainties of feminism, that is to say, the notion that the nature of our sexual pleasures and preferences will in some way enable us to speak with a particular voice. This kind of view no longer has currency among feminists who have taken seriously the insights of psychoanalysis or indeed among cultural analysts more generally who have engaged with the theoretical implications of difference and diversity.

But there is a paradox here. I am refusing the earlier comforts of a clear voluntaristic voice, of a unified subjectivity, of a simple correspondence between our circumstances and how we think. Yet, nevertheless I am claiming that there is some connection. The purpose of this introduction has been precisely to assert a relationship between who we are, how we live in the (post)modern world, and what we have to say. So, I am insisting on a link between history, desire and knowledge. The point is that these factors can never be arranged into any predictable unity. Outcomes are always uncertain. Why and what we speak is inflected by such disparate and fragmented phenomena, by psychic experience, politics, theory, that we can never disentangle the complex strands of causation. There can be no 'feminist voice', no single reading of a particular text. We make our way haphazardly, idiosyncratically, not only through the quagmire of our own experiences but also through those of others.

This introduction, the commentaries between chapters and the chapters themselves, will in the end acquire meaning only through the prism of the readers' own conscious and unconscious life. Readers will differently note and respond to transformations in my preoccupations and my style of exposition. They will detect emphases I am unaware of and will react to my inventions, obsessions and denials according to the pattern of their own psychic registers. Whatever sense or pleasure they extract from the text will be a consequence of the interaction of their personal narrative with the one that I offer here. And of course these two narratives do not stand alone. They in turn are the outcome of other histories and imaginings whose boundaries and endpoints are as arbitrary as those of this piece of writing.

So although this introduction may expand the meanings of the chapters that follow, it does not fix or contain them. Although it connects the chapters to each other by elaborating their context, it also disrupts the notion of a coherent whole by drawing attention to the complexity of the way meanings are produced and the intricate and unruly elements at play in the formation of our intellectual selves.

Notes

1. Among authors who have discussed some of these intellectual formations and transformations are Perry Anderson (1969); Juliet Mitchell (1971); Dick Hebdige (1988); Stuart Hall (1988a); Meaghan Morris (1988); Mike Featherstone (1988). See also Chapter 2 in this volume.

2. Basil Bernstein has drawn attention to changes in the classification of knowledge in the context of schooling (1977). For the impact of feminism on existing disciplines see, e.g., Ann Thompson and Helen Wilcox (1989); Lyn Pykett (1990); Terry Lovell (1990). For discussions of 'truth' see, e.g., Foucault (1980); James Donald (1989); the 1988 postmodernism issue of *Theory, Culture & Society*, 5 (2–3).

3. See, for example, Ann Oakley (1981); Heidi Hartmann (1979); Meaghan Morris (1988).

4. Among those who have addressed these questions are Zygmunt Bauman (1988); Douglas Kellner (1988); Nancy Fraser and Linda Nicholson (1988); David Harvey (1989); Barbara Creed (1987); Dick Hebdige (1988); Lisa Appignanesi (1989); Craig Owens (1985); Mark Poster (1988); Jean-François Lyotard (1984); Steven Connor (1989); Meaghan Morris (1988); Toril Moi (1990); Kobena Mercer (1990); Stuart Hall (1990); Homi Bhaba (1990); Mitra Tabrizian (1987).

5. See, e.g., Linda Nicholson (1990); Teresa Brennan (1989); Jacqueline Rose (1986); Carolyn Steedman (1986); see also Chapter 8 of this volume.

6. See, e.g., Juliet Mitchell (1975); Juliet Mitchell and Jacqueline Rose (1982); Julian Henriques et al. (1984); Laura Mulvey (1989); Lynne Segal (1990).

7. See Chapters 2, 8 and 10.

8. See, e.g., Stuart Hall (1987); Kobena Mercer (1990); Kobena Mercer and Isaac Julien (1988); Pratibha Parmar (1989); Trinh T. Minh-ha (1990); Mitra Tabrizian (1987, 1990). Mitra Tabrizian, Isaac Julien, Trinh T. Minh-ha and Pratibha Parmar are all film-makers as well as theorists.

9. See, e.g., Jeffrey Weeks (1985); Simon Watney (1987); Elizabeth Wilson (1985, 1990). See also *Perverse Politics: Lesbian Issues* (1990) a special issue of *Feminist Review*, 34; Richard Dyer (1990); Kobena Mercer and Isaac Julien (1988).

10. Where it is addressed it tends to be in the context of biography or psychoanalysis, see, e.g., Sigmund Freud (1986); Peter Gay (1988). For tentative explorations into the relationship between identity and politics see, e.g., Paul Hoggett (1989); Rosalind Minsky (1990). Among those who have attempted to make connections between identity and intellectual

work are Angela McRobbie (1980); Cora Kaplan (1983); Lynne Segal (1983a); Dick Hebdige (1985); Stuart Hall (1987); Marian McMahon (1991).

11. 'Nationalism, Racism and the Other', ICA conference London, 11 May 1991.

2

FROM UTOPIAN TO SCIENTIFIC FEMINISM? CRITICAL ANALYSES OF THE FAMILY

With the development of the new wave of feminism in the late 1960s and early 1970s, 'the family' became a central focus of concern. It was perceived as the key institution in the determination and perpetuation of women's subordinate status. Thus, politically and theoretically, the new feminism distinguished itself from earlier feminisms which, it was felt, had tended to concentrate exclusively on women's rights and opportunities in the public sphere. The new feminism also developed its politics and theory in reaction and relation to the New Left, with which it had, and continued to have (particularly in Britain), a close association. In neither of these traditions had the family appeared as a critical arena.

So the initial attempts to understand women's oppression through an examination of the family were voyages of intellectual exploration and discovery. What made them uniquely dangerous and exciting was that they were rooted in and had implications for the way in which everyday lives were being lived. Thus not only did they emerge from the struggles to make sense of the complexities and frustrations of personal experience, many were also polemical and prescriptive in that they insisted on challenging the nature of existing familial relations.

What is interesting is that from these marginal, experiential and oppositional beginnings, feminist ideas about domestic life were, over the course of a few years, to become established as a new 'discourse' – a consolidated body of knowledge, institutionalized in feminist writing – which exercised power to define, regulate and disrupt modes of thinking and behaving. The process of this transformation is not easily theorized, and I shall do no more than draw attention to it.

What I shall do in this chapter is to document some of the key ideas which appear in the early critiques of the family and attempt to place them in a political and theoretical context. I shall indicate the way in which some of the early concerns were developed in subsequent and more elaborated feminist work. Certain themes were neglected in the early writing and received only perfunctory treatment in the intervening years; I shall draw out and analyse some of these gaps. I shall also discuss the utopian in feminist thought and the way in which this has shifted over the last fifteen years from the sphere of 'the family' to that of 'sexuality'. The morality inevitably embodied in some of the visionary writings and politics emerges as a kind of moralism, in that covertly it sets standards of personal conduct. I shall look at the contradictory impact that this phenomenon has had.

My choice of texts to illustrate these trends is bound to be selective, and my representation of them will be to some extent determined by my participation in this history. Thus I shall refer not only to what was written, but also on occasion to my memories of how the material was received. Overall, the emphasis will be on uncovering those aspects which can illuminate our understanding of the present rather than on attempting a total reconstruction of what was written and happened between 1969 and 1972 – the years on which I shall primarily focus.

'The personal is political'

It is by now a commonplace to point out that feminism centre-staged the personal in a way that was unprecedented in political movements. It argued, first of all, that personal experiences were not individual isolated phenomena but the product of social circumstances which affect women in a systematic fashion. This was to be exposed in consciousness-raising groups through the examination of what had hitherto been considered too trivial to discuss in political terms: the minutiae of daily life. The other component of this centring on the personal was that private life became a legitimate object for 'public' scrutiny and evaluation.

It is from these two strands that the majority of the early critiques of the family were composed. In style they varied considerably. Many were founded on the experience of motherhood. Some were statements of despair or revelation. Others were more analytical, and I shall discuss the theoretical propositions in these later on. Here I want to concentrate on aspects of the political content and impact of the work (though, of course, it is impossible to draw a definitive line between the political and the theoretical). There is no doubt that in addition to trying to explicate personal experience, these articles had in common a major polemical objective: their overwhelming intent was not to engage in academic debates or to fill in the gaps in existing disciplines (which I shall argue became a dominant characteristic of subsequent analyses), it was rather to raise political consciousness so that people would act to change their lives. Thus a large proportion of these articles explicitly challenged the existing form and ideology of the 'nuclear family' – that is to say, the close and closed domestic unit composed of adult heterosexual monogamous couple and dependent children in which women were isolated from each other and responsible for child-care and housework – and frequently ended with proposals for alternative household organization.

The utopian vision

This imagined alternative household amounted to a utopian vision. In general, it proposed a unit much larger than the nuclear family; the pooling of labour, resources and responsibility; the abolition of power and economic dependency; the erosion of 'possessiveness' in personal relations both between lovers and between parents and children; and most importantly, the abolition of gender differentiation. This was not to be merely an alternative mode or a way of dropping out – part of the 1960s' counter-culture. A reorganization of this kind, it was often argued, would have multiple ramifications; it would in the end undermine the very foundations of capitalism. Many of the ideas were not new. Notions of pooling resources and eroding the economic power of the patriarch were present in nineteenth-century utopian and socialist schemes as well as in the ideals which informed the early development of the kibbutzim in Palestine in the first part of this century. Critiques of 'possessiveness' in personal relations were products of debates which culminated in the 1960s, though they started much earlier. In relation to children, the dominant influence was the anti-family perspective of Laing and Cooper.[1] Their proposition that children actually suffered from (became products of) excessively protective and insistent parenting was transformed from a negative critique of mothers, and appropriated by the early feminists in order to justify women's interest in loosening maternal bonds. Critiques of possessiveness in sexual relations were rooted in the counter-culture of the 1960s and neo-Reichianism, but were again transformed in order to illuminate the double sexual standards which operated both inside and outside marriage. Reich's theories about the politically conservative effects of sexual repression in children were made gender specific as part of a broader explanation for the more accommodating behaviour of women. Most important as well as specific to this new utopian vision was the insistence on the abolition of gender differentiation, particularly in housework and child-care. Men were to engage in the domestic sphere on equal terms with women.

It was this aspect which was quite unique in the history of socialist thought on the family. The dominance of ideologies about 'the natural' seems to have prevented the abolition of the sexual division of labour within the home from ever having been imagined. As a concept, it was absent from most early feminist writing. Sheila Rowbotham, for example (not a mother at the time), in her otherwise inspiring article 'Women's liberation and the new politics' (first published in 1969), was remarkably moderate and traditionally socialist in her proposals for the family (Rowbotham, 1972). She argued for more nurseries, launderettes and municipal restaurants rather than the entry of men into the domestic sphere. Margaret Benston (whose analysis of domestic labour I shall refer to later) also argued for the socialization of child-care, cooking and so forth rather than increasing men's share of household responsibilities (1969). For many women in the early women's liberation movement, the issue was marginal to their lives. Yet for others, particularly those of us with young children, the issue of domestic responsibility was of overwhelming significance; the family was not only of theoretical interest, it was the sphere in which oppression was most excruciatingly experienced. Mothering was the linchpin.

Anna Coote and Beatrix Campbell have identified two key events which they claim were responsible for the mobilization of women and their recruitment to feminism in the early days; these were the women's equal-pay strike at Ford's in 1968 and the Koedt article on 'The myth of the vaginal orgasm' in 1969 (Coote and Campbell, 1982). I suspect that one could produce dozens of women for whom the moment of illumination was prompted by another instance. For me, and probably many other mothers, the key influence was a relatively uncelebrated article, 'Child-rearing and women's liberation', written by Rochelle Wortis in 1969 and presented as a paper at the first Women's Liberation Conference in Oxford in 1970 (Wortis, 1972). It was probably the first feminist critique of Bowlby's theories of maternal deprivation. In a measured academic style, Wortis pointed out that in some societies 'multiple attachments are the norm', and that what a child requires is a stable, sensitive, stimulating environment which can be provided by two or more people, male as well as female. Her conclusion was programmatic and polemical:

> If the undervaluation of women in society is to end, we must begin at the beginning, by a more equitable distribution of labour around the child-rearing function and the home. . . . Men can and should take a more active part than they have done until now. . . .
> The creation of alternative patterns of child-rearing . . . is as much a political problem as an educational or psychosocial one. . . .
> We cannot wait for the revolution before we change our lives, for surely changing our lives now is part of the revolutionary process. (Wortis, 1972: 129–30)

In today's climate, in which these ideas have become quite routine, it is hard to conceive the powerful impact this kind of analysis had. Notions about the dangers of maternal separation were so pervasive at the time that they had become part of common sense and were simply not questioned. The idea that men *must* take an equal part in child-care, and that this was not only *not* a trivial demand but part of the revolutionary process, seemed daring and exhilarating. It seemed a blindingly simple solution to the apparently irreconcilable needs of mothers, for time, and young children, for the kind of loving and consistent care rarely available in nurseries. (At the time, nursery provision was in any case only available to approximately 10 per cent three- to five-year-olds, and practically non-existent for children younger than this.)

Yet, as I have already pointed out, an equal division of labour and responsibility between men and women within the domestic sphere was not always given priority or even considered in the emerging women's liberation movement. Indeed, even among those women for whom the experience of mothering and domesticity was totally enveloping, there was no consistent acceptance of the revolutionary nature of the rearrangement of domestic life. For many, it continued to appear as an individual solution, in spite of the rhetoric of the personal as political. The assertion that family change was political implied a substantive reassessment of what, for socialists, counted as politics. And this was only just beginning to happen.

These contradictions were manifested in another paper given at the Oxford conference, written by Jan Williams, Hazel Twort and Ann Bachelli (1972). Each being the mother of two children, they presented an angry account of the 'martyrdom' and isolation of marriage, motherhood and housework and insisted that neither improvements in domestic technology nor women's entry into the labour market could offer a solution. Neither, interestingly, could men's equal participation in child-care: 'Man as mother as well as man as house-slave is no answer' because this would 'extend oppression'. The answer lay in communal living. Yet this also had limitations in that ultimately it remained an 'individual solution': 'Living in a commune must not be envisaged as a resolution to the housewife problem. . . . However women live . . . their militant work must be governed by the imperative need to rouse the consciousness of their silent submerged sisters' (Williams et al., 1972: 35).

The emphasis on communal living was equalled, then, by their emphasis on the importance of consciousness and personal change. The problem was stated incisively: 'The oppression that every woman suffers is deeply in her, she first has to realize this and then to fight it.'

Consciousness and change

Williams et al. share with many other writers of the period the conviction that once ideologies of motherhood and child-care, so deeply internalized by women, were exposed as concepts which served only to subordinate them, the process of restructuring family life could be embarked upon. Not without a struggle, of course. But there is no doubt that it was felt that change depended largely on the *voluntarism* of women. We could do it if we wanted to. It had not happened before because we had been numbed by our conditioning. Because our new-found 'consciousness' had revealed to us the nature of our oppression as women in such a rapid and powerful fashion, it was assumed that the task was merely one of extending these insights to other women.

Yet, of course, these insights were not always unambiguously received, even among those women already committed to the women's liberation movement, precisely because they demanded not only a self-critique, silent or spoken, of a substantial portion of previous identities, but also because they implied a visible reorganization of domestic practices. Thus, for example, debates about the 'glorification of motherhood' were not unproblematically illuminating. The dilemma was not only to recognize our own complicity in tolerating what was suddenly so patently intolerable, but also how to distinguish between what of our old lives had to be jettisoned and what was worth keeping. How, for instance, were we to reconcile our rational critiques of a concept like maternal instinct with what seemed to many of us an indissoluble knot of passion for our children? And as I have already said, these early feminist critiques implied a change of practice as well as consciousness. This meant not only changing, but being seen to change. Although explicitly critical statements were not often made, it was clear that we both internalized the new criteria and used them as a basis for evaluating each other's living arrangements and relationships.

The following is an example of how this used to happen. Between about 1970 and 1972, women from the Belsize Lane Women's Liberation Group (of whom I was one) and our households were among a number of people who gathered on Hampstead Heath each fine Sunday to picnic and play volleyball together. These gatherings were significant because the truth about the division of child-care within our living units was made quite public. Both men and women were, in a sense, on trial. If young children ran on to the volleyball pitch and disrupted the game by crying for comfort from their mothers rather than their fathers or 'other friendly adults', we could feel quite exposed. This sort of occurrence seemed an almost shameful demonstration of our inability to progress beyond the stage of consciousness raising.

The political concern with consciousness and change found its theoretical expression within the early critiques of the family in their regular emphasis on 'conditioning' and 'socialization' as the key process in the construction of our acquiescence. The problem was to explain why we had failed to imagine that things could be otherwise. As Sheila Rowbotham put it:

> Women have been lying low for so long most of us cannot imagine how to get up. We have apparently acquiesced always in the imperial game and are so perfectly colonized that we are unable to consult ourselves. Because the assumption does not occur to us, it does not occur to anyone else either. (1972: 5)

And Williams, Twort and Bachelli: 'Most of all it has been a sheer impossibility to imagine ourselves being involved in change of any sort' (1972: 31).

Biological explanations were rejected early on. Freud's theories were unacceptable mainly for the concept of penis envy and the manner in which his psychoanalytic principles had been adapted in postwar US therapy, which, at its crudest, aimed to adjust a woman to the circumstances of her life. A third reason, though never as explicitly stated, was Freud's emphasis on the importance of the early development of children, which generated in its wake ideologies of appropriate maternal care. These rejections left us with a relatively non-contradictory and undynamic account of the development of femininity: sex-stereotyping arose from a process which included expectations, rewards, and identification with parental roles within the family; it was compounded by toys, schools and the media in 'society'. At the time, this model seemed sufficient. First of all, it explained cross-cultural variations (an area much researched in those days in order to substantiate our arguments against those who posited 'the naturalness' of gender difference and domestic organization; see, for example, Oakley, 1972). Secondly, it seemed to be confirmed by our experience of personal transformation. As a profoundly 'social' explanation, it provided the opportunity for social intervention. It seemed, at this point, that ultimately the construction of gender difference was subject to our control.

In isolating men's entry into the domestic sphere, communal living and consciousness, as the three key political features in the early texts, I have not exhausted the personal and programmatic elements in them – that is to say, those aspects which appealed directly to our sense of possibility and change. Some of the more 'analytical' features of the articles, such as, for example, reference to the nuclear family as a unit of consumption (to which I shall return later) were also subject to political resolution within the commune (see, for example, Crockford and Fromer, 1972). The texts were not *mainly* polemical and prescriptive. Yet, because they were so often rooted in our own domestic and emotional experiences (in a way in which analyses of women's class position, say, were not), they must be read in relation to the changes that were attempted as well as the relative failures of these attempts.

Trials and limitations

Before addressing the problems encountered in the practical implementation of the utopian vision, I want to examine more closely some of the proposals that were made. A general schema of the alternative household has been presented. Here I shall look at Shulamith Firestone (1970). I have singled her out because her '"dangerously Utopian" concrete proposals', as she herself called them, are the most detailed. In part of a lengthy section she argues for household contracts:

> A group of ten or so consenting adults of varying ages could apply for a licence as a group in much the same way as a young couple today applies for a marriage licence, perhaps even undergoing some form of ritual ceremony, and then might proceed in the same way to set up house. The household licence would however only apply for a given period, perhaps seven to ten years, or whatever was decided on as the minimal time in which children needed a stable structure in which to grow up.
>
> Children would no longer be 'minors' under the patronage of 'parents' – they would have full rights . . . [For example] the right of immediate transfer: if the child for any reason did not like the household into which he [*sic*] had been born so arbitrarily, he would be helped to transfer out. An adult . . . [who might wish to do so] might have to present his case to the court, which would then decide as do divorce courts today. . . . A certain number of transfers within the seven year period might be necessary for the smooth functioning of the household . . . however the unit . . . might have to place a ceiling on the number of transfers in or out, to avoid depletion, excessive growth, and/or friction. (1970: 232, 234)

Considering how difficult it is for two people to commit themselves to each other and to sustain a relationship, the likelihood of ten people, 'of varying ages', simultaneously deciding that each others' nine best friends are also theirs, and that they are prepared to in effect 'marry' them for about ten years, is far fetched to say the least. Implicit in Firestone's argument is the strange idea that all the individuals in this household will make decisions to undertake responsibility for children at the same moment, so that at the end of the contract all the children will be seven to ten years old, and old enough to make decisions about where to live next (to form their own contracts perhaps?). It is also assumed that the abolition of the category of minor will enable a child to reject its 'parents'. At the age of two or three? How are the 'ceilings' to the number of transfers to be determined and enforced? What happens if everybody wants to leave and nobody is prepared to continue to take responsibility for, say, four babies? The problems, of course, are legion.

Firestone's programme was both more visionary and a great deal less grounded in the *experience* of child-care and families than were the British equivalents. (Hers were perhaps set further in the future?)[2] All the same, this brief excerpt illuminates some of the problems that had to be confronted by those who attempted to implement the new ideals. It is quite impossible to describe all the difficulties and contradictions here. Among the most acute and time consuming were probably those which arose from the lack of rules and criteria available to help negotiate the new contexts in which traditional relations, expectations and modes of behaviour had been called into question. Thus, in one celebrated commune in north London, an unwillingness to claim rights over property (rooms) or people (lovers) meant that everyone regularly fell asleep around the kitchen table. Living with several people was no guarantee of more intimacy. On the contrary, it often led to an increase in personal reserve. Nor was the promise of reducing domestic commitment borne out: demands and confrontations were often multiplied. Then there were the problems of unreconstituted consciousness: little girls still wanted to be princesses; principles about reducing mother–child bonds and sharing out the cleaning were sabotaged by uncooperative men; biological mothers occasionally reasserted proprietorial rights over their children and took them from fellow-members of the collective household with whom they had formed close ties. Traditional emotions like guilt, jealousy, dependence and resistance died hard (see also Clarke, 1983).

I certainly do not want to give the impression that all the experiences were negative and unproductive. In some cases satisfying solutions were worked out. What I want to stress are the tremendous difficulties encountered in attempting to live out the ideals. It was thus that the limitations of voluntarism became increasingly apparent. Gradually the utopian visions, with their implicit moral imperatives, were referred to with more scepticism; the optimism started to fade. Yet it still seemed impossible to develop a theory and critique of the family without conceptualizing alternative forms. An article which I think exemplifies the dilemmas of this transition period was written by me at the end of 1971

(Nava, 1972). Here I want to draw attention to its conclusion in which, in the style of the period, I offered the utopian proposals. 'How do I visualize the new ideal?' I speculated. What I, in fact, set out was more detailed than Wortis or Williams et al., and far more constrained by what seemed *possible* than Firestone. What the proposals took into account were precisely the trials and failures of the previous few years. It was an attempt to reconcile the ideal with what our limits seemed to be. Group living, I suggested, was 'one *possible* alternative' to the limitations of the nuclear family; housework and child-care should be shared 'as equally as *possible*' (emphases added in 1982). Although a few moral imperatives remain – 'Marriage should be abolished' and 'children should not be economically dependent on their parents but on the group . . . all money and property should belong to the group' – these are tempered by an acknowledgement of the persistent nature of traditional personal relationships.

There is no doubt that in principle I passionately supported the idea of collective households. They seemed the only way of avoiding the negative aspects of the family while simultaneously retaining domestic life as a source of warmth and security. Although particularly vital for women with young children, this way of living appeared capable of providing a solution to everybody's dilemmas. Yet, in spite of believing this, I concluded the article with a sceptical interrogation of the voluntaristic assumptions which had become so widespread:

> What chance is there for any real change? On a personal level the way we live lags far behind our theories, old responses and resistances persist. . . . Are we capable of acting upon and changing not only our ideas and our environment, but also our feelings? (Nava, 1972: 43)

The problem remained 'in our heads', but was far more complexly and deeply embedded than we had anticipated. But it was still *women's consciousness* that was given priority as an object of political analysis and strategy. In my article there was no specific reference to the reluctance of fathers/husbands (as well as others, both men *and* women) to act upon their support for the principle of collective child-care, nor to the exercise of power by men.

Contradictory repercussions

The particular emphasis in the early family critiques on change in consciousness and on programmes for prefigurative lifestyles (although crucial to the momentum of the movement and to the recruitment of women to it, in that consciousness-raising groups undoubtedly provided immediate rewards not available in more orthodox political organizations) thus also contained certain conceptual and political weaknesses. As I have already indicated, the complexity of psychic life, the resistance of men and the hazards of collective living were underestimated.

In addition, I would want to argue that ultimately the emphasis on personal change created limits to the political effectivity of the critiques. As prescriptions, they were pertinent mainly to (some) women in the movement. To the vast majority of women outside, they remained largely irrelevant. This is not to say that the analyses did not advance the debates both inside and outside feminism. They did. Outside the movement, it was to the Left in particular that the arguments were directed.

This historical association in Britain between the women's movement and the revolutionary Left – the determination to force the Left to take the politics of women's liberation seriously – was, I think it can be argued, another constraint. It was one of the factors responsible for the relative failure of the feminist family programmes to formulate proposals for welfare, legal and fiscal reform – to make demands of the state. Within revolutionary politics of the late 1960s, policy proposals of this kind were condemned as reformist and liberal, and were neglected.

However, this is certainly not to suggest that feminist political activity was confined only to 'changing the way we live'. Women in the movement were particularly active in a number of areas which emerged directly from the family critiques. Examples of these were the organization of collective child-care, crèches at conferences (the first in which men looked after the children was at the 1970 Oxford Conference), and community nurseries (for which demands were sometimes made of the local council). The first refuge for battered women was set up in 1971 (within five years, there were over fifty throughout Britain). This type of political activity was defined as grassroots organization and thus escaped the label of 'reformist'. (Consciousness-raising groups had a more ambivalent response from the Left. They were sometimes virulently attacked by both men and women: feminists were described as 'objectively agents of the reactionary ruling class' who inhibited the revolutionary activity of the working class.)

Another consequence of the alignment of the women's movement to the revolutionary Left was its rejection of the capitalist press. This meant that feminist ideas were never really popularized. Accounts of women's liberation on the women's pages of the national press were invariably distorted, since we refused to write them ourselves, and then used as evidence of the implacable opposition of capitalism to the movement. In pointing to what I consider were some disadvantages arising from the early connections with the Left, I certainly do not want to exonerate the press, which undoubtedly many times deliberately misconstrued what we had to say; I am arguing that to get them to report it right was not a priority. Nor do I want to suggest that anti-reformism was a strategy developed only out of the revolutionary politics of the previous decade. Over and over again in the women's movement, it was justified by reference to what was then conceived of as the failure of the suffragist 'single-issue' campaign, the failure to continue the struggle once the vote had been won (though subsequent research proved this assumption to be incorrect). Thus, in the early days, it was feared by some women that to fight for and win abortion on demand, for example, might be to defuse the broader political momentum of the movement. In this respect, Britain in the late 1960s and early 1970s was different from the United States. It had no equivalent to the active yet fairly traditional liberal feminist organizations, like the National Organization of Women (NOW), which although disregarded by socialist and radical feminists, were all the same successful in achieving reforms of significance for the lives of women outside the movement. In sum, the point I want to make here is that the *political* orientation of these early critiques, their demands for personal change rather than reform, can be argued to have limited their success in reaching beyond the confines of the movement in spite of the extraordinary intensity of the effect on those women within it.

I would like to draw attention to another unanticipated and adverse consequence of the particular personal and political emphases in these early family critiques. For several centuries family life has been subjected to moral evaluation (by the Left as well as by the Right). The complex interaction between this traditional moral resonance, criticized by feminists but ultimately only inverted rather than totally abandoned, and the feminist concentration on the personal, resulted in an unprecedented political phenomenon: the legitimation of judgements on the *person* and her *life*, in addition to her ideas and the political effectivity of her actions. This politicization of the personal was probably the major moral contribution of feminism. Its impact was enormous and led to an expansion of what counted as politics in both conceptual and practical terms. It was undoubtedly a progressive phenomenon; yet its effects were at the same time very contradictory. Both the confessional mode of consciousness raising and the elevation of domestic life into an object available for scrutiny and assessment (in which good conduct could be awarded the metaphorical badge of the 'good feminist') were also profoundly *moralistic* and ultimately inhibiting. They emerged as a transmuted form of regulation.

So an inevitable aspect of the underbelly of the utopian programme, with its embedded assumptions of voluntarism and its particular analysis of consciousness (which took little account of the unconscious), is revealed as a moralistic censure of those who failed to achieve or attempt the vision. I am not suggesting that this censure was explicitly voiced in most instances. It was much more likely to take the form of self-criticism and guilt. Sisterhood in those days was more supportive than today; in the face of extensive external opposition, differences within the movement were minimized where possible. Paradoxically, it was perhaps precisely this mutual support (which, of course, in some ways contradicted yet also coexisted with the principle of public scrutiny), and therefore the lack of persistent investigation, which allowed these 'failures to live up to the ideal' to be attributed to individual inadequacies rather than collective theoretical and political errors (that is to say, the limitations of voluntarism and the difficulties of group living). In this instance, personal troubles were not transformed into public issues, they were not properly theorized. It was then supremely ironic, but perhaps to be predicted, that our attempts to overthrow the existing moral basis of family life succeeded only in shifting its axis. And as I have already suggested, the persistence of the moral ultimately inhibited further development of this strand of the family critiques. The visionary terrain was gradually evacuated.

I would want to argue that this occurrence marked a kind of crisis in feminist discourse on the family. It both provoked and demanded new ways of thinking about the problem. Thus, in the work that followed this period, the prescriptive was largely absent. Although moral and political considerations continued to act as underpinnings, they ceased to have the visibility that they had previously had. Subsequent writing tended to be analytical rather than polemical. Of course, the failure of the vision to resolve the dilemmas of the domestic lives of feminists was not the only factor to contribute to this change of style and direction. The year 1972 has been pinpointed as the one which saw the decline of post-1968 euphoria, the counter-culture and the first stage of the women's liberation movement (Weeks, 1981; O'Sullivan, 1982). With it came an increasing recognition of the need to extend the field of study, to develop both a more rigorous general theory and specific histories of operations and relations within the family and between the family and other social spheres. The shift from the visionary terrain and from a concern with the minutiae of daily experience was also a positive response to the tougher political context of the 1970s. In addition, there was an expansion of academic feminism in which the personal and the programmatic had no place. These factors combined during the 1970s with a more general social acceptance of marital dissolution and variations in domestic organization (to which, of course, feminist ideas had contributed).[3] One could speculate that the decline of feminist moralism in relation to the family was part of a wider transformation in which aspects of family life were decreasingly objects of moral evaluation.

The moratorium on prescription returned the organization of domestic life to the sphere of private unaccountable decision-making, though not necessarily to its nuclear form. It remains, of course, an essential feature of personal life to be negotiated by all feminists, and is undoubtedly negotiated with a changing battery of insights, principles and demands. But no longer is a single arrangement of living or child-care specified as the most apposite or correct in the struggle to advance the position of women.

Voluntarism and sexuality

To conclude this section I want to draw attention to a more recent development within feminism which seems to echo many of the dilemmas I have already discussed. The decline in moral imperatives and assumptions of voluntarism in relation to domestic organization was followed a few years later by an upsurge of similar imperatives and assumptions in certain feminist accounts of sexuality (predominantly those of some radical and revolutionary feminists). In common with most other recent work on the subject, these accounts reject the 1960s biological-drive model in which sexuality was constantly pitting itself against societal constraints (though inconsistently, they often appear to hang on to these in their comments on male sexuality). They also reject psychoanalytical explanations[4] which emphasize the part played by the unconscious in the construction of sexual desire. In the manner of the early critiques of the family (though with a different object), these more recent feminist critiques have stressed the oppressive nature of both traditional and 'permissive' heterosexual relations, and have prescribed politically correct alternatives. For the critics of the nuclear family, the commune provided the utopian solution; similarly, for the critics of traditional sexual relations, the solution has become political lesbianism – that is to say, a distancing from 'male' modes of sexual expression and from relationships with men in order to advance the feminist struggle. Underpinning this ideal is the assumption that sexual desire is subject to rational political choice, echoing the voluntarism present in the family prescriptions.

Again, in the same way that private child-care arrangements were exposed to political scrutiny and judgement, women's sexual preferences have now become an indicator of the 'good feminist' – a legitimate object of political evaluation. In contrast, however, because positions within feminism are so much more polarized than fifteen years ago, there is no longer an impetus to minimize the censure for the sake of unity and sisterhood. In this recent expression of feminist utopianism, judgement is not always confined to 'incorrect' expressions of sexuality; it can be extended to include the whole woman. All aspects of her political contribution to the movement become available for criticism. This is not only a kind of sexual reductionism, it has become a new form of regulation.

Thus, as with the family critiques, I would want to argue that the effects of the voluntarism embodied in the political lesbian prescriptions must ultimately be inhibiting. Beatrix Campbell has suggested in an extended discussion of the subject that 'they deny any [feminist] political practice within heterosexuality and don't safeguard specifically lesbian culture and sex. They *prohibit* the formulation of a feminist sexual politics' (Campbell, 1980: 18). At this point I have no explanation to offer for the displacement of the moral from the domestic sphere to the sexual. Whether or not the limitations of voluntarism and the contradictions of sexual life will become apparent – whether or not this approach to sexuality will undergo a decline to parallel that of the early family prescriptions – remains to be seen.

The theoretical contributions

A unique feature of the early women's liberation movement was its insistence on the fusion of the theoretical, the political and the personal. For the purpose of this chapter, I have attempted to unravel these strands, though no easy division can be made between them, and here my intension is to focus on the family critiques primarily as a body of theory. This will include looking at general assumptions and influences, and distinguishing between those areas of concern which subsequently were developed into major debates, and those which were dropped.

One of the significant characteristics of most of the early writing was its theoretical eclecticism. A number of different approaches were drawn on in order to tackle prevailing ideas which stressed the universality and inevitability of existing roles within the family, and the harmonious 'fit' between the nuclear family unit and modern industrial society. However, the overriding feminist concern was not to pinpoint the deficiencies of existing theoretical perspectives. It was to create a coherent explanation of all aspects of women's oppression, one which took into account the way the family operated economically and ideologically and the way in which it was experienced. For this project, theoretical purism was not a priority, and as well as focusing on diverse areas, the work combined a range of theoretical approaches (though differences between socialist and radical feminists were as yet uncrystallized). It also varied in its sophistication.[5] All the same, there were certain consistent patterns which emerged and continued to have political and theoretical consequences.

One of these was the notion of the family as a unit, a unity encompassing different but complementary functions (Mitchell, 1971). This view was taken on by feminists from existing analyses and was then inverted. So, instead of being wholly good, the family became wholly bad. The tendency was to consider all aspects of it oppressive for women. Implicit in this kind of approach is the notion that progress can only be achieved if the family is totally destroyed. Minor reforms which benefit women tend to be undermined. Also undermined, I think, as a consequence of this totalistic view, are the positive features of parenting and intimacy which can occur in family life.

More important and more influential theoretically and politically was the feminist concentration on ideology as a *source* of women's oppression. In the late 1960s and early 1970s, this was in contrast to most Marxists, for whom the economic was the prime determinant of other aspects of society. But as Juliet Mitchell pointed out: 'There is nothing less "real" or "true" or important about the ideological than there is about the economic. Both determine our lives' (Mitchell, 1971: 155). And although women's relation to the economy was always of concern, it was overwhelmingly *ideologies* – of femininity, of wifehood and motherhood – and the influence of these in all spheres which were the focus of feminist scrutiny and attack. This insistence on the determining nature of the ideological contained two elements: it implied a recognition, on the one hand, of the power and persistence of ideologies which justified the subordination of women; and on the other, of the strength of ideas as a motor of change. As a theoretical proposition, it produced reverberations that extended beyond feminism to influence developments within Left social theory over the following decade.

The weakness of the feminist emphasis on ideology as the source of women's oppression was that it probably obscured the substantial material benefits that accrued to men as a consequence of their position within the family. Theoretical attention to this came much later. During the early period, the concept of male supremacy and chauvinism was certainly present in the political rhetoric as well as in small group discussions. Yet, at a more analytical level, the matter was either undiscussed or men, too, were perceived as victims of the ideologies of masculinity and femininity.

Children and mothering

As has already been indicated, the aspect of the nuclear family which received most consistent attention in the early texts, and was considered by most feminists of the period as absolutely central to any analysis of the position of women, was the socialization of children. Within this general area, ideologies of motherhood and child-care were subjected to the most historically specific, detailed and frequent criticism. The particular focus was almost always Bowlby's theory of maternal deprivation (see, for example, Wortis, 1972; Mitchell, 1971; Nava, 1972; Sharpe, 1972; Oakley, 1976). First postulated during the 1940s and widely popularized during the 1950s, it suggested that the separation of young children from their mothers, even for relatively short periods, could result in permanent damage and delinquency (Bowlby, 1953). Although Bowlby's hypothesis had been subjected to considerable academic criticism, mainly because his studies were conducted on children in institutions, and he himself had withdrawn certain arguments and qualified others, it was not until the feminist onslaught that the pervasiveness of the ideology at a popular level started to decline. Dr Spock rewrote sections of his celebrated baby manual (1963) initially one of the greatest culprits in this process of popularization, in response to feminist pressure. Within a few years, the issue had ceased to be of significance in most feminist discussions of the family. Yet in the initial stages there is no doubt that it was crucial. Several of the texts argued that, in the postwar period, the ideology of maternal deprivation had operated to justify the closure of nursery schools and the exclusion of women from the labour market. They also pointed out that women who stayed at home to look after their babies were, in addition, available to carry out the important job of unpaid cook and housekeeper for their husbands and school-age children – workers and future workers. Thus present in an embryonic form was an understanding of women's contribution to the reproduction of the labour force, a perspective which was developed and became dominant among Marxist feminists later on in the 1970s. What is interesting is that these conclusions were originally arrived at through an examination of the 'myth of motherhood' and *not* through an analysis of the reproduction of the relations of production.

The argument continued by suggesting that the effects of the 'myth' were not only to confine women to the tedium and isolation of the home, but also to curtail their activities in all other spheres. As a consequence of this exclusion, many women (as well as men) 'glorified' the role of wife and mother. Furthermore, the 'myth' was perpetuated within the family, since this was the primary site for the socialization of children into their gender roles; and boys and girls, it was argued, patterned their behaviour on the parent of the same sex, thus assuring a continuation of women's subordinate role.

By about 1973, the ideologies of motherhood and child-care had lost the centrality they had held in the early texts. Since then there has been little theoretical discussion of these issues. This is not only because the critiques were so forcefully made in the initial stages. It is also because an intellectual pursuit of the issues encounters political dilemmas: they do not always lead in the right direction; they are not completely subsumable within the feminist framework. So although the early critiques of Bowlby were absolutely correct in pointing out the absurdity of assuming that only mothers could care adequately for children, this was primarily an assertion about the interests of mothers. The interests of children, their dependency and vulnerability, have never really been explored within *feminist* theory. Various related explanations for this are possible: there are the political fears that too much concern about the needs of children could feed into the anti-feminist backlash; at a personal level, the issue might be too contradictory to face; finally, a satisfactory feminist theory of children's needs may simply not be possible. Where the question has been addressed, the tendency has been to designate the work non-feminist, in that women's interests are not given priority (Hodges, 1981).

Another prominent feature of the early texts which remained relatively unexamined after the initial years, yet which, in contrast to the previous issue, might well yield more to feminist investigation, is 'the glorification of motherhood'; that is to say, the insistence of many women (outside the movement) that family life and motherhood can be both rewarding and a source of authority. This phenomenon has tended to be constructed as 'false consciousness', an inability to recognize the real nature of oppression. And although some of the early texts touched on the complex nature of the attachment of women to the home – for example, 'Some women resent their husbands' increased participation in the home and see it as an intrusion into the one area where previously they held some autonomy' (Nava, 1972: 39) – it has perhaps been felt that a proper examination of this area would also add grist to the anti-feminist mill. In fact, I think that the feminist failure to look sensitively at traditional (though, of course, highly contradictory) sites of women's power, like the family[6] and physical attractiveness, has proved a theoretical and political error. Theoretically, the failure emerges from the perspectives which view the family as a unit that is wholly bad for women, and women's physical adornment as invariably part of their objectification. Politically, this insensitivity might well have curtailed the expansion of the movement.

Totally absent from the early writing was any discussion of youth as a category within the family, and the complex interaction between gender and generational relations. The emphasis in youth studies was on boys and street culture (McRobbie, 1980). It is only in the last few years that attention has been focused on adolescent girls, and on the specificities of the regulation of young people within the domestic sphere as well as on the street (McRobbie and Nava, 1984).

The absence of attention to adolescence within the family also high-lights another gap. The early texts focused exclusively on the domestic as a context of care for very young children (probably a reflection of the authors' personal circumstances). The periodicity of family life was not taken into account: but children grow and have changing needs, they become increasingly capable of making practical, emotional and financial contributions. The difficulty of establishing the point at which the fulfil-ment of children's needs amounts to exploitation of adult (maternal) labour, and the nature of this, has barely been touched on in feminist theory (the exception is Leonard, 1980).

The economy

The issue of domestic labour was categorized both under 'wifehood/motherhood' and 'the economy of the family'. Most often in the early texts it was subsumed under the former. Juliet Mitchell (1971), for exam-ple, although drawing attention to the material value of housework, does not include it as a significant component of any of her four structures (production, reproduction, socialization and sexuality). It was the *experience* of housework that tended to be emphasized, its triviality and privatization.

Those accounts which situated domestic labour in the economy derived mainly from socialist women who were not prepared to relinquish the primacy of the economic in determining women's position. For example Margaret Benston in Canada (1969) argued that housework was a pre-capitalist form of production, it constituted the economic base of women's subordinate status; women were not only discriminated against but exploited; unpaid labour in the home contributed to the profits of capitalists. Jean Gardiner, in a paper entitled 'The economic roots of women's liberation', given at an International Socialist women's con-ference in 1970 and reported by Sue Sharpe, argued that: 'The labour of the worker and his wife is appropriated, the one directly and the other indirectly, by capital' (Sharpe, 1972: 140). These were the earliest attempts to construct a Marxist analysis of the value of housework and its relation to capitalism. The objective was to fill in the gaps in Marxist theory and also to force the issue of women on to the socialist agenda. The work culminated in the mid-1970s in what has become known as the domestic labour debate (see Himmelweit, 1983).

Some of these ideas penetrated the family critiques that emanated from within the early women's liberation movement, but were not characteristic of them. For example, Sue Sharpe (1972) addresses the question of the value of women's labour to capitalism but concentrates predominantly on how this was expressed at the level of ideology. Sharpe also proposes that the family constitutes a 'subordinate mode of production', though without specifying what this means. Whether the family was a 'pre-capitalist' or 'subordinate' mode of production, or whether it was merely characterized by 'different relations of production', also became a major issue in the domestic labour debate.

A quite different materialist approach to these questions was demonstrated in Christine Delphy's pamphlet, *The Main Enemy*, which was published in France in 1970, though not translated into English until 1977. In it, Delphy argues that the family constitutes a *distinct* mode of production, which coexists with capitalism, in which the labour of women is appropriated by *men*; the emphasis is on relations of exploitation *within* the unit of the family. Delphy's analysis undoubtedly continued to have theoretical reverberations for longer than any other text of the early period. It formed a major plank in the debates about the relationship between capitalism and patriarchy which were to preoccupy feminist theorists at the end of the 1970s. The reason her work was both so influential and contentious was because she insisted on focusing on the benefits of women's unpaid labour which accrue to men rather than capital (see also Phillips, 1981).

In the early British texts, however, discussions of the family and the economy concentrated, on the whole, on the contribution to capitalism made by the family as a unit of consumption. Within this women were the principal agency: 'Aspirations to accumulate such commodities as televisions . . . cars etc. are repeated in every single family, providing the immense consumer market necessary for [capitalist] production. Advertising gives the poor housewife the full works' (Sharpe, 1972: 139). The assertions about the importance of the family as a unit of consumption were relatively unsubstantiated at the time, and as a theoretical avenue this has remained largely unexplored. Yet as Michèle Barrett (1980) has suggested, this approach might very well prove more fruitful in demonstrating the support of capitalists for a particular family form than either the domestic labour debate or the reproduction of the labour force theories. An examination of one further 'economic' feature of the family – the unequal distribution and control over the wage and commodities (including food) within the family – was not to emerge until later, and has recently produced some very interesting research (Oren, 1974; Land, 1981; Whitehead, 1981).

Reproduction and sexuality

Reproduction and sexuality are the remaining spheres of significance in the early critiques at which I want to look. These were both accorded a wider range of theoretical interpretations (as was the economy) than child-care and motherhood, over which there was considerable uniformity.

For Shulamith Firestone (1970), reproduction constituted the crucial as well as indisputable biological difference between men and women. It formed the material basis for the subordination of women. Only through the development of artificial reproduction would the oppression of women and the biological family end. Firestone's theory tends towards technological as well as biological reductionism. As Rosalind Delmar (1972) has pointed out: 'There is no reason why within present institutions, [reproductive] technology should not be used as a further instrument of women's oppression.' This aspect of Firestone's work is more a feat of the imagination than an analysis which offers guidelines for the development of political strategy.

Reproduction was identified by Juliet Mitchell (1971) as one of her four structures of women's oppression. She points out that reproduction, sexuality and socialization, all located in the family, are historically and not intrinsically related. The twentieth-century decline in the importance of the reproduction of children is accompanied by the increasing importance of their socialization. These observations formed the cornerstone of her theory, in that she argued that modification in one structure was likely to be offset by reinforcement in another. What was required was a simultaneous transformation of all four structures – what Mitchell, after Althusser, calls a *unité de rupture*. This theoretical assertion was characteristic of the unitary view of the family and women's oppression to which I referred at the beginning of this section. Its implications are anti-reform: improvements in one structure are likely to be cancelled out by renewed disadvantage in another. This is a hydraulic model reminiscent of Reich and (some would argue) Freud, in that it suggests a fixed amount of oppression circulating in the body politic: push it from the hands and it will reappear in the feet. More recent work sees the family as a site on which material, legal, ideological and psychological discourses intersect, but between which there is no necessary correspondence (Donzelot, 1979; Bennett et al., 1980). For example, changes in family law have no predetermined effects upon, say, ideologies of child-care.

Interestingly, the issues of reproduction and control over fertility were quite often neglected in the early feminist discussions of the family.[7] In the first years of the movement, 'free-contraception and abortion on demand' was a major slogan and area of struggle, but on the whole it was defined as a battle between women and the law and the medical profession, rather than one which concerned patriarchal authority within the family. New perspectives on this were developed towards the end of the 1970s: 'The characteristic relation of human reproduction is patriarchy, that is, the control of women, especially their sexuality and fertility, by men' (McIntosh, 1977). The problem then became one of specifying the different forms of this control and their relation to production (McDonough and Harrison, 1978; Edholm et al., 1977).

Sexuality in the early critiques remained overwhelmingly influenced by the theoretical assumptions of libertarianism. In these, sexuality was constructed as a drive. Its repression created the submissive personalities required by capitalism. (Subsequent contributions rejected the biologistic assumptions of this early work and stressed the social construction of sexuality.)[8] What was added to the libertarian approach by the early women's liberation movement was a signalling of the contradictions between the demand for sexual freedom for all and the continuing double standard by which women were condemned if they exercised this 'freedom' as freely as men. (Or, indeed, if they chose not to exercise it at all.) It was pointed out that the ideology of monogamous marriage applied, in effect, to women only. In this framework, it was considered that the natural sexuality of children was also subjected to repression and should be allowed free expression.

But the critique was not confined to inequalities in degrees of freedom. It was pointed out that the very nature of female sexuality had been defined in terms which suited the desire and pleasure of men. The notion (based largely on Freud) that vaginal and clitoral orgasms were distinct, and that sexually and emotionally 'mature' women experienced the former, was revealed as mythology by the clinical research conducted in the United States by Masters and Johnson. Koedt, in 1969, was probably the first to incorporate this into a feminist analysis (Campbell, 1980). Thus the clitoris as *the* source of the female orgasm was established as a major political issue by feminists from the very beginning of the new wave.

In many of the early discussions of sexuality, pleasure was not related to the 'nuclear' family form, though Pat Whiting (1972) examines married women's (lack of) experience of it. Although her general perspective remains within the 1960s tradition, with its emphasis on the 'liberation' of sexuality, unlike others she does address the issue of lesbianism as an alternative to oppressive and unpleasurable heterosexual relations: 'More women [who were previously married] are taking the gay position believing that equality can only be worked out by two similar partners. These women . . . state quite categorically that the male is not necessary for women's complete sexual satisfaction and happiness' (Whiting, 1972: 212). Whiting was more prepared than most writers of the period to perceive sexuality as a political arena of contestation between women and men, and not merely as a phenomenon which had to be liberated from moral and political constraints deriving from tradition and the political and economic organization of society, that is to say, from *beyond* the family.

Some other developments

In this evaluation of the early contributions on the family, I have indicated the direction of subsequent work where this developed directly out of the earlier propositions. A number of significant approaches of the 1970s hardly appeared, even in embryonic form, in the early critiques and therefore have not been mentioned. I shall refer to them briefly.

Although the organization of claimants' unions and resistance to the transparent sexism of social security policy towards cohabiting women formed an integral part of early women's liberation movement politics, the part played by state policy in reinforcing a specific family form was examined in detail only later in the 1970s. Hilary Land pointed out that: 'The British social security system, by perpetuating inegalitarian relationships, is a means of reinforcing, rather than compensating for, economic inequalities' (1976: 108). And Elizabeth Wilson looked at the way in which ideologies of femininity and the family influenced social welfare policies, and how these in turn amounted to 'no less than the state organization of domestic life' (Wilson, 1977; see also David, 1980).

The 1970s also saw a considerable amount of research into historical variations in familial ideologies (Davidoff et al., 1976; Hall, 1979). Other writers drew attention to the importance of distinguishing between familial ideology and current 'household form' which only infrequently resembled the breadwinning father and dependent mother and children of the ideal typical nuclear family (McIntosh, 1978; Barrett, 1980). Several authors wrote about the very substantial violence perpetrated by men against women (and children) within the family, though interpretations of this phenomenon, and of what the appropriate strategy to overcome it should be, varied (Pizzey, 1974; Hanmer, 1977; Weir, 1977; Radford, 1982).

In 1974, Juliet Mitchell argued for a more complex understanding of the child's acquisition of femininity and masculinity within the nexus of familial relations. She was the first to reassert the value of Freud, and in particular his theory of the unconscious, for feminism (Mitchell, 1975). Nancy Chodorow (1978) in the United States, also addressed herself to this problematic. She differs from Mitchell in that her explanation for the construction of masculinity and femininity lies in the *social* arrangements of child-care, in which women mother (and thus make it amenable to change), rather than in the universal nature of the Oedipal conflict. Almost invariably, it is women with whom young children form primary emotional bonds and from whom they must separate as they mature. It is this asymmetrical early environment which determines personality differences between men and women, and women's subordinate status. Chodorow's argument implies that the key to rupturing existing gender relations lies in the creation of new patterns of parenting in which men participate equally.

Probably the most significant theoretical project with a bearing on the family was the attempt, in the late 1970s, to establish a definition of patriarchy and its relation to capitalism. This was a highly complex debate which, to simplify it grossly, was about whether the oppression of women was determined primarily by their relation to capitalism or to men. Patriarchy remained a relatively descriptive concept which was employed in a variety of ways to refer to the subordination of women as a category in relation to men. Because some early radical feminists used it to designate a social division between men and women both more deep-rooted and more influential than the division between classes in capitalist society, it was on the whole rejected by Marxist and socialist feminists. This is not to say that Marxist and socialist feminists remained uncritical of the failure of Marxism to examine the specificity of women's position. They were, however, unwilling to take on an explanation for the subordination of women that could not ultimately be incorporated within a Marxist framework, which (at its crudest) posits that all aspects of the social totality are in the last instance determined by the capitalist mode of production. In this kind of analysis, the sexual division of labour in the family and discriminatory state legislation, for example, were explained in terms of their relation to capitalism; the benefits for men tended to be ignored.

Significant among the critics of this kind of perspective were Heidi Hartmann (1981) in the United States and Christine Delphy (1977) in Europe. Hartmann, who characterized herself as a feminist socialist, refused to give capitalism priority and insisted that Marxism was unable to explain the particular oppression of women. This could only be done by reference to gender hierarchy – patriarchy. For Hartmann, patriarchy and capitalism were two distinct systems whose interrelations varied at any given historical moment. Each could determine the other. Delphy's propositions (already referred to in the 'economy' section of this chapter) were not dissimilar to Hartmann's and formed the foundation of the radical feminist position in the British capitalism–patriarchy debate. With Diana Leonard, she argued that the family, as a distinct economic system in which women's labour was exploited by men, coexisted with capitalism but was not internal to it (Delphy and Leonard, 1980). It was the organization of labour within the family which constituted the material basis – that is to say, the most significant determinant – for women's oppression in other spheres. Because Delphy and Leonard called themselves radical feminists, their analysis was often erroneously confused with those of revolutionary and some other radical feminists (who stressed essential biological differences between men and women, and politically argued for separatism from both men and the Left). This confusion (as well as the influence of orthodox Marxism in Britain) might well have been responsible for the reluctance of Left feminists to consider Delphy's propositions carefully. Hartmann's work was not received as critically by socialists either in the United States or here.

Inevitably, these are highly caricatured representations of the theoretical positions taken up in the debate (see Phillips, 1981 and Beechey, 1979 for further discussion). Although in my opinion these positions are best imagined situated along a continuum rather than entrenched in opposing camps, there were all the same important differences between those feminists unwilling to relinquish the idea that capitalism was the ultimate beneficiary of women's subordination and those who argued that it was men. In the end, the effect of the debate was probably to draw out more clearly the distinctions between feminists at opposite ends of the continuum.

In the period of the early women's movement, a far less developed theoretical and political polarization had existed. Socialist feminists *did* draw attention to male violence and radical feminists *were* concerned with the exploitation of women in the labour force. As I have already argued, these early feminist theories were, on the whole, developed in conjunction, in order to map out an unexplored terrain. The project was a collective one. Differences between theories can often be accounted for through an examination of the perspectives with which historically they were associated. Thus, in their analyses of women, feminists in the United States were more inclined to establish analogies with caste and race (see Dunbar, 1970) than were feminists in Britain, whose close association with the Left led them to give priority to questions of class and the relationship of women's liberation (a non-class movement) to the working class (Bachelli et al., 1970).

The development of different tendencies within feminism in subsequent years contributed to a greater refinement of the feminist problematic; yet the abrasive theoretical and political encounters between tendencies sometimes forced a retreat into increasingly defensive and abstract positions formed *in opposition* to those of other feminists. Energy was often dissipated within the movement instead of being directed into engagement with the world 'outside'.

What now?

Over the past decade, the family has been broken from its idealized image as a unit and a haven and exposed as a site of domination and exploitation. This has not happened only within the confines of the movement. The ideas generated there have been increasingly disseminated and popularized. There has been a massive output of writing and the establishment of several feminist publishing houses. The feminist magazine *Spare Rib* had in the 1980s an estimated readership of 100,000. Women's magazines as different as *Cosmopolitan* and *Woman's Own* regularly have articles which seriously address feminist issues. These have combined with the impact of activists in teaching, community work and trade unions to the point where feminist ideas have, in many instances, become part of a commonsense way of viewing the world.

Recent theoretical work has tended to move away from the schematic analyses which characterized the capitalism–patriarchy debate of the late 1970s, and has instead concentrated on the specificities and contradictions of femininity and family life. The component parts of women's subordination do not inevitably coalesce to form a coherent whole. Nevertheless, a recognition of these contradictions and of the limitations of voluntarism in our personal lives must not allow us to absolve the domestic sphere from further radical critiques. It remains one of the key sites on which womanhood is acted out and perpetuated.

Yet, politically, the specific circumstances of women's lives are often still not taken into account in the formulation of policies, even by the Left. This is one of a range of factors which has contributed to a shift in feminist political activism during the early 1980s. Large numbers of women previously engaged primarily in relatively small-scale and local feminist campaigns have joined the Labour Party. The specification of ideals, the popularization of feminist perspectives, and grassroots community organization – however important – are no longer considered sufficient. Feminist objectives have expanded to include the formulation of *realizable* strategies for concrete reforms which can ensure a redistribution of resources and new legislation to promote and protect the interests of women (Coote and Campbell, 1982). These must be achieved in order to create a base – a precondition – from which to readdress the issues of consciousness and ideology, and redress the balance of power and privilege.

Notes

1. For a discussion of these ideas see Segal (1983b).

2. In the last few years the utopian in feminist thought has more often been expressed in fiction. See for example Marge Piercy (1978).

3. Between 1970 and 1979 the divorce rate trebled for those under twenty-five and doubled for those over twenty-five. The decade also saw a phenomenal increase in the numbers of people who chose to cohabit rather than marry, though precise figures for this are not available.

4. Psychoanalytic theory has more often been used by socialist feminists in order to understand sexuality. See for example *Feminist Review*, 11 (1982) and *M/F* 5 and 6 (1981), though there are also important differences between these two journals.

5. Juliet Mitchell's *Women's Estate* (1971) is in a different league from the rest.

6. An exception to this is Valerie Walkerdine's fascinating article 'Sex, power and pedagogics' (1981) in which she looks at the way small girls in nursery schools are the subjects of a variety of contradictory discourses. Within the domestic they exercise considerable power over small boys.

7. For example, in Michelene Wandor's collection (1972) it is hardly mentioned in the articles that focus on the family and only really receives attention in the section entitled 'Crime and the Body Politic'!

8. There are two main approaches within this general category. The first is adopted by writers influenced by Foucault and certain readings of Freud (see the journal *M/F*). The second is influenced by the interactionist perspective of Gagnon and Simon (see Stevi Jackson, 1978).

COMMENT

From Utopian to Scientific Feminism?
Critical Analyses of the Family

'From Utopian to Scientific Feminism' is a historical piece, a version of my own history, written from the perspective of the early 1980s. As an attempt to look backwards and analyse feminist texts of an earlier moment in relation to the intellectual approaches, politics and personal histories of the period of their production, it anticipates the project of this collection. Like a play within a play, the chapter refers back – as I do here – to a piece I wrote a decade earlier in order to unpack and reflect upon developments in feminist debate.

And as all histories do, it tells us not only about the late 1960s and early 1970s – the moment under scrutiny – but also about the vantage point of the early 1980s. In this respect it lends itself to a more textured reading today than when it was first published. Although it remains, as it was in 1983, a comment on the conviction and conceptual strengths and limitations of the women's liberation movement during the late 1960s and early 1970s, it provides additionally for readers today an overview of theoretical developments across the whole of the 1970s as well as a contemporary perspective on early 1980s feminist moralism and political lesbianism.

In this respect it sketches in a political and theoretical backdrop for the chapters that follow, and particularly for '"Everybody's Views Were Just Broadened": A Girls' Project and Some Responses to Lesbianism', a polemical piece of work written two years earlier which argues in a much more controversial fashion against certain feminist positions. In comparison 'From Utopian to Scientific Feminism' is more considered and academic – despite the provocative critique of voluntarism and sexuality – reflecting precisely the shift it describes from an engaged and utopian feminism to one that is more analytical and distanced.

In the process it registers the growing critique of totalizing theory (or meta-narrative as we are more likely to say today), the impossibility of feminist demands and the importance of psychoanalysis to our understanding of subjectivity and contradiction, thus already illustrating the trajectory I outlined in the Introduction. In drawing attention to the passage of the feminist agenda into popular culture it also demonstrates the increasing permeability of academic boundaries and the growing importance of cultural studies. At a theoretical level therefore, if I had written this piece a decade later it would not have been very different (though after the demise of municipal socialism and the recent shift to the Right I would have had less faith in the Labour Party). I would, however, have had to address, even if tangentially, the implications of my own and other feminists' changing consciousness about the family.

During the 1970s, obsessed as we were with the inequalities of child-care and the *constraints* of family life and couple relationships, we could not have anticipated the resurgence in the late 1980s and early 1990s, both within and beyond feminism, of the positive aspects of parenting and cohabitation. For many feminists of the first wave who postponed childbearing partly as a consequence of the early critiques, this last decade – the period of their late thirties and early forties – has been an anxious time of indecision and sometimes disappointment. For those of us who already had young children in the early 1970s and struggled then to establish larger units of one kind or another in order to cope with the frustrations of child-care, the rewards of older children and extended households have been very substantial. We are mostly glad we did it when we did.

These recent developments in life cycle and popular consciousness, along with changes – however modest – in ideas about masculinity and fatherhood (Segal, 1990) and the critiques by black and Third World feminists of the narrowness of focus of the early work (Tang Nain, 1991) are issues which would have been addressed had I written this article today.

3

A GIRLS' PROJECT AND SOME REPONSES TO LESBIANISM

Part I

> It's nice to get it out into the open and talk about lesbianism to girls of our
> own age – because you just don't normally.

> These friends are really open-minded, they've made me think about things. If
> you'd have talked to me about lesbians before I started going around with this
> lot, I'd have said, 'How disgusting' and all that. But now it don't bother me.
> They're just like other people, aren't they? They should just get on with it if
> they want to.

> If I went in and told my mum I was pregnant she'd most probably thank the
> stars above her, you know, like: 'She's all right after all.'

These are some of the comments made by girls who attended a 'girls'
project' in a London youth centre in the spring of 1979. Many issues
which were of interest to the girls were raised during the course of the
project. Lesbianism was one of these, and is the one which will be focused
upon in this chapter. But it is useful first of all to present some general
information about the project, its objectives, and about the girls who
attended it.

This particular project was organized by a group of local teachers,
youth and community workers and parents (all of whom were women)
and consisted of ten evening sessions. It was designed for girls only, in
order to provide them with the opportunity for thinking about subjects
which were of special concern to them (as girls) and were rarely covered
by the school curriculum or normal youth centre activities. Films, plays
and improvisation were used to examine such topics as girls at school;
families; health; work opportunities; relationships. The sessions included
discussion and practical workshops, simple electrical and plumbing skills
were demonstrated and girls were encouraged to participate in the music
evening. Overall, the project was intended to familiarize girls with some
of the basic questions raised by feminism; but importantly it was also
intended to create a time when girls could meet on their own, develop a
sense of solidarity with each other and enjoy themselves.

Between eighty and a hundred girls came to at least one evening session.
About thirty attended on a regular basis. These ranged in age from thirteen to seventeen and came from a number of different schools; some
were middle class, others working class. At the organizing stages it was
expected that many girls would attend the project without becoming
conscious of its connection with ideas developed in the women's

movement. In fact it emerged that most of the girls were aware of the feminist orientation but were not deterred by it. All of them, to a greater or lesser extent, were already challenging conventional ideas about the sort of behaviour which is considered appropriate for girls. In interviews afterwards many girls told me that what they had valued most about the project was the discovery that other girls felt the same way about various aspects of their lives. They said their ideas had been clarified, they had found the sessions fun, made new friends (age differences between girls were considered insignificant) and learned some new skills. In addition the girls had become more sensitive to the ways in which their problems were often the same as those of adult women.

Thus there were many effects of the project, which during a short space of time had covered a broad range of issues of relevance to girls. For the purpose of this chapter I want to concentrate on the dimension of lesbianism. The subject of homosexuality was first raised in a play performed at the project, and then discussed by the girls. This session continued to have reverberations for a long time afterwards; in the interviews I discovered that not only had it made the girls think differently, but in some cases it had substantially changed their lives. This is the reason I have chosen to focus on it. I shall first sketch out the background to the relevant session of the project, and then look at what the girls themselves had to say about their responses to it.

All societies define the boundaries of acceptable behaviour for men and women; within these, certain types of behaviour are approved, others merely tolerated. In our culture, lesbianism falls outside the boundary of what constitutes tolerable behaviour for women; it is taboo. Homosexual women have been forced to conceal the fact, or alternatively, have been obliged to suffer extreme disapproval. Most have chosen to hide it. With the rise of the women's movement in the late 1960s, behaviour that was previously taken for granted was questioned. It was pointed out that there was nothing 'natural' about sex roles and the sexual division of labour (they varied from one culture to another), and that existing arrangements tended to benefit men. The 'naturalness' of sexual preferences and prohibitions was also called into question.

This is the kind of analysis which, in a very general way, underpins one of the plays shown at the project. The performance of *Is Dennis Really a Menace?* by Beryl and the Perils,[1] was the trigger for the initial discussion on homosexuality among the girls. The play is harsh, and very funny indeed. Through naive cartoon characterization and presentation, the authors/performers introduce subjects which are normally unspoken in public situations. They look in particular at the different ways boys and girls (and men and women) feel about and act out their sexuality. The play is controversial as well as funny, but the girls considered it one of the highlights of the project and enjoyed it very much. The discussion after the performance lasted well past the time the sessions usually ended.

Lisa:[2] At first the play made me a bit embarrassed, but after a while it was all right. It was acting things in front of you that made it different. When you talk about it with your mates, it's not the same.

As the discussion continued it emerged that many of the girls were made uncomfortable by a relatively small section of the play about lesbians: between jokes, a serious but fleeting (two seconds at most) kiss had occurred between two of the women. Here is part of the discussion that followed the performance:

Lisa: I'll be honest, right. The bit that really embarrassed me was the bit about homosexuality. I don't know why. It's not a subject that I talk about at home, or even with my mates. You sort of shun away from it.

Jill: Yes, you pass it by. You get to talk about everything else, but you just pass that by.

Lisa: I feel a bit of a hypocrite though sometimes. I've seen girls kissing each other on the street and that, you know, and when you talk about it with a group of mates, you think, yes, why shouldn't they, if that's the way they feel. But if you're walking along and see something like that, you sort of turn round and say, 'Ooh, isn't it horrible, how can they do it!' It makes you feel a bit of a hypocrite. You've got to have a lot of guts to say your point of view. I think every girl knows that every other girl wants to say something about homosexuality, but they all know that each one is going to be embarrassed, and they don't want to be the first to bring it up.

Not much more was said about homosexuality on that occasion. The girls continued to talk for another hour about the way in which boys are under pressure to act tough, about how some boys discussed girls in sexual terms, about relationships, fears of the dark and rape, and so on.

About three months later I talked to Ruth and Eva about the project and about that evening. Ruth was seventeen, Eva was fourteen, both their mothers are feminists so they were already familiar with some of the issues that were raised. They had very vivid memories of their responses to the play.

Ruth: That was the best session for me. The discussion was really good.

Eva: It answered a lot of questions, I don't know what they were, but it answered them. I knew that if the boys would give me half a chance, I'd relate better to them than I did before.

Ruth: It gave me a kind of strength. It was saying, 'Everyone thinks like that, you're not alone in the world.'

Their response to the lesbian content of the play was more ambivalent:

Ruth: I noticed that everyone was scared. It's not so much thinking about it in yourself, it's 'What are they thinking, the person sitting next to me, how do I react so that I don't embarrass myself?' Everyone is so aware of each other.

For boys and girls there is a constant process of checking out in order to assess the status of particular ideas and ways of behaving among their friends.

Eva talked about what she thought about the play.

> *Eva:* I must admit that when I first saw it I began to get a little defensive. I'd
> never seen anything like that before. When they talked about lesbians, I
> didn't know what I felt – I think I felt a little defensive. But when we started
> talking about it in the discussion afterwards, it was a lot better. Everyone was
> talking about it, they didn't feel so shy anymore.
>
> *Ruth:* I think it's very heavy, that play. When the woman was discussing it with
> the psychiatrist, that was really good. When the psychiatrist said, 'If you
> could take a pill to make you straight, would you take it?' And she said back
> to her 'Well if you could take a pill to make you gay, would you take it?'
> I loved that. That brought a lot about lesbians out into the open. But when
> the two started kissing, I think it was very frightening. I mean even me; I'm
> around lesbians all the time, because lots of my mum's friends are, and I see
> them kissing all the time. But those two, standing there in front of
> everybody, having people actually meant to be watching them, it was *very*
> strange . . . so if I felt like that I can imagine how the others felt . . .

For Ruth, the acting exposed aspects of her private life to the judgement
of the other girls. She felt personally threatened. But she was right to
suppose that the anxieties were greater for the others.

Lesbianism continues to be a very taboo subject, particularly the overt
defiant lesbianism represented in *Is Dennis Really a Menace?* Having it
talked about in the play made many of the girls feel uneasy, but having
it acted out, seeing two women kiss (even if ever so fleetingly) was worse
(and not comparable to moments in the play when the women performers
portrayed men, and acted out sexual situations with other women which
depicted heterosexuality and were therefore unproblematic). But the very
fact of watching the play and discussing it afterwards seemed to break
down some of the taboos and ease the situation. As Eva said, 'When it
did come out, it made me feel a lot better inside.' Tentatively the girls
were beginning to ask themselves why sexual relations between women
(and as a consequence, the exclusion of men from the sexuality of women)
should pose such problems and be such a forbidden topic. As a subject
for discussion the standing of lesbianism had shifted slightly; it had
ceased to be unmentionable.

At about the same time, I interviewed Lisa and her friends. For them
the impact of that evening at the project was far greater than it was for
Ruth and Eva. 'We talked all the way home, talk, talk, talk,' they said.
Lisa was fifteen, the group of girls she hung around with were Jo, also
fifteen; Carol, sixteen; and Maria, seventeen. There were some others in
the group who had not attended the project. All of these girls and their
families had known each other for many years, they lived on a housing
estate in part of the borough which was reputed to be a tough working-
class area. Most of the girls' evenings were spent at their local youth club,
or sitting on the wall outside it. They looked and dressed like other girls
from the working-class areas in their part of London, but in other
respects they were not so typical. This was partly because of their very
good relationship with the youth leader at the club, Jenny, who had a lot
of confidence in the girls and encouraged them to do things they would
otherwise have been unlikely to do.

Carol: Jenny doesn't act as though we're a bit thick, she talks to us as if we're people. She doesn't talk down to us. That's how she gets us to do things.

Although many of the young people who went to the youth centre were in non-academic CSE streams, Jenny had convinced them to do O-level maths and other exam subjects at the centre after school. The girls had made films and videos with her using professional equipment; she had involved them in the administration of the centre and encouraged them to sit on the Borough Youth Committee. Quite often she talked to them about feminist and socialist ideas, and it was through her that they had heard about the girls' project. Altogether Jenny was a very important influence in their lives.

Carol: It was mainly through Jenny that we thought about anything at all really. But it developed more at the project. I really liked it there, because it made everybody think more, just about the things you do every day. Everybody got talking . . .

Later Carol said:

Jenny has talked to us about feminism, but she's never really said much about lesbians.
Jo: Nobody ever does. It's just not talked about. At school in sex lessons it's always a man and a woman. . . . 'And when you go out with a boy, this'll happen and that'll happen', and things like that. What if you don't go out with a boy? What happens then?
Carol: I was just *hoping* and *hoping* it would come up at the project . . . I thought it would.

The discussion after the performance of *Is Dennis Really a Menace?* at the project, during which the subject of lesbianism had been raised very briefly and in very general terms, had enabled Carol to talk about her own feelings to her closest friends for the first time.

Carol: It was after the session that I could first tell the others about me, because I knew then what their reactions would be, a bit. I've known I was a lesbian since I was twelve or thirteen, I used to write it in my diary, but I didn't know what to do . . . I never told anybody till after the project.

The girls described the walk home on the evening when Carol told them.

Lisa: We was together when she told us, walking along . . . I was looking at her . . . because we knew Carol was before she told us.
Maria: We just sort of guessed it.
Lisa: I was thinking to myself, is Carol going to turn round and say, 'Well, so am I'?
Maria: We tried to get her to talk about it . . . . Then she told us.
Carol: They just ignored it at first, didn't make any comment on it . . . it wasn't till the next night, when we was a little bit drunk that they all started talking about it. . . . There was Maria, Lisa, Jo, Sophie, Gill, Karen . . .
Maria: That night was funny, because you see it was all so new to us, right. Because you think, ooh, lesbians, yuk, funny kind of people, homosexuals. But then, someone you've known since you were about that high and grown up with, well you think, mmmm, no, there's nothing wrong with them, there's nothing different with them, you know . . . . First it was twenty

questions: What's it like? We used to be a bit, what did she call it? Patronizing, she called us. That annoyed us first of all, but we were, when you think about it now, we were being patronizing, saying, 'We're good, we've accepted it.' Whereas we shouldn't have been like that, we should have said, 'So? So what? All right, you're gay, that's it.' We shouldn't have thought to ourselves, we're really good and that. Because we were so close we could talk about a lot of things a lot more.

The seven girls spent the evening exploring the meaning of Carol's disclosure. The next step was to decide what to do about it.

Carol: After I told all my friends, I wrote off to a sort of gay group, Parents' Enquiry, but that wasn't much good. They kept telling me there was nothing to worry about. I wasn't worried anyway really. I've never thought I was disgusting or anything like that. So then I went to Grapevine,[3] to the gay teenage group.
Jo: We had to drag you up there, didn't we?
Carol: I was so scared, I wouldn't go by myself.
Jo: The group's mixed, you meet once a week and talk.
Maria: You don't have to be gay to go there, we went along with Carol. But that one bloke gave me an awful look the other day, I don't think he liked me because I'm straight. But it's not right for him to have prejudice against me, whereas I haven't got any against him.
Carol: It was all blokes there practically.

Carol didn't feel that she and the homosexual boys had much in common.

Carol: So then I started going to the discos. I met Elaine because she put an ad in *Gay News*, just to start writing. You lot didn't know that, did you? That was the first time I bought *Gay News*. Then we met, and we liked each other sort of straight away, it was good it was. I've been going out with her for five months now, I hadn't been out with anybody before. We used to go out a lot to discos, because my mother wouldn't let Elaine in the house at all – not even for half an hour.

There are very few places where gay women can go and feel comfortable.

Carol: We really only like going to the discos because you don't have to worry about everybody looking at you and coming up to you. Even in a gay pub, it's full of blokes and weirdos sitting there staring at you. I hate it.
Jo: When Carol told us she was gay, we started going to places with her, to the gay discos.
Maria: She said to us one night, 'Why don't you come up? They're not going to jump on you.'
Lisa: To tell you the truth, honestly, when I walked in there I was shitting myself, I really was, I thought everyone was going to be staring at me. I didn't want people to think that because I went up there I was a lesbian.

But it turned out to be comfortable for women who are not lesbians too.

Maria: We used to just go up there. I got to like it. It was the atmosphere that's completely different from what you get in a straight disco – when you get the boys down that end and the girls down that end, with about three people dancing in the middle and that's it. And you sit there. And you're afraid to get up and dance by yourself in case the boys start laughing . . . This is really different. They do come on and that down there, but you don't care because that's a woman, and that's it, you could face a woman and it wouldn't bother you. I mean, if they started anything, you wouldn't be afraid to argue back.

Lisa: Whereas with a bloke, you'd think, bloody hell . . .

Maria: Because they'd always get back to you in some way or another; blokes get violent with you.

Jo: Since I've been going down there I haven't seen a single fight. Go to a disco around here and it's guaranteed there's going to be a fight that night.

Things started to change for Jo as well.

Jo: When we started to go to discos with Carol, I used to sit there and think: my God, I'm really enjoying myself, and I shouldn't be because I'm straight, I should be out there with all the boys, and that. For about two weeks my mind was really confused, I didn't know what I was going to do. Then I thought: there's only one way I'm going to find out. I can't go through life thinking: I'm straight, I'm straight, when I've got a little thing in the back of my mind saying, 'No, you're not really.' So I just tried it. And here I am, I'm still alive. [*Laughter from all the girls.*]

Lisa: And you ain't got pink spots on your face or nothing.

Jo: I caught the measles through it.

The girl Jo met at the disco was Christine whom she had first met at the project. Christine was seventeen and was on a Youth Opportunities Programme placement with a cabinetmaker. When I talked to Jo, she and Christine had been together for three months.

Jo: One night up at the disco, I met two of my teachers. I couldn't believe it. And because I'm always bunking off, they said, 'Perhaps we're going to see a bit more of you now.' At first when I saw them, I tried to hide. I said, 'Cor, look, there's my teacher', and I went straight to the toilet. I didn't think: they're here for the same reason as me, they're lesbians too. I just thought: ooh, what have I done!

It often seems to be quite difficult for girls to realize that older women have the same experiences as themselves. This is one of the ideas that the project helped to break down; it was recognized that age is not always a significant difference.

All Jo's friends, including Carol, were very surprised when Jo started going out with Christine, because she had always gone out with boys before (whereas Carol had never felt that she was heterosexual). It is possible that because lesbianism was no longer quite so taboo, Jo's expression of it was to some extent a gesture of solidarity with Carol, a confirmation of their group friendship as well as an exploration of her own sexuality. In addition it could be interpreted as a kind of resistance to the acute sexism of the local male culture.

Maria and Lisa firmly defined themselves as 'straight', but they both agreed with Jo about the boys in the neighbourhood:

The boys around here have got to be such big hard men, they really are enough to turn you off. Especially when they're all together, then they feel they've got the right to act tough.

When confronted by aspects of the boys' culture that they disliked and wanted to challenge, Maria and Lisa, as heterosexuals, were not prepared to consider the strategy of resistance that Jo had opted for. In their relationships with boys, they had to cope with quite profound contradictions; they wanted to go with them, but they had little respect for most of the ones they knew.

> *Maria: Sometimes* some of them have good ideas: when one of them actually does say something intelligent, you can't believe it.

Jenny, the youth worker, told me that in her experience, the boys rarely explored their own private lives and found it almost impossible to talk to each other about personal matters. While they were in the club, they were also less likely to discuss issues of general social and political interest than the girls.

> *Lisa:* There's one of them, he's really clever, he knows a lot. But he's National Front. I think to myself: what a fucking waste, you've got those brains, but you're stupid. All he wants is to be one of the boys, work at the post office, get someone pregnant, marry them.
> *Maria:* When we argue with them and get the better of them, they don't like it.
> *Lisa:* Sometimes they just use violence, like chuck things at us in the street.

Maria and Lisa and the other girls down at the club had often had negative and frustrating experiences with the boys. This probably contributed to the sympathy and sensitivity they were able to feel towards Jo and Carol.

Lisa talked about how many people seemed to think that if a woman was a lesbian she was going to make advances to all other women and behave in a sexually aggressive way.

> *Lisa:* I've got this teacher who said, 'Beware of lesbians, they follow you down the street.' She was talking a lot of bullshit. I mean just because someone's a lesbian, it doesn't make them a different person, right. It doesn't stop us being mates. I mean, if Jo or Carol came up to my house and I'm wearing my knickers and bra, I don't think they're going to start ripping them off or something, I don't think I've got to cover myself up.
> *Maria:* Where I work, people think like that too. They are very ignorant of the facts of being gay.
> *Lisa:* Personally, I think there's a lot less risk of a lesbian attacking you than what there is of a bloke.

But although Lisa was quite emphatic in her statements of support during her conversations with me, Jo and Carol felt that in fact she was still very ambivalent; most of the time she seemed to accept them, but sometimes she didn't. Perhaps this was because Lisa was still in the process of making up her mind about a lot of new things. She hadn't been part of the group as long as the others, and her parents were far more strict. So coming to terms with lesbianism wasn't all straightforward. It wasn't consistently easy for any of the girls down at the club to accept the changes.

> *Jo:* I went down to the club one night and said, 'I don't go out with Christine no more', and they were all so pleased: 'I knew Jo would go back out with boys again', and things like that. And I just sat there. Because really I *was*

still going out with Christine. And I told them. And they all got embarrassed and laughed it off.

Carol: That really showed what they were thinking though, because if they were so pleased that she was going back out with a bloke, that shows that they're not all that keen on her being a lesbian in the first place.

Carol's interpretation may well have been correct. Under the circumstances it's not difficult to understand why the girls down at the club reacted in the way they did: supporting Jo and Carol was not easy, it involved them in many confrontations. The hostility towards lesbianism from most people in the community was considerable. In Carol's experience men seemed particularly threatened and angered (although some were prepared to defend them, as the following incident shows).

Carol: Elaine and me went to this straight party. We'd kept separate most of the night because we didn't want to start any trouble. We were standing in the hall and Elaine put her arms around me, and we just hugged, and then we split apart. Then this man came over and said, 'Are you two lezzies?' And we said 'Yes.' And he said to me, 'I'm going to put your head through that brick wall.' A great big fat pig he was. Then this bloke leapt up and said, 'Oh, she's with me, it's all right.' But we had to go. They asked us to leave.

It is worth noting that the man who protected Carol did so by denying her lesbianism. The kind of aggression shown by the first man at the party was not uncommon.

Carol: It's nearly always blokes who come up and start taking the piss and threatening to kick your head in and that. I've never had a woman come up to me and say, 'You make me feel sick.'

Jo talked about some of the initial reactions of the boys around the club.

Jo: When some of the boys found out I was a lesbian, for two days running we had eggs on our heads. Everywhere we went it was, 'Hello, Jo, fucking dirty lezzie', things like that.

Carol: Practically every time I walked past, if I was on my own or with Elaine, they went, 'Oh there goes the lezzie.' It's only one boy now, Reg, he's the worst one, he just keeps kicking me and poking me. Not hard, but it's just so aggravating. The first time they saw me with Elaine they said, 'Oh, you're not a lesbian are you?' And I said, 'Yes.' They said, 'We don't believe you, you'll have to kiss her.' They wanted a show, so we just ignored them.

Jo: One day me and Christine was kissing at the bus stop, we didn't realize some of the boys were there. And they goes, 'Oh my God, they are!' they walked off really disgusted. Scared them off. So next time they come near us and we don't want them, all we have to do is to start kissing.

Carol: They're pathetic, they go on about cucumbers and things like that, because they can't imagine it in any other way.

Carol laughed at the boys' assumption that sex necessarily included penetration and at their ignorance of the different ways in which women experience sexual pleasure. 'Sex between women is much more equal,' she said.

In spite of the opposition they encountered, the girls no longer attempted to deny their lesbianism. The exception to this is that Jo refused to tell her mother. Jo's mother, Ann, and Carol's mother Margaret, had been best friends since their children were babies, and both had been separated from their husbands for many years. They were very upset when they discovered that Carol was gay.

> *Jo:* They took it really badly. They thought it was wrong. Carol's mum was really frantic.
> *Carol:* I told her in the end, because she half knew. She had a mad fit to begin with. She was going to take me to see a psychiatrist. She went down to the GP to get a letter, and he told her, 'It's no good taking her somewhere unless she wants to change.' But as I don't, she changed her mind. She still has the odd fit though; the first time I wanted to stay out all night, she came up and got me and battered me up in the car. She's all right now, but she doesn't talk about it. Ever since that first day when she sat down and talked to me for a while, asked me some questions, since then she's just ignored it.

Carol felt that Jo's mother, Ann, was more understanding than her own. Jo said that was because Carol wasn't Ann's daughter.

> *Carol:* Her mum was good, she was talking to me, being more kind than my mum. It was pretty amazing really. One day I was just sitting there, and she started asking me what women do when they're in bed. I never expected her to ask that, it was just because she's never known and she wanted to know. I was really stunned. It was really good, just talking about it *properly* . . . but she did say she thought once I'd slept with Elaine I'd go off it. Pathetic that was! As though I'd go off it after that. [*Laugh.*]

In the months that have passed since Carol first told her mother and started going out with Elaine, things have begun to change, people have become more accepting.

> *Carol:* I'm getting so used to being able to say it and talk about it to my friends. Practically everybody who knows me knows now. I don't have to watch what I say any more.

For a long time Jo wouldn't tell her mother, although Carol thought she should because Ann knew anyway.

> *Carol:* Jo's mum said, 'Is Jo?' I didn't know what to say because Jo doesn't want me to tell her, so I said 'No.' But Ann wouldn't go mad, I know, she told me.

But in the end Jo did talk to her mother about it, and Ann later told Jenny, the youth worker, that she had felt much closer to Jo ever since. Carol's mother isn't so upset about it any more either.

> *Carol:* She knows what we're doing when I stay out, she doesn't like it very much, but she accepts it now. I don't stay out very often. I suppose I can't expect her to let Elaine stay the night, she wouldn't let me if it was a boy, not in the house. But she does let Elaine come up in the evenings now, so we don't go out so much.

The boys down at the club are changing too.

Carol: Most of the time they're all right now, just every now and again when they get bored, they start taking the piss.

Robert was one of the boys who had thrown eggs at Jo and Christine.

Jo: When Robert was on his own he was fine really, he used to come up and say, 'Hello Jo, how are you?' But after the eggs thing, I used to look at him as if I didn't know him. That got him really annoyed, so then when he was with his gang he got even worse . . . but he's come to since. He's eighteen now, I think they must get better when they get older. The other day, me and Sophie was sitting on the wall and he came over. We just ignored him. Then he said, 'I don't go around with the others any more.' So we said 'Why not?' And he started pouring it all out. He sat there and tried to have a serious talk with us, he said he realized how silly he'd been, and if we wanted to go with girls, we should go with girls. Things like that. He said he was fed up of going round with silly little kids. Then he actually *apologized*! We couldn't get over it. We just sat there and looked happy . . . so I say hello to him now.

Jo added that she thought the other boys had quietened down now too, they all seemed to be getting used to it.

So through having the courage to persist in publicly expressing their sexual preferences (which was possible partly because of the sensitive support they had received from their friends and a few adults, and partly because of their contact with feminist ideas), Carol and Jo had in a very short space of time managed to alter the way other people in their community thought about lesbianism. It had been accommodated, transformed from being a taboo into being a relatively commonplace topic of discussion, not approved of, but tolerated.

A substantial hurdle that remained was the assertion of Carol and Jo's homosexuality in the context of work and school. Both recognized that this would be much more difficult, because they wouldn't be able to rely on long-standing friendships which could act as a foundation for the restructuring of ideas about lesbianism in the way that they had been able to do in their community. Carol had just started her first job.

Carol: I don't know what's going to happen at work. Everybody round here knows now, but I'm going to have to go through the whole thing again. It was different with that lot, because I knew them. I'll tell them at work eventually I should think, because they're bound to start asking things like, 'What did you do at the weekend?' And I'm not going to lie to them, I'm not going to make up a boyfriend or anything like that. . . . You know, in spite of everything, I've never really thought: Oh I wish I wasn't. I don't know why it's never bothered me. The way I've been brought up you'd think it would. But it just never did.

We know very little about how girls of any class are brought up, behave and think. Youth studies have confined themselves almost exclusively to boys, and clearly a lot more work is necessary. There has been almost no consideration of the specific ways in which girls are regulated, either by parents in the family or by boys in youth clubs and on the streets.[4] It is quite probable that the confidence, courage and perception shown in the face of a very difficult situation by the girls I have written about is not typical. All the same I believe that these girls represent a growing number who refuse to consent to prevailing ideas about how they ought to think and behave, not only in the field of sexuality but in relation to all areas of their lives. An examination of what is not typical is worth while not just because it is interesting in itself, but also because it helps us understand the nature and processes of what *is* typical. In this case it can, for example, lead us to challenge the claim that 'femininity' is deeply embedded in the culture and that change occurs only very slowly. The second and related point which I think emerges from the experiences of these girls is that small interventions (like youth work and girls' projects) can have quite extensive repercussions. There is a ripple effect; though exactly how this works and why it takes place at some times and not at others is difficult to know.

Before concluding I want again to emphasize that in this section I have chosen to deal with one aspect only of these repercussions. In the interviews with the girls they talked at length about their families, schools, work, boyfriends, books and their future. Finally I would like to draw attention to the general assumptions that feminist ideas have most pertinence for and impact on middle-class women. It is clear from the expressions of the working-class girls who attended the project that they have been as affected as girls from middle-class homes. As Lisa said, 'When it comes to things like this, no matter what background you come from, most of us feel the same.'

Part II

These interviews with Carol, Jo, Maria and Lisa took place in the summer of 1979; Part I of this chapter was written at the beginning of 1980 and can stand on its own as a discrete entity. Because publication was delayed, I decided two years later to return to some of the girls for further interviews, and to write Part II as a rather lengthy postscript, thus transforming the original piece of work into what is in effect a kind of longitudinal study. This has allowed me not only to document some of the changes in the lives and thoughts of the girls which have occurred over the two years, but also to re-examine certain points made in the initial article, and raise new ones.

The material in this section is based mainly on interviews with Maria and Carol, each on her own, during the summer of 1981. In the course of the interviews I showed them the article I had written and told them that I intended to write a postscript which I would also show them on completion. I have also included information gathered from conversations with Jenny which took place at different points during the interim period. In my description and analysis of these most recent events, I have attempted to maintain a continuity of approach and style; however since the intended readership is no longer the same as it was for the original article,

I have also raised certain questions at a slightly more theoretical level.

I shall start off by returning to the proposition made in Part I which was deduced from what the girls themselves said in 1979. This was that small interventions like youth work and girls' projects could have quite extensive repercussions, and that lesbianism had ceased to be taboo and had become in some ways tolerated within the community in which the girls lived. This kind of claim, in order to be fully substantiated, requires widespread interviewing and observation within the community. Since this was not possible, I decided that the most fruitful approach was to ask the girls and Jenny for their opinion on the matter. Maria's response was emphatic:

> People's views did change a lot. Everybody's views were just broadened.

She talked about how she and many of her friends could no longer take heterosexuality for granted.

> *Maria:* Since Jo and Carol, I've never thought of anybody as 'straight'. You shouldn't assume that anyone is just heterosexual.

When Maria said she was convinced that the views of all those involved had broadened as a result of the discussions and confrontations triggered by Carol's and Jo's lesbianism, she was perhaps referring principally to the people of her own age who attended the youth centre; from her account it appears that these were mainly girls, though she also made a specific reference to a boy whom she felt had changed. The overall impression that emerges is that the greatest and most painless changes took place among the girls' own (female) contemporaries. However, Maria also talked about the conversations she had had with Carol's and Jo's mothers and with the women at the local shop where she used to have a Saturday job, and told me that she felt that their opinions had altered too.

When I asked Jenny how she felt about the assertion that there had been a slight shift in attitudes among the people of the community in which the youth centre was located, she agreed, and in her answer referred mainly to the adults. She was very close to several of the mothers in the neighbourhood, among them Jo's and Carol's. Most people in the area had lived there a long time and knew each other well, and Jenny felt that in the period after Jo and Carol told people they were gay, there were a number of serious discussions about homosexuality among them. Many of the women came to terms with it, she claimed, though not always easily. On one occasion they even defended it. About a year after Carol and Jo had started have lesbian relationships, Carol's mother, Margaret, gave a birthday party for one of Carol's younger sisters and asked Jo to help out. One of the children who went to the party was the young daughter of a man named Reg who used to live on the estate and had known Jo's and Carol's families for many years. When Reg discovered, shortly after the party, that Jo had been present at it, that (as Carol put it) 'this "disgusting" lesbian had been near his daughter', he went back to Carol's house, and although Jo and Carol and their mothers tried to reason with him, he could only shout. He threatened to beat the girls up and come back with his mates to burn the house down. Jenny told me that many of the women on the estate rallied angrily to the defence of the girls over this and vowed never to talk to Reg again. She interpreted the event as evidence of Margaret's and Ann's greater tolerance towards lesbianism, and since it was Ann (Jo's mother) who told her about the incident, she was obviously in a good position to make this kind of assessment. Carol, however, was a little more sceptical: 'It's true they were great at the time, that they were really angry, but I think they were defending us more as their children than as lesbians.'

It is impossible to establish the precise nature of either Ann's or Margaret's motives on this occasion, or of their more general responses to Jo and Carol's lesbianism, because in the case of both women, their feelings about their daughters' sexuality was affected by a number of disparate factors. There certainly is evidence to indicate that Margaret has changed a great deal since her first panicky attempt to get Carol to see a psychiatrist and her initial point-blank refusal to have Elaine in the house. Margaret had been brought up as a Catholic, and the reservations she continued to have seemed a great deal to do with her anxieties about all unsanctioned expressions of sexuality. For her, homosexuality was included in this category. Carol described to me how Margaret eventually made the decision to allow Elaine to stay over in her daughter's bed.

> *Carol:* I thought she'd never do it. But one night nearly two years ago, it was my seventeenth birthday and Elaine was there, my mum said, 'Come on, I'll take you to the pub.' So we went to the pub and got really pissed, and my mum was telling Elaine all about me when I was a baby. Then I said, 'Well, Elaine's got to go now, to get her last train,' and Mum said, 'Oh, no, it's OK, she can stay, but she can't stay in your bed.' All right. But she did, we just collapsed we were so pissed. But then Mum said, 'Well OK, Elaine can stay at weekends, silly her going all the way home. But she'll have to stay in your bed and you can sleep with me.' And I said, 'OK.' It seemed reasonable enough, I just thought I'll work it up from there. But when it came to it – the first Friday – I couldn't stand it, it was worse than her going home because at least then she was twelve miles away, but being fifteen foot down the corridor, I couldn't stand it. So I said to my mum, 'I'm going in there to sleep with her.' And she said, 'If you do that, Elaine can never stay again.' So I said, 'What is it you mind?' And she said, 'Well, it's not right, is it, sex in your mother's home.' So I said, 'What did you do with Bill (the bloke she used to live with) when he used to stay? You slept with him, you didn't just cuddle him and go to sleep.' And she said, 'Ah, I knew you'd throw that back in my face.' Because she felt really guilty that she'd had a man living there. Well, then I started getting a bit bold and said, 'You just don't like sex very much, you think it should be done when you're married. But we're not going to get married, are we?' I think she didn't really like sex, because she thought it shouldn't be done in your mother's house, because it wasn't 'decent'. I kept saying, 'Why, why, why is it wrong?' And she just said, 'Well you're not supposed to, it's not decent.' And I said, 'Of course

it's decent, people do it all the time.' So we talked about it for about three hours. All night. About her attitudes to it and why I couldn't sleep there. I mean it's bloody stupid that she doesn't let my sister's boyfriend stay over either.

In the end, she just cried, and she said, 'Go on, go in there, go on, go in there,' in a really martyred tone. And I said, 'All right then Mum,' and just went in there. And after all that, Elaine was asleep! But it was really good, I'm glad that I talked to Mum like that. We were just talking for hours and hours. After that she let Elaine stay at the weekends.

Different factors influenced Jo's mother, Ann. Her feelings about her daughter's lesbianism were complicated by the fact that Jo's relationship with Christine was often unhappy.

Carol: Initially Ann was upset because Christine was a woman, but I think she would have come to terms with it in the end. But because Christine hurt Jo so much, that's what put her completely off the idea. I mean Jo was really hurt by the whole affair. It was horrible to see it and not be able to do anything about it.

It is important to point out here that Christine was not interviewed and in all likelihood would have had a quite different version of these events. In spite of this, I feel Maria's and Carol's opinions must be documented because it was clear that they considered the nature of the particular relationship to be one of the most significant developments of the past two years. Both of them had a lot to say about it.

Carol: It was incredible; before, Jo was always bubbly and lively, but for the two years she was with Christine she never made one friend, because Christine was so bloody jealous.

Maria: Christine was really messing her about with other girls. Jo found out that it wasn't all nice, she found out all the grotty bits – that women can be just as bad as blokes at times.

Carol: I think Christine was the nearest Jo could have got to a bloke, in her attitudes to women. You can't just assume that every lesbian is also a feminist, or thinks of women in any different way from how a man would. And you know, I think that Jo and I both just assumed that at the beginning.

This appears to be a harsh criticism of Christine. It must not be forgotten that Jo was prepared to engage in the relationship for two years, and that almost certainly there were positive factors in it for her to which Carol and Maria did not refer, or perhaps chose not to see. To them, as well as to Ann, it was the negative aspects that appeared paramount. They told me that at one point Jo was so miserable about Christine she took an overdose of sleeping pills and alcohol and had to go to hospital.

Maria: That drove Ann really mad. She didn't want Christine ever to come to the house. If Christine had even attempted to knock on the door Ann would have smashed her one.

It seems pretty clear that Ann's feelings about lesbianism were coloured by the particular relationship Jo was involved in. Carol insisted that Ann's hostility didn't necessarily imply hostility towards lesbianism in general. She mentioned again how moved she had been when, right at the beginning, Ann had talked to her seriously about lesbian sex; and although she wasn't convinced that at the time of the burning threats Ann and Margaret had defended Jo and herself as lesbians rather than as daughters, all the same she maintained that significant changes had taken place in the attitudes of their mothers and of other people – it was not that anybody approved, but people had become more tolerant and 'were forced to think more, mainly'.

In this respect, Carol agreed with the points about change made in Part I of this chapter and understood that these claims were quite modest. In addition both Maria and Carol told me that there was no question that the trigger for the interrogation and declaration of lesbianism among the girls in the group was the performance of *Is Dennis Really a Menace?* at the girls' project, and the discussion that followed it.

> *Carol:* God knows when I would have told them otherwise.

There is also no doubt in their minds that Jenny has had a tremendous influence on their lives. Carol said, 'It was Jenny who made us realize there were alternatives.' Jenny was both supportive and encouraging.

> *Carol:* She pushed us into going to the project in the first place.
> *Maria:* She got it into our minds that if you're a woman, don't let them look down to you. You've got your rights. I was thinking about that the other day – we really used to have some rows with people. Since we've stopped coming to the youth centre so much – because everyone has split up – our views have changed. We're not all into it as much as we used to be. It's not women, women, women, all the time. At one time I was a fanatic. Now, it's give a little and take a little. I still read *Spare Rib*, though not all the time. But on the subject of lesbianism my views haven't changed.

Thus, the girls – now young women – had (predictably) made a number of transitions in their lives since the summer of 1979. In some respects the events which had taken place two years earlier continued to have repercussions and a direct influence on the way they thought and behaved. In other respects the effects had been modified by new experiences.

Maria, Carol, Jo, Lisa and their other friends from the club were no longer as close to each other as they had been that summer.

> *Carol:* Since then we've all drifted a bit. That was the closest we ever got, it was really intense.

Both Carol and Maria said that reading through this article aroused very vivid memories in them. With hindsight Maria was able to analyse what underlay one aspect of the confusion and excitement that she and several of her friends had felt when they started to consider the idea, in response to Carol's and particularly Jo's experiences, that sexuality was not fixed.

> *Maria:* It was really confusing, because every single one of us – we didn't admit it at the time, not till months or a year later – but everyone of us had sat down and actually thought, could I ever be gay?

For some of the group the assumption that sexual preferences are immutable continues to be questioned, as can be seen from Maria's and Carol's descriptions of the general developments in their own and in Jo's and Lisa's lives over the last two years. Maria, now nineteen and the oldest of the group, had just spent two years training to be a hairdresser. She told me she had really enjoyed it, and was now looking for work. For about a year, she had been going out with a man she had met at college.

> *Maria:* We've had our rocky patches now and then. At one time I said, 'Yes, this is the bloke for me', and I lost all my ideas and interests. It was really weird, I was becoming the girl I didn't want to become. You know what I mean? Like I was looking up to him for everything, letting him decide where to go. . . . But now I'm getting my ideas back again, and I'm starting to think on my own. And I still think that there could be the possibility that one day I could have a relationship with a woman. I don't know. Just see what happens. I don't think I'd not want to have it, I'd like to experience it. But just at the minute I'm quite happy as I am.

Lisa had left school at Easter and was working in a large office.

> *Maria:* She really enjoys it, she's really good at her work. She's been going out with a bloke called Dave for about two months. If you spoke to Lisa now, I don't know what she'd say, but I think she'd say, 'Well, I'm definitely straight, and that's it', because she's getting on so well with Dave.

Jo (now seventeen) had just got a job in a restaurant. When her relationship with Christine finally ended she started going out with Mike, the boy she had been going out with when she first met Christine. A few months ago she had a miscarriage, and now she and Mike are trying for a baby again.

> *Maria:* I used to go round and talk to Jo's mum. Once she said, 'Do you think Jo will change back?' And I said, 'Well, I don't know, I don't know.' I mean Carol, she always will be gay, but with Jo I always had this strange feeling that she'd get back with Mike. When her mum first heard she was pregnant, it was another shock to her. Her mum hasn't stopped having these shocks with Jo. Every time I go over there she says, 'She's doing my brain in again.' But I think she's quite pleased.

Maria talked about the changes in Jo.

> *Maria:* It's like she's never been gay, just like she's been with him all the time. She rang me up one day to tell me. I knew she hadn't been getting on well with Christine. She rings up and goes, 'I didn't realize it then, but I realize it now, it was just a phase that I was going through.' She goes, 'I regret it now.' I said, 'Well you shouldn't regret it' . . . I think she's happy enough now.

Jo wouldn't come with Carol when we arranged to do the interview. Carol said caustically, 'Pretty obvious why she won't.' Although she didn't say so, I think that one of the reasons she was so angry with Christine for hurting Jo was because it had meant that as a consequence she had lost Jo's companionship – she felt more isolated. Carol said that she and Jo still got on well, but that they rarely saw each other any more because they went out to different places.

Carol: She sees one of my younger sisters down at the pub. The thing is that because Jo was with Christine and got so hurt, she won't even consider having a relationship with a woman again. Never. It's completely out of the question now, because of Christine. She won't even come for a drink with me somewhere where there might be gay women. She just won't. Well, she says one day when she's drunk, she might.

This clearly reluctant concession to Carol seems to indicate that although Jo now appears firmly and defensively heterosexual, she has not totally denied the significance in her life of sexual relationships and friendships with lesbians. It is also worth noting that Jo's actual relationship with Christine, which I described when I discussed her mother's response to it, was quite different from what she had anticipated it would be. My interpretation two years ago, in which I suggested that Jo's lesbianism was in some measure a resistance to the sexism of the local male culture, has turned out to be far too simple. Jo was obviously not able to jettison totally the pervasive assumptions about gender roles within relationships – about passivity and activity – any more than Christine was. In fact paradoxically Jo and Christine seemed more tied to them in the context of their lesbian relationship, at least at a visible level, than Jo appeared to be in her relationship with Mike. One could speculate that Jo's pregnancy represented cast-iron evidence of her femininity and so freed her to be less passive in other respects than she was while she was with Christine.

Maria: Being with Christine calmed Jo down. In that relationship, Christine was the more domineering one. Before, Jo would always say what she wanted to say, and she's like she used to be now.

Carol is working for a bank; she has been there two years and has been promoted, but she finds the work boring. She would like to do something more challenging, though she is not yet sure what. Her colleagues at work know that she is a lesbian and a feminist and seem accepting, and her relationship with them is quite good in spite of the fact that they have little in common. They have elected her as their Union representative because they know that she is prepared to argue for what she believes in. Carol is still going out with Elaine. It has been two and a half years now and they continue to get on very well with each other, although about a year ago they broke for about three months.

Carol: I wasn't glad at the time, but I'm glad now, because when I met Elaine . . . I met her straight away, and I often thought what would it be like to just go out on my own and meet people. It was terrible when it happened, but after a month or so, even though I was sorry not to see her, I was glad, because it gave me the opportunity to make friends of my own and not just friends of hers.

Carol talked about the effect that Jo going out with Mike again had had on her own mother.

Carol: Up until that happened my mum had thought well, right, this is the way she is, and just accepted it. But as soon as Jo started going out with Mike again, it was like, will it happen to you?

Then she added:

I'm not saying it won't, but it's not very likely in the near future anyway.

She was aware that for most of the people who know her this would come as a surprise and that compared with two years earlier it indicated a change in her feelings.

> *Carol:* I was thinking that I'd changed when I read the article. But it was early days then, wasn't it? I was preaching, I was very enthusiastic about everything. I think I'm gay now. But I'm not going to say that in twenty years time I'd never have any relationship with a man. It seems unlikely, but I'm not ruling it out. That would be rather a stupid thing to do I think.

So what other points are to be drawn from these new conversations? In this section I want to consider some methodological issues which emerge from the particular nature of my relationship with the girls and, at a more general level, from the dilemmas of feminist research. Secondly, I want to look more specifically at the way in which the impact of feminism on the girls has combined with the more general process of maturation and the influence of significant adults to produce certain effects. Finally I intend to examine some of the ways in which the new material ties in with the conclusions arrived at in the first part of this chapter.

First however, I want briefly to refer to the terminological issue which has political and theoretical ramifications. Interest in working with younger women and girls and recruiting them into the women's movement is a relatively recent phenomenon, as is theoretical interest in generational distinctions. Feminism of the early 1970s was concerned principally with women in the family and in the workplace. Although there was concern about sexist educational materials[5] and a few relatively isolated attempts were made at presenting feminist issues to adolescents,[6] it is only since the late 1970s that we have seen a general shift of concern towards younger women and girls, in the form of youth work directed specifically at girls, conferences and newsletters for workers with girls, journals set up by girls, anti-sexist programmes in schools, and so on. And it is out of this section of the movement that the problem of terminology has arisen: are females under eighteen years of age 'girls' or 'young women'? For some of the women (young and old) involved in these activities, it seems as inappropriate and derogatory to call these people 'girls' as it has been to call adult women 'girls' for those in the mainstream of the move-ment.[7] Yet, as is obvious from this chapter, it seems to me useful and indeed necessary to maintain at times a conventional distinction between adults and younger people. It is true that this form not only describes but in some measure reinforces generational differences and power relations, while simultaneously minimizing the significance of gender as a unifying principle. But the implications of doing away altogether with the conceptual categories of 'boys' and 'girls' would be I think to obscure the specificity of the social construction of youth and childhood – the distinct oppression and denial of independence to which young people are subject in all spheres. So I have retained the use of 'girls' to describe the young females in this chapter, particularly in the discussion of the periods during which they are still at school and economically dependent; though in doing so I am certainly not denying the importance, especially for political organization, of the similarity of the subordination and interests which exists between women and girls.[8]

Next I want to discuss two related methodological issues: the nature of my relationship with Carol, Jo, Maria and Lisa; and the questions raised by feminist research of this kind. My relationship with the girls was in the first instance superficial. I met them every Thursday evening over a period of ten weeks (they all attended practically every session) and chatted to them no more often than to any of the other girls, though in a sense the contact was special in that they knew I was a good friend of Jenny. When, a couple of months later, I went to interview them to find out their impressions of the project, Jo, Lisa and Maria chose to talk to me together. (Carol was not at the club that evening.) The interview, which lasted two and a half hours, was far more animated and wide ranging as well as longer than any I had had with other girls from the project; and it became clear later, as I read over the transcript of what was said on that evening, that they were working up to the point where they could tell me about this pretty momentous occurrence in their lives. I was the first adult they had confided in, and they were both excited and remarkably forthright. That summer I had one further very long interview with Jo and Carol. So our initial hours of contact were very limited, and I do not pretend in any way to have been a very significant figure in their lives. On the other hand, precisely because I was relatively remote from their everyday world, yet also one of the organizers of the project and a friend of Jenny, I was perhaps ideally placed to be the one to listen to their story. And of course I was not neutral as I listened, my position was a partisan one. Although I didn't say very much, it must have been clear that I was full of respect for their courage, for their clarity and subtlety of thought, for the support they offered to each other, and for the way in which they challenged in general what girls are supposed to do and say. It is quite possible that my response and my situation placed me into the category of supportive adult (along with Jenny) and so in some small way affected the mode in which their subsequent lives were lived out.

This phenomenon, in which the researcher affects the outcome of the research in which she is involved, is of course not unique; however it remains important to acknowledge it. Ann Oakley (1981: 58), in her article 'Interviewing women', has referred to 'the mythology of "hygienic" research with its accompanying mystification of the researcher and the researched as objective instruments of data production' and urges that this: 'be replaced by the recognition that personal involvement is more than dangerous bias – it is the condition under which people come to know each other and to admit others into their lives'.

'Intimacy', she argues, is not possible without 'reciprocity'; that is to say that the interviewing process must offer some personal satisfaction to the interviewees. This is both in order that, as feminist research, it be effective and valuable so that it facilitates the making visible of women's experiences and thus makes a contribution to the sociology of women; and, as importantly, in order that it be politically justifiable so that interviewees do not consider themselves exploited as a source of data, but on the contrary feel that the intervention has been positive in relation both to their own lives and to the lives of others in their situation.

With these criteria in mind, I want to refer to the comments made by Maria and Carol on the text of Part I. Both said they thought it accurate, really interesting, and were pleased it was going to be published. Carol was enthusiastic about the idea of writing a postscript; she said that she and her friends were amazed that anyone should consider that what they had to say was important enough to write about. On an earlier occasion Jo had said that she saw no reason to change her and her friends' names for the article (though on this I decided to override her judgement). When Maria told me how much she liked the article she added that she thought most people of her age would understand it. At the end of my last interview with her, having explained to her the hazards of this kind of research for feminists, I asked her whether she felt she had been 'used' at all.

> *Maria:* No, no, not at all. I feel sort of – you know – sort of proud in a way. I was in a really bad low all day today, I've cheered up a lot now.

I now want to examine the specific forms that the young women's ideas and behaviour have taken as a consequence of their association with feminism. Of course in this chapter I have barely referred to areas like work and politics, but in the realm of sexuality and maturation feminism has combined with a more general adolescent rebellion to produce certain kinds of outcome in the lives of these girls. Their refusal to concede to orthodox processes of sexual categorization – that is to say their refusal to accept that sexuality must be heterosexual or indeed fixed – has, it seems to me, two components. On the one hand, this refusal is linked to a generational resistance to the status of youth, which in its specifically gendered form is likely to be expressed in the arena of sexuality (rather than, say, street crime) and can include pregnancy and motherhood as a means of subverting parental and school authority. This is certainly not to suggest that all adolescent expressions of sexuality are of this kind but, rather, that the adoption of an 'adult' form of sexual behaviour is probably the most common strategy employed by girls in their confrontation with the social constraints of adolescence. But this strategy is limited by its failure to challenge the subordination of femininity; its paradoxical nature lies in the fact that it frees girls to some extent from the regulation of adults while simultaneously reinforcing their (highly probable) regulation by the boys with whom they have sexual relationships. And it is precisely this contradictory quagmire that the girls I interviewed were helped to negotiate because of their contact with feminist ideas. Through their refusal to consent to heterosexuality as the only valid form of sexual expression, they were able, as young women, to engage in *both* rebellious *and* autonomous behaviour.

But in addition, and this is the other component, because the girls' refusal to consent to orthodox processes of sexual categorization derived (in part) from an understanding of feminist principles, they were also able to make sense of Jo's unfortunate relationship with Christine; they felt that Christine was not a feminist, she behaved like most of the men they knew. Feminist principles, however, as is well known, are not uniform, and it looks as though Jo's experience with Christine was one of the events which contributed towards the shift that can be detected in the young women's attitudes over the two years. I am not suggesting that they were conscious that these moves within the spectrum of feminist politics and theory were being made. All the same I think there is evidence of a rejection of an essentialist position, which identifies all women as essentially wonderful, to one which recognizes that some women, even if they are lesbians, are not; and therefore to a position in which the social nature and fluidity of gender construction are implicitly understood. And perhaps it follows that if not all women are wonderful, some men might be. It is this phenomenon which helps to explain the most striking feature to emerge from the second round of conversations: Maria, Carol and Jo have made it clear that for them sexual preferences are not fixed; neither heterosexuality nor homosexuality are assumed.

Finally I want to return to one of the dominant themes of both Part I and Part II. After examining the content of the second round of interviews I believe that justifiable grounds continue to exist for arguing that certain changes took place as an indirect consequence of the influence and support of a feminist youth worker, and of the discussions and implicit support of women workers and other girls engendered at a girls' project which ran for ten weeks only. Although these changes, mediated by the actions of the girls, are complex and contradictory, I think they cannot be denied. To do so seems to me to be taking on board the conceptual approach adhered to by certain sectors of the Left in which the state and ideology, defined in both capitalist and patriarchal terms, are perceived as so monolithic that no inroads can be made.[9] Yet we are all aware that over the last twelve years the women's movement and the ideas that the movement has generated have had a very substantial impact. But we have grown accustomed to assuming that this impact has been confined mainly to middle-class university-educated women, that is, to those who have articulated that impact and been politically involved in the mainstream of the movement. Yet it is quite possible that participation in the movement is no indicator at all of its influence. And perhaps the description of the events in these girls' lives constitutes an exemplar of how the process operates.

Notes

1. A video of the play has been made and is available from the National Association of Youth Clubs, PO Box 1, Blackburn House, Nuneaton, Warwickshire CV11 4DS.

2. The real names of the people quoted in this chapter have been changed.

3. An advisory centre for young people in north London which deals with personal and sexual problems. For a while Grapevine's premises were being used by the Gay Teenage Group for their meetings. For further information about the group, now called Lesbian and Gay Teenage Group, contact 071 263 5932.

4. These points are expanded in Chapter 4.

5. See Northern Women's Education Study Group (1972).

6. For example, the Women's Theatre Group worked primarily in schools and youth clubs from 1974. One of their plays of that period, *My Mother Says I Never Should*, was published in Michelene Wandor (ed.) (1980).

7. An issue of *Girls Line* advertises a 'feminist drama workshop for young women aged nine to twelve'. For another interesting example of shifts in language use since the late 1960s, see *Shrew* (1970) the journal of the Women's Liberation Workshop, in which feminist demonstrators are called 'girls' by other feminists.

8. For a longer discussion of the relative significance of gender and generational distinctions, see Chapter 4.

9. For example, see Althusser's (1971) reference to the radical teacher as a kind of ineffectual hero.

A note of interest to end up with. I worked on this chapter on and off for over a year and a half and it was only as I was typing up the final clean copy that I realized that the two fictional names I had given the mothers in the story – Ann and Margaret – were virtually those of my own mother: Anna Margareta!

COMMENT

A Girls' Project and Some Responses to Lesbianism

This proved an extremely contentious article, not as might have been expected for youth service and education authorities, but among feminists and women youth workers. Here I shall give a brief account of this troubled history and draw attention to some of the political and theoretical issues at stake.

My personal involvement in the girls' project, which is described in the text, and my subsequent decision to write about it, is an example of local intellectual work. Given my domestic responsibilities and the turbulence of my life at the time, the idea of confining my research to something specific, manageable and located in my neighbourhood, yet at the same time innovative and in feminist terms worth while, was appealing. Youth work and girls seemed initially a relatively innocuous option. I could not have anticipated that writing about this area would prove so problematic.

The focus on sexuality was not part of my original design. It emerged in the course of post-project interviews with the girls concerned and subsequently became the subject of the article in response to a specific request from the editors of a book about feminist issues for girls. This aspect of the research was thus written up (as Part I of the chapter included here) and accepted for publication. At a later date, however, one of the editors had second thoughts and the piece was excluded from the collection for which it had been written. The reasons why emerged slowly and messily. Interestingly there were no criticisms of the tone or content of the piece. The issue ultimately boiled down to the fact that the editor concerned had been persuaded, in line with revolutionary feminist thought at the time and the views of a few women associated with *Working with Girls* newsletter, that only lesbians and trained youth workers with girls could be permitted to write about lesbianism and girls' work.

Despite the objections from myself and others, the decision was final, so the following year I wrote a postscript – a Part II – to the article in which I addressed some of the criticisms that had been made of the first part. The expanded version was finally published in *Feminist Review*, 10, in 1982. The correspondence which followed its publication and my reply appeared in *Feminist Review*, 13, 1983, and are printed in the following pages. The initial statement was written by the editorial collective of the journal (of which I was not yet a member).

Letters about Mica Nava's Article and Her Response

We have received a number of letters about the article by Mica Nava that we published in *Feminist Review* Number 10 last year: '"Everybody's Views Were Just Broadened": A Girls' Project and Some Responses to Lesbianism'. We are printing two of them here, together with a reply by Mica Nava. These two present the main general points of criticism that were made.

We were aware when we decided to publish the article that it had been the object of a campaign of criticism and that it was not included in the book for which the first part of it was originally written. Some of the criticisms stemmed from disputes going on among professional youth workers; others, such as the question of whether a heterosexual woman should write about lesbians or a middle-class woman write about working-class girls, were of more general concern. Nevertheless we decided to publish the article because we rejected these criticisms and felt that the article made a valuable contribution to feminist thinking.

It records a form of outgoing feminist activity that is very different from that of professional youth work but that has lessons for all sorts of women's movement projects designed to present feminist ideas to a wider circle of women. It is appropriately hesitant in its interpretation of the girls' responses, but it does demonstrate that the project – and particularly the performance of *Is Dennis Really a Menace?* by Beryl and the Perils – triggered off discussions of lesbianism among the girls, both heterosexual and lesbian, that had never happened before. It provides an insight into how this group of girls thought and talked about sex and social life and a refreshing contrast to the dominant image of girls as hapless victims of sexist culture and sexist media who retreat into a world of talk about boys and fantasies of romance. Here we have a self-selected bunch no doubt, but a bunch of girls who though subject to all sorts of pressures are nevertheless thoughtful, independent, capable of helping themselves and each other.

Those of us who are older have a right and need to read, and write, about girls. It is an important concern of the movement that so many of each generation reject women's liberation and enter into the traps of romance and marriage, deference to men and motherhood as a career. It affects us all, and for our own sakes we need to explore what can be done to change it. Our concern does not necessarily begin and end with their interests and viewpoints.

We have stated that 'we do allow heterosexual women to write about lesbians and vice versa'. This does not mean, of course, that we would publish anti-lesbian material; and we do not consider Mica Nava's article to be so. She reports some derogatory comments made about Christine, a lesbian, by some of the other girls, including another lesbian. She makes it clear that Christine would 'have had a very different version' had she been interviewed, but reports the comments because they reveal a great deal about the standards and experiences of the other girls. This is not anti-lesbianism, though it may be personally hard on Christine as an individual. Many feminists do not accept a rigid division between lesbian and non-lesbian. On our own editorial collective, at least six out of the sixteen women are full-time lesbians, but others have lesbian relationships or have done in the past. We support the right of lesbians to organize separately as lesbians, but not the right of a particular group of lesbians to dictate to the rest of the women's movement or to dictate our editorial policy. To have a political disagreement with certain lesbians is a very far cry from being anti-lesbian.

Feminist Review **Editorial Collective**

Dear Feminist Review,
You wrote recently in your editorial:

> Most of the articles in this issue of *Feminist Review* – if not all of them – are politically
> controversial. We make no apology for this, indeed we see the journal as useful in
> provoking debate among feminists on contentious issues. If you disagree with an arti-
> cle, please write and say so. The *Feminist Review* collective obviously takes respon-
> sibility for the choice of questions raised in the journal. It also takes decisions on who
> it publishes and we know some feminists disagree with those decisions (for example,
> we do not publish work by men, but we do allow heterosexual women to write about
> lesbians and vice-versa). (*Feminist Review*, No. 10)

The paragraph continues but we were brought to an angry halt by the final
phrase and write now an open letter of protest against the anti-lesbianism
expressed in your editorial policy. It is anti-lesbian because of the complete
failure to acknowledge that heterosexual women inhabit and perpetuate the
very heterosexual world which oppresses lesbians and suppresses lesbianism.
Heterosexual women are in a direct power relationship to lesbians and it is
absurd to imply as you do that there is some equivalence in the status of
lesbians and heterosexual women which makes it allowable without qualification for them to write about us.

You justify it on the grounds that some utility of the journal lies in provoking
'debate on contentious issues'. We hold that this is sidestepping the issue.
Such a policy, masquerading as radical and again without qualification, finds
cousins in the failure to act against the continuing legality of fascist groups to
operate in our communities, mythologies of academic neutrality (a quality
which is often mistaken for scholarship) and other examples of abdicated
responsibility. Yet, you state, you take 'responsibility for the choice of questions raised' and for 'who' you choose to publish. What responsibility have
you shown to the women (lesbians) who are the subjects of this editorial decision and how on earth do you propose to be responsible for what is now well
beyond your control – the interpretation by readers of a heterosexual woman's
interpretation of lesbians?

There are ways in which we can talk about each other in settings over which
we have control. Articles for public consumption are not one of those ways.
Lesbians have had to labour for some time with images of ourselves and our
experience which are romanticized, held up as a great challenge to 'capitalist
patriarchy' and otherwise sanitized by observers who have little or no
experience of what it involves to be lesbian all day, every day for the rest of
our lives in a heterosexual world. This world permits little rest from a struggle
not to be tolerated but to *be*.

To this end we insist on control over our own struggle within and without
the women's liberation movement. The autonomy we exercise is exactly
parallel to the autonomy exercised by the WLM and black movements and we
demand that you respect that autonomy by altering your editorial policy.

Birmingham Lesbian Offensive Group

Dear Feminist Review,
The Camden Girls Project disassociates itself from Mica Nava's article
'"Everybody's Views Were Just Broadened": A Girls' Project and Some
Responses to Lesbianism' (*Feminist Review*, No. 10), even though some young
women who have been and still are involved in the Project as users and
workers are discussed in the article.

There are confusions about the aims of this article which might easily be
read as confusion of the aims, activities and achievements of Girls Projects.

The writer of the article does make it clear that she is writing about a few hours interviewing with a few individuals, but at the same time appears to want to draw dubious conclusions about the links between feminism, Marxism and Girls Projects.

Mica Nava's comment 'interest in working with younger women and girls *and recruiting them into the women's movement* is a relatively recent phenomenon' implies a lot of things we would wish to take issue with. The Management Group of the Camden Girls Project would describe itself as feminist. We therefore endeavour to ensure that feminist principles and practice are fundamental to the theory and practice of our Project. We do not see these principles as being the same as standard feminist behaviour against which every young woman must be measured. We believe in creating and supporting an environment in which young women might feel free(er) to explore their own identity and lifestyle. We are *not* in the business of creating a production line, rolling out feminists or lesbians. Neither is there a structure and organization for young women to roll off a production line on to!

Mica Nava writes: 'small interventions (like youth work and girls' projects) can have quite extensive repercussions' and then in a confused fashion asks herself 'how this works and why it takes place at some times and not at others'.

Quite simply, the scale of intervention she is talking about cannot have the 'extensive repercussions' she lays claim to. While it is true that the content of *any* play, youth project, school curriculum, comic, TV programme, etc. comes from political ideology and makes political statement, it takes much more than one play or ten nights on a Girls Project for girls and young women to explore and challenge their sexuality and politics. Yet Mica Nava implies that it only took one play for the girls and young women to change their sexuality – like kids with a new toy they want to try it out. We would be guilty of ageism and classism if we thought the working-class girls and young women who are the users of our Project were that malleable.

This article is voyeuristic and dubious. *'An examination of what is not typical is worthwhile not just because it is interesting in itself . . .'* written by an unacknowledged heterosexual academic who should have acknowledged her isolation by listening to the women working on the ground rather than choosing to maintain an isolated position which has effectively obscured their work. The Camden Girls Project is for all young women in Camden and managed by heterosexual and lesbian women. We are responsible (jointly with Islington Girls Project) for management of the Young Lesbian Group, but consider it improper for heterosexual women to document this area of our work.

To say that 'Jo's' lesbianism (or any other woman's) is a 'resistance to . . . sexism' is to undervalue and deny the full content and context of lesbian relationships and to ignore the prejudice and conditioning which underlies heterosexist attitudes that measure all relationships by their own standards. Further, to later document and validate what are obviously anti-lesbian attitudes and behaviour ('they felt that Christine was not a feminist, she behaved like most of the men they know') is in itself anti-lesbian and an attempt to set standards of what is a right-on feminist. Such anti-lesbianism must raise serious doubts as to the validity of the whole article.

We know how pleased most people are to be given space of any sort in 'the media' – particularly those sections of the community who do not usually have that access, so it is not surprising that 'Maria' and 'Carol' agreed to being discussed in the article. But why wasn't 'Christine' (the other lesbian) asked? We know that few people with power (usually white, middle class, often academic, mainly heterosexual, males, but here it is a woman) are going to divest themselves of power to those sections of the community who do not have that access, rather than rip them off. Mica Nava should either have helped those young women document their experience, and the analysis of that experience, themselves, or have been much more conscientious and explicit about all the potential implications and repercussions of the article.

Lastly, we would ask Mica Nava to check her sources – the National Association of Youth Clubs do *not* organize annual conferences for women doing youth work with girls. The reference made is clearly about the Women Working With Young People conferences which are organized by feminist youth workers who, unlike Mica Nava, work co-operatively and collectively for themselves and other feminist youth workers, with support from NAYC and other organizations.

In sisterhood,

The Management Group
Camden Girls Centre Project

Dear Feminist Review,

The letter from the Management Committee of the Camden Girls Project makes similar points though in a less abusive and inventive fashion, to several I have received since 1980 when I wrote Part I of my article. For those who have read it, it may come as a surprise (as it did to me) that this piece should prove so contentious for other feminists. For those who have not and want a brief résumé: it is not a great deal more than an edited transcript of conversations with a group of girls who talk about their own responses, and those of the members of the community in which they live, to the fact that two of them become involved in lesbian relationships (though one subsequently goes back to her original boyfriend) partially as a consequence of a discussion after a play at a girls' project. In responding to the letter from the Camden Girls Project I shall consider some of their specific accusations, but I mainly want to discuss what I take to be the more important underlying assumptions.

I am not sure why the women on the management committee of the Camden Girls Project should find it necessary to disassociate themselves from my article. They had nothing to do with the girls' project I wrote about and I have had nothing to do with theirs. In my article I make no reference to the Young Lesbian Group, contrary to their claim.

The girls' project of which I wrote was organized quite independently and preceded the establishment of the Camden Girls Project by some months. Ours, which lasted for ten weeks, was set up and run by an unpaid collective of four teachers, a community relations officer, myself (on the basis of being a local parent and having been a member of the Women's Theatre Group for some years) and only one youth worker (who was not in contact with the organizers of the Camden Girls Project). The group I was involved with was consulted before I wrote up the article and then again before publication, as were the girls about whom I wrote. The project we organized adopted a similar format to the Hackney Girls Project which had taken place the year before and was as far as we knew the first of its kind. Both of these were more pedagogical in style (and the content of the sessions perhaps more overtly political) than I understand the Camden Girls Project to be. There the emphasis is on continuous personal interaction between youth workers and girls over a long-term period, and making available to girls club activities from which they have hitherto been excluded. I think it is to this difference of approach that the third paragraph in the letter refers. Although distinct, both types of project seem to me valuable in feminist terms.

The point about whether the project of which I wrote provoked a change in the lives of the young women is dealt with at length in the article and is not worth reiterating here. The accusation that writing about young working-class women necessarily entails 'ripping them off' is also dealt with in the article. If readers refer back to the article over these issues, they may at the same time like to place the phrases that have been quoted in the letter in their proper context. In this way they will be able to assess for themselves the justice of the interpretations that have been made by the authors of the letter.

The Management Group go on to accuse me of being an 'unacknowledged heterosexual'. It is true that in the article I did not consider it relevant to state my sexual preferences (if that is what the complaint is about). However the young women whom I interviewed were quite aware that I have relationships with men (as are most people who know me) and nevertheless chose to confide in me.

The next accusation levelled against me is that I am anti-lesbian. This is apparently because I report and subsequently allude to a statement made by Carol, the young lesbian in the story: 'You can't just assume that every lesbian is also a feminist.' To deduce that I am anti-lesbian because I chose not to exclude this is absurd. I would never dream of accusing the authors of the letter of being anti-women merely because they make critical comment about one women (i.e. me).

The authors of the letter go on to ask why I didn't interview Christine. There were several people who were referred to in some detail in the article and were not interviewed; probably most important among these were the girls' mothers. If I had been able to talk to them, to Christine, to the boys, there is no doubt that the story would have been more complete. It was obvious to me that Christine might have a different version of the events and I make this point quite explicitly in the article. However all accounts are bound to be selective, as well as constrained by time and money factors. My principal objective was to produce an accessible piece of writing for girls and young women (not an academic audience) which might help to open up an important and much neglected area for discussion. Unfortunately, the article was excluded from the book it was originally written for (which was aimed at a young audience) as a consequence of pressure from some of the women who are continuing to attack me.

I think that there are two important general convictions held by the authors of the letter which underlie and fuel the more specific criticisms that have been made. The first *appears* as a hostility towards academic or intellectual women. However, part time or ill paid, academic women are considered closer to men; however many classes they may teach or women's studies courses they may struggle for, their endeavour is thought less worth while than that of 'on the ground' youth workers; women researchers are accused of 'ripping off' the subjects of their research regardless of the nature of their work. The implication is that by contrast youth workers have more authentic and committed relationships with their clients. The history of the contradictory part played by state employed welfare workers is glossed over. Because of their contact with the 'real' working-class world it is felt that youth workers are able to make a greater political contribution. But not only that – and this is where the apparent anti-academicism is revealed as part of an attempt to defend and enhance professional status – it has been my experience that a few feminist youth workers feel strongly that only *trained* youth workers are properly equipped with the expertise to 'work' with girls and set up girls' projects. Thus the project I was involved with must, by definition, be inadequate because it was initiated and organized without the official sanction of those qualified youth workers in charge of overseeing work with girls. Yet this kind of attempt at professionalization contradicts certain fundamental feminist tenets. These are: first, the demystification of expertise; and secondly, the commitment of all feminists to extend the struggle by forming alliances with other women whether young or older. Thus in order to be more acceptable in feminist terms, what is actually a staking out of the professional territory of girls' work becomes transformed into a criticism of those women who it is felt are encroaching upon it. The defence is transformed into an attack. The focus of the attack in this instance seems to have become 'academic women' who are perceived as being able to offer, in writing, interpretations of work with girls (and with young lesbians) which threaten to elude the control of the authorities in the field.

The other key conviction which has motivated the attack on me is stated quite explicitly in the letter from the Birmingham Lesbian Offensive Group [BLOG] and echoed in the letter from the Camden Girls Project. This is that only lesbians can write about lesbians. In answer to this I want to point out first of all that of the six young women I interviewed, four were heterosexual and one was bisexual. Only one of the group continues to identify herself as a lesbian, and she has written a letter in which she states quite clearly that she supports the way I wrote up the story.

Furthermore the notion that only lesbians can write about lesbians assumes that sexual preferences are fixed, that differences between heterosexual and lesbian women are quite definitive and so significant that they justify the creation of divisions within the women's movement. According to those who hold this view, women must be *either* lesbian *or* heterosexual. BLOG in their letter imply that this categorization is as simple and fundamental as those which are based on biological differences between reproductive organs and skin colour – of sex and race. But this is to confuse desire with physiology, and many women in the women's liberation movement refuse to position themselves in one camp or the other. Other women may feel that the sex of the individuals they desire is likely to remain constant (whether male or female) yet do not consider this of such overriding significance in their lives that it must determine whom they make social and political alliances with. Although I do not deny for a moment that heterosexual women have many privileges in a heterosexist society, it could be argued that the differences between them and lesbian women are no greater than for example between women with children (whether lesbian or heterosexual) and women without. Childless women are, among other things, likely to be a great deal better off materially than are mothers. Yet I don't think many mothers would insist that we construct divisions within the movement on these grounds. At a time of political reaction, when the gains we have made are threatened daily, the women's liberation movement is in danger of being rent apart by internecine warfare. The sex of those we share our beds with has been elevated by some women into the single most important measure of the nature of our feminism. As an issue it has acted to obscure matters of power and dependency within couple relationships; it is also rapidly becoming the issue which might irrevocably divide and undermine the movement. Surely it is more urgent to form a united front and to direct our energies into the struggle against the world 'outside'.

Mica Nava

'A Girls' Project and Some Responses to Lesbianism' and the letters which it provoked address some of the questions about the relationship of theory to practice and about the nature of divisions within feminism of that moment which were also referred to in Chapter 1. These are not unchanging, however, and the particular conflicts described here were to be defused over the following years as youth work with girls became more commonplace and as young lesbians increased their visibility and networks of support. In this widening context single articles and small interventions assumed less importance. At the same time the moral righteousness which was so pervasive – and often so debilitating – within feminist circles in the late 1970s and early 1980s also declined somewhat.[1] The conviction that there was a single political truth and that different approaches threatened the purity of the feminist project eased a little as feminists felt less beleaguered and feminist ideas became established and popularized through teaching, magazines, TV dramas and other cultural forms. So in today's climate in which a plurality of feminisms coexist it is difficult to imagine why a relatively modest article such as this should have proved so contentious.

Interestingly, at no point in the course of the conflict about who was entitled to write about lesbianism and youth work were the interests of the potential readers of the piece taken into account. This was partly because it would have been politically inexpedient to do so, but it was also because audience as a theoretical category had not yet found a secure place on the cultural agenda. This was to change over the next decade with the growing recognition that 'a text's unity lies not in its origin but in its destination' (Barthes, 1977: 148). The piece has also dated in its use of language. This echoes a point made in the text itself (see p. 61) in which I comment on changing uses of the word 'girls'. The use in the article of the word 'homosexuality' to describe lesbianism was not considered controversial in the dispute, although today it would be because of the way it homogenizes the experiences of men and women. The fact that 'lesbian' is now the uncontested term well beyond gay and left cultural circles is evidence both of the linguistic influence of feminism and of the redrawing of lines of difference.

There is one other point I want to raise now in this return to the writing and reception of 'A Girls' Project and Some Responses to Lesbianism'. It is an admission. When I re-interviewed Carol in 1981 for Part II of the article she told me that her mother's boyfriend had sexually and physically abused her and her younger sisters. I suppressed this from the article because it seemed extraneous to my argument and because a reference to it might have appeared to give it explanatory force in relation to Carol's sexual preferences. To mention it could have had the effect of pathologizing lesbianism, and this was not something I wished to do, particularly in the context of the political confrontations I describe above. Looking through the transcript of the interview with Carol for the purpose of writing this passage in 1990 I see that we discussed the question – I asked her if the experience with her mother's boyfriend had put her off men – and she insisted quite appropriately, detecting what conclusions might be drawn from an affirmative answer, that many heterosexual women also had experiences of this kind.

So what sense should be made of this confession about omission? It is first an indication of feminist political imperatives about lesbianism current at that time. These were expressed in a poster popular among feminists which challenged prejudices about lesbians and gays by inverting them and applying them to heterosexuals: 'What exactly is HETEROSEXUALITY? . . . and what causes it?' it asked (Wakeman, 1975). To consider the possibility of specific psychic and early biological determinations was taboo because this could render lesbianism 'unnatural' and confirm mainstream misconceptions. Secondly, my omission is evidence of how embryonic was the recognition at that point of the extent and gravity of child sexual abuse. This was to emerge later. If Carol had confided to me thus a few years on I would have found it untenable to exclude some discussion of it from the article despite the contradictions that it might have raised. The moral dilemmas produced by such situations are discussed at length in Chapter 6, 'Drawing the Line'.

Finally, the omission is evidence of what is well established in cultural studies, though less accepted in sociology: the impossibility of objectivity. It confirms the intellectual movement of the last decade which I refer to in the Introduction, towards increasing scepticism about the possibility of 'truth' and 'authenticity', towards the insistence that, as Angela McRobbie put it in an article in which she discussed in general terms some of the issues raised by this particular controversy: '*Representations* are *interpretations* . . . they employ selective devices such as highlighting, editing, and inflecting . . . [which] invariably produce new permutations of meaning' (McRobbie, 1982: 51). The account of the girls' responses was of course shaped by me. The suppression of Carol's abuse from the narrative – whether this was experienced by her as traumatic and determining or not – is a poignant reminder of the constructed nature of all ethnography.

Note

1. There seems to have been a recent revival of divisions encompassing a much broader section of the population in relation to pornography; see *Feminist Review*, 34, 35 and 36 (1990).

4

YOUTH SERVICE PROVISION, SOCIAL ORDER AND THE QUESTION OF GIRLS

Mixed provision is . . . in reality predominantly male . . . but is described as mixed . . . as no one actually excludes the girls. (Camden Area Youth Committee, 1982: 7)

In this chapter I look at the development of the youth service in Britain as a form of provided leisure and at the historical marginalization of girls within this. An examination of these issues illuminates both the part played by youth work provision in the social policing of young people and the distinctive mode in which girls are regulated. I also look at the consequences of these phenomena for contemporary youth work, and draw out some of the implications of the different kinds of politics and practice embedded in feminist youth work with girls. I shall start by making some general observations about the study of youth and about the shifting and sometimes contradictory definitions, relations and location of young people.

During the last fifteen years an enormous amount of work has been done in order to refine our understanding and analysis of the social position of women, and a study of the specific attributes of girlhood has been included in this project. Over the same period, the field of youth studies has also expanded and a considerable amount of research has been done into the particularities of the situation of young people. It is by now a commonplace to point out that this second body of work has been predominantly about boys – usually white, urban, working-class boys – and that girls are rendered visible only where they are pertinent to the experience and perceptions of the boys.[1] In these studies a critical analysis of the relationship *between* boys and girls rarely appears. But much feminist work has also failed to address this terrain: it has concerned itself either with the culture and circumstances of girls only, or – as has generally been the case in sociological and psychological studies of childhood, youth and schooling – it has compared boys and girls. The different educational performances, the different positions of boys and girls as subjects in an adult world, have been contrasted. But the power relations which connect and define boys and girls as distinct categories, and which vary according to the context or discourse in which they are situated, have tended to be neglected. Yet the relationships *between* boys and girls and *between* masculinity and femininity are of considerable importance. In this chapter I draw attention to the way in which aspects of these relationships become apparent in the course of a more general examination of the provision of leisure facilities for young people.

Another common absence in the study of youth is an analysis of gender difference in the relationship of young people to adulthood. Distinctions between girlhood and adulthood and the transition from one to the other have been presumed to be the same as those between boyhood and adulthood. Youth *in relation* to adulthood has been understood as a category undivided by differences of sex, race and class, that is to say by all those differences we immediately look for *within* the categories of youth and adulthood. Yet these are issues which cannot be taken for granted. Differences of age and class may not have the same significance for women as they do for men; class, for example, has been a more significant divider of women at some historical conjunctures than at others. These are questions which again are pertinent in a study of the youth service and also have particular implications for feminist youth work with girls.

Historically youth has been an enormously variable category, and of course still is. Not only, for example, is there no agreement about which age group constitutes 'youth' (manifested in the fluctuating age of entitlement to half-fares, educational grants, marriage and the vote), over recent years young people have contradictorily been defined as the mainstay of industries such as music and fashion (both as consumers and producers) and simultaneously as in need of supervision, control and training. Dominant preoccupations and perceptions about young people are neither constant nor coherent. They shift, as do institutional definitions and the structural location of youth, in relation to other changes. Thus in a period of recession and unemployment a number of new attributes of youth are produced and exposed to scrutiny. One of the most striking of these is that young people who are unemployed or on government training schemes (and who tend to be working class) are dependent upon the income of their family of origin for an unprecedented length of time. With the raising of the school-leaving age in the early 1970s and the youth opportunity programmes and unemployment of more recent years, there has in effect been a prolongation of the period of childhood – of young people's dependency and of parental responsibility and control.[2] The decline in the material power of young people has led to a decline in their importance as consumers. Since so few jobs are available, 'adult' comportment and 'respectable' appearance become increasingly irrelevant. The possibilities of moving away from home, of travelling (even to the centre of town) recede. Not only are young people increasingly dissociated from the culture of employment and from financial resources of their own, they are confined to the local street and family culture of their schooldays.

This process of infantilization which has occurred over recent years has increased the relative importance of the informal activities and relations of the street, of leisure, the youth club and the domestic sphere.[3] These are contexts which are differently structured from those of employment, consumption and schooling, and which when examined can illuminate aspects of gender and generational relations not immediately visible in studies of the economy and education. Youth culture of the street and club is relatively unshaped and unsupervised by adults; it thus both transforms and exposes relationships within the category of youth. The current economic climate, then, when combined with the feminist critique which, as well as stressing the need to focus on girls, has always emphasized the importance of the domestic sphere, indicates also the need for a much closer examination of the activities and regulation of boys and girls within the *home*. As a subject, the domestic lives of young people has rarely been considered of significance either in studies of the family or in studies of youth. In contrast, urban street culture has featured prominently in the sociology of youth for some time now.[4] It would therefore be misleading to imply that the contemporary context of unemployment, riots and recession is alone responsible for the current focus on young people and their 'leisure' – this preoccupation has a very long history. Nevertheless present-day political circumstances both centre-stage these issues and offer new ways of looking at them; it becomes possible to postulate theoretical links between youth on the street, youth service provision, and the regulation of young people within the family. An examination of gender differences in these domains will be the project of this chapter.

The development of the youth service as a form of provided leisure

It is no longer new to draw attention to the fact that anxiety about the visible presence of youth on the streets has been not about youth in general, but about working-class male youth. Concerns expressed about dirty and unruly children during the period of rapid urbanization and social dislocation prior to the imposition of compulsory education in the nineteenth century, in which insurrection appeared a constant possibility, were mainly concerns about boys (Mayhew, 1968; Stedman Jones, 1976; Gillis, 1974; Walvin, 1982; Pearson, 1983). Late nineteenth-century and early twentieth-century attempts to regulate the leisure time and supervise the moral development of disorderly working-class youth were on the whole directed towards young males (Blanch, 1979; Gillis, 1974; Thompson, 1975). In nineteenth-century representations of youth subcultures, youth unemployment, youth as rioter, youth in opposition – in the imagery of youth as a problem – girls were usually invisible. As Blanch has said, '"youth" [is a] term with strongly masculine and delinquent connotations' (1979: 103; see also Hebdige, 1982).

The development of the present youth service and the creation of special provision for young people outside formal schooling can be interpreted largely as a response to these 'masculine and delinquent connotations' of youth. Towards the end of the nineteenth century, with the advent of compulsory education, working-class children were displaced as a problematic and disruptive genus by post-elementary-school 'youth'. Gillis (1974) has suggested that this was the period of the emergence of the social category of 'adolescence'. The period also saw the emergence and consolidation of voluntary youth organizations and clubs which acted as a complement to schooling; in addition to religious and moral guidance they offered a form of out-of-school surveillance and social policing by members of the Church and middle classes. A founder of the Working Boys' Clubs wrote in 1890 that the clubs provided 'wholesome recreation' to those who would otherwise be likely to have only 'vicious and degrading pleasures' (quoted in Simon, 1974: 70). The objectives of the Boys' Brigade were stated in 1883 to be 'The Advancement of Christ's Kingdom among Boys, the promotion of habits of Obedience, Reverence, Discipline, Self-Respect and all that tends towards a true Christian manliness' (quoted in Simon, 1974: 64). Blanch (1979) has argued that during this period coercive measures were increasingly used to suppress street subcultures and control the spare time of young people by directing them into 'provided leisure forms'. Most of these provided activities were not only moral and religious in content, they were also unquestionably militaristic, and had the aim of cultivating the *esprit de corps* considered to be lamentably lacking in the poor – that is to say, patriotism and discipline. Underlying the provision was an attempt to contain street problems and delinquency among mainly working-class boys; an additional objective however, was to combat the seditious influence of workers' social and political clubs. Youth provision was thus part of a much wider attempt to create moral and social cohesion, to win consent. Brian Simon has concluded that the youth movement initiated in the latter part of the nineteenth century was a 'reaction to the problems of a particular period, to a particular and a menacing social crisis' (1974: 71). Its aim was predominantly to 'preserve the established order in Church and State by educating the masses in manners and morals and up to political responsibility, which meant, of course, acquiescence' (McG. Eager quoted in Simon, 1974: 61). It attempted to capture and regulate boys and young men both physically and morally.

Under these circumstances youth provision in the late nineteenth century was directed towards girls only when it was considered that they lacked domestic and moral surveillance and instruction. This would arise either when they were away from home, as domestic servants, which was very frequently the case, or when their own homes were considered inadequate for the purpose, and it was felt that they required not only training but protection from the 'temptation' that their 'precocious' financial independence could expose them to (Dyhouse, 1981: 105). Girls were also singled out for special educational and youth service provision where it was felt that they could in consequence contribute to the enterprise of 'civilizing' the working class by transmitting back into their 'demoralized' and 'deficient' familial environments their newly acquired bourgeois domestic and religious values (Nava, 1984; Dyhouse, 1981). In the early part of the twentieth century, a period in which bad mothering was often held responsible for the decline of the British race and empire (Davin, 1978) the emphasis in girls' clubs was on developing the maternal skills considered so inadequate (Dyhouse, 1981; Davin, 1978; Blanch, 1979). Overall however, provision for girls was minimal compared with that for boys. For example, Blanch has estimated that in Birmingham in 1913, the number of girls attending Street Children's Union clubs amounted to only 1 per cent (1979: 117). Although there was a considerable increase in these figures subsequently, on the eve of the First World War it was still considered inappropriate for girls and women to spend their leisure time outside the confines of the domestic sphere.

Since its inception during the latter part of the nineteenth century and the early twentieth century, youth work has continued to aim at exercising some form of supervision over the leisure time of poor and working-class youth, particularly in urban areas, and at coping with oppositional culture and potential delinquency. 'In the 1920s and 1930s . . . the youth service . . . was seen as offering some defence against poverty, depression and disease, and as helping to bring some cohesion into a society whose values were widely thought to be under threat' (HMSO, 1982: 4). This is not to say that the objective of recruiting the 'deprived' has always been successful. Blanch points out that in the early part of the century, although 'the children of unskilled and semi-skilled parents were thought to be more in need' (1979: 116) it was predominantly children from the more prosperous and respectable sectors of the working and lower middle classes who attended clubs. And Pearl Jephcott (1954: 110–11) bemoaned the inability of youth organizations to attract the 'below-average' child from the 'below-average' home.[5]

In this respect the authors of the Albermarle Report (HMSO, 1960) distinguished themselves by insisting that the youth service was 'not a negative, a means of "keeping them [youth] off the streets" or "out of trouble"' (p. 35). They argued that the state should provide facilities for young people who did not benefit from the amenities available to those in full-time further and higher education – that it should in effect equalize the distribution of resources. Nevertheless, these progressive claims were backed up by drawing attention to the growing rates of delinquency – 'the crime problem is very much a youth problem' (p. 17) – and to the increase in the numbers of young people in the population, particularly male young people, because of the postwar 'bulge' and the abolition of National Service (p. 13). Thus it too envisaged the youth service as a means of combating the effects of 'disadvantage' and of coping with the entry of '200 000 young men between the ages of 18 and 20 [into] civilian life' (p. 13). In 1969 the HMSO report *Youth and Community Work in the Seventies* also presented an argument against the custodial tradition in youth work, yet all the same emphasized the need to establish contact with 'young people at risk' as well as to 'integrate immigrant adolescents'.[6]

So although wide variations exist in the style of provision available in the 1980s, from highly traditional boys' clubs and uniformed voluntary organizations[7] to informal youth and community centres, on the whole the youth service today continues to act as a non-compulsory extension of formal schooling which attempts to deal with some of the problems generated by unemployment, failure and disaffection in school, 'inadequate' homes and potential insurrection. Much of the more progressive youth provision of the last decade has been quite successful in exerting a counter-attraction to the freedom of the streets. Many young people have benefited through the provision of facilities, excursions, camps, the presence of often sympathetic adults in a less structured environment than the school, the provision of space for meeting friends away from the constraints of the family and off the streets. All of these are concrete gains. Nevertheless this kind of softer practice remains predicated on a welfarist cultural-deficit model which conceptualizes certain sectors of youth as in need of supervision, protection and 'life skills'; which, in short, tends to hang on to the notion of certain sectors of youth as a problem.

The recognition of the ways in which youth work is still directed at winning young people who would otherwise – or do – constitute a problem, points to the part youth work continues to play in the maintenance of control and consent. The massive increase in expenditure over the last few years on Youth Opportunity Programmes (YOPs) and more recently on the Youth Training Scheme (YTS) at a time of general cutbacks in the public sector serves to endorse this perspective. According to documents drawn up by the Conservative government's Central Policy Review staff in February 1981 (before the riots) and leaked to *Time Out*, YTS has among its purposes the removal of unemployed young people from the street in order to minimize the possibility of disorder and dissent. It is stated that 'The effect [of long-term unemployment upon young people] in terms of attitudes to work and opportunities for crime and other forms of social disruption is undoubtedly a matter for justifiable concern' (*Time Out*, 20–26 May 1983). Evidence in support of this proposition is contained in government plans to withdraw supplementary benefit from those young people unwilling to participate in YTS (*The Guardian*, 6 August 1983). In drawing attention to some of the considerations underlying the creation of government youth schemes I do not wish to suggest that the youth service constitutes a monolithic united apparatus which has as a sole and conscious objective, class and generational control. However it is being proposed that the youth service be made a more cohesive institution and be more tightly linked to YTS (HMSO, 1982). The Thompson Report also points out that in the last decade four private members' bills in parliament have attempted to make the youth service both more comprehensive and mandatory (HMSO, 1982: 7). Yet to suggest that youth work is only, or principally, about the policing of young people is to conceptualize it too narrowly and to fail to take account of its multiple aims, and of the diverse and sometimes conflicting politics and practice of different regions, agencies and individuals. For example the resistance of some youth workers to the constraints under which they operate, their participation in struggles to organize politically, to improve provision and to win social and political enfranchisement for youth, has been considerable and cannot be categorized in such a way. All the same, in the context of this argument it is necessary to emphasize the fundamentally regulatory and coercive features of state provision for young people in order to be able to illuminate the particular position of girls both inside and outside the youth service.

Gender differentiation in the youth service and the regulation of girls

So how do girls fit into this kind of analysis of the objectives and effects of youth service provision – or indeed into the category of youth? First of all it is necessary to emphasize the *marginality* of girls and women in today's youth service. As could perhaps be predicted, national provision for girls is far below that of boys. The Thompson Report says:

> As regards . . . young people aged 14 and over, the evidence suggests that, in terms of membership of youth groups of all kinds, the boys outnumber the girls by about 3:2, and that in terms of their participation in activities and the use of facilities, the boys are much more conspicuous than this proportion would suggest. (HMSO, 1982: 63)

An ILEA report, *Youth Service Provision for Girls* (1981) shows that girls' membership of voluntary and statutory clubs averages about one-third that of boys.[8] This does not include the 24,000 membership of the London Federation of Boys' Clubs, of which there is no girls' equivalent. The report also points to the 50 per cent decline in membership among girls over fourteen, as well as to the slight increase among boys of the same age. But, as the quote from the 1982 Thompson Report suggests, membership figures give no indication of attendance, participation in activities and use and distribution of resources. In some 'mixed' London clubs, even those with a positive policy towards girls, attendance ratios are often as low as twelve boys to one girl. Indeed, as the Camden Area Youth Committee Report *'Out of Sight'* on provision for girls suggests 'Mixed provision is the term used to describe what in reality is either predominantly male, or sometimes all male work, but is described as "mixed work or mixed provision" as no one actually excludes the girls' (1982: 7). In fact girls' access to activities and facilities is so limited in most clubs, it seems not unreasonable to speculate that a primary reason for establishing or converting to mixed clubs in the first place, was to increase their attractiveness to *boys*. As one male youth worker told me, 'the boys are so much easier to handle when there are girls present'. In terms of resources, the ILEA report calculated that some boroughs were spending an astonishing five times as much on boys as on girls (1981: 9).

More remarkable still are the 1982–3 figures for resources grants paid to registered youth organizations in Islington, an inner London borough with a reputation for being progressive. These indicate that only 2 per cent of the total amount was allocated to girls-only groups (this includes organizations such as the Girl Guides), 32 per cent went to boys-only groups, and the remaining 66 per cent was allocated to mixed groups, which as we have already seen, are predominantly male. Women as workers are also marginal in the youth service. It has been estimated that only 25 per cent of full-time paid staff are women, and that at officer level the figure declines to less than 10 per cent (HMSO, 1982). Most youth and community training courses pay little attention to the issue of work with girls (*Working with Girls*, 14, 1983: 2), and the recent Thompson Report (HMSO, 1982) while devoting a small section to work with girls, has been criticized for failing in the rest of the report 'to reflect in any substantive way the views, or specific needs of women and girls . . . the Review Group – a predominantly male group – produced a document which reflected a very male view of what the Youth Service . . . is or could be' (Janet Paraskeva Hunt, quoted in *Working with Girls*, 14, 1983: 15).

Certain questions and conclusions emerge when this evidence, about the under-representation of girls and women and the paucity of resources available for them, is combined with the analysis of the development of the youth service which was made earlier. If youth provision is indeed largely a response to the 'delinquent connotations' of 'youth', then the implication is that girls are not in need of the same kind of regulation as boys. From this it follows that nor are girls properly 'youth'. These are distinct points which will be developed separately.

Historically girls have presented far less of a street problem than boys. Delinquency figures have always been far lower than for boys. Girls are less likely to be involved in gangs and riots, and confrontations between them and the formal state apparatus of law and order occur less often. They are also less likely to be politically militant, to take part in industrial action and demonstrations.[9] As Wilmott (1966) naïvely stated on page one of his study *Adolescent Boys of East London*, 'In general girls pose less of a problem to adult society; partly for this reason, partly because resources were limited, we decided to confine the study to boys.' This association between boys as a problem and the unequal distribution of resources and attention is echoed in Jephcott (1954: 116) when she protests that girls' club activities are often jettisoned in favour of activities for boys because 'girls are less delinquent' and do not need to be kept out of trouble. It reappears in the Thompson Report's minimal coverage of discrimination against girls, and indeed in its assertion that the term 'work with girls' is misleading in that it might convey the impression that girls were a 'problem' for the youth service (HMSO, 1982: 62), a comment made without any apparent consciousness of the way it serves paradoxically to justify and confirm girls' marginality. This approach must be compared with the substantial concern shown throughout the same report about racism in Britain, and about the need to nurture multiculturalism. Since girls are not considered a problem, unlike black youth, they get less attention in the report and fewer recommendations are made to increase provision for them.

However it is not only that girls are less insurrectionary than boys, they simply do not occupy public spheres to the same extent. Girls are less of a problem on the streets because they are predominantly and more scrupulously regulated in the home. On the whole parental policing over behaviour, time, labour and sexuality of girls has not only been more efficient than over boys, it has been different. For girls, unlike for boys, the *principal* site and source for the operation of control has been the family. These are very general assertions and of course the form of this control has not been uniform. Class and cultural variations even within Britain are very substantial. But on the whole working-class girls (the sisters of the boys to whom youth provision is most often directed) spend far more time at home than their brothers, whether still at school, on the dole, at work or on a youth training scheme. Their leisure time is far more likely to be spent in their own house or their friend's (McRobbie, 1978), in contrast to the boys whose spare time is more likely to be spent in public places – in the street, the club, the local café – doing nothing (Corrigan, 1979). Working-class girls are also expected to take on a larger share of the labour and responsibility in the domestic sphere. As a detached London youth worker has observed:

> An aspect of girls' lives which was noticeable is the isolation in which some girls live and the amount of domestic chores they have to do. Many girls were only to be seen on their way home from school, on errands to the shops, in launderettes or minding younger siblings during holidays or evenings. One activity almost *all* girls do is babysitting, paid and unpaid, for friends, neighbours and relatives. It appears that for girls there are few social outlets. (ILEA, 1981: 65)

Girls' sexuality is subjected to far greater scrutiny and vigilance, and they are frequently just not allowed out, not even to youth clubs. Indeed a recent survey of girls aged fourteen to fifteen in several north London schools (ILEA, 1981: 71) showed that 16 per cent never went out in the evenings without their parents, and that 33 per cent went out only once a week. Where moral panics about girls have arisen, and social service intervention into the terrain of the familial has been considered justifiable, this has usually been (as in the nineteenth century) because parental authority over domesticity and sexuality has appeared inadequate. These claims are confirmed by Annie Hudson's research on the relationship between girls and welfare service professionals. She points out that whereas boys in trouble are likely to be referred to social services 'by the formal agents of social control (predominatly the police) the behaviour of girls is often . . . the source of consternation for families. The processes of control are more subtle, hidden and diffuse' (1983: 6).

These processes of regulation are not only in operation within the family; they also occur in schools, in clubs and on the streets. In the public and less structured context of the youth centre, the regulation of girls is largely enforced by *boys* through reference to a notion of femininity which incorporates particular modes of sexual behaviour, deference and compliance (Wood, 1984; Cowie and Lees, 1981). In this culture outside the home, girls are observers of boys' activities and boys are observers and *guardians* of girls' passivity. The ability to exercise this control does not usually reside within the individual boy. Such power is located in groups of boys (and girls) who, through reference to certain discourses and categories – like 'slag' and 'poof' – are able to ensure 'appropriate' masculine and feminine behaviour. It is therefore not only through the family, but also through the interaction of girls with boys outside it, that the femininity and thus the policing of girls is assured.

In this way we can begin to see that the lack of equal youth service provision for girls cannot merely be attributed to oversight, partiality or tradition. A substantial part of the explanation must lie in the fact that, since girls have not constituted a street problem to the extent that boys have, a need to devise informal ways of containing and supervising them has simply not arisen on the same scale.

Conflict and difference within the category of youth

This differential regulation of boys and girls inside and outside the family (reflected in differences in youth provision) is one of a range of phenomena which point to the inadequacy of the conceptualization of youth as a unitary category. As I have already said, it is not new to point to the failure of most 'youth' studies to take any account of girls. But it is not only that in examinations of 'youth' and 'children' girls are invisible or marginalized. In these studies girls are simply unproblematically subsumed under the general category that defines one group of people to another, that is to say youth to adults. This approach obscures differences within the category. Emphasis on youth as a period situated between childhood and adulthood has resulted in the neglect of gender as a *relational* concept – of power relations *between* boys and girls.[10]

To refer again to the case of youth work, it is not just that (male) administrators fail to provide equal resources for girls, or provide resources which reinforce traditional gender roles; that parents demand the presence of their daughter in the home; that most male workers (and many female workers) encourage or tolerate the subordination of girls in their clubs. It is also, very importantly, that *boys* lay claim to the territory of the club, and inhibit attempts by girls to assert their independence from them, to speak, to act, to disrupt conventional forms of femininity and masculinity. The manner in which this inhibition and control is exercised by boys over girls is quite complex. Paradoxically girls on the streets and in clubs are less likely than most boys to become victims of physical attack by (other) boys, precisely because they are *girls*, precisely in order to preserve definitions and boundaries of masculinity and femininity. These observations do not undermine the notion that power relations are structured into sexual difference, but suggest that in a public context it is not necessarily physical violence which enforces sexual dominance and control over youth club territory.[11] Of course boys often physically disturb girls' activities, physically appropriate facilities and exercise power through their ability to project the *threat* of physical assault, both over girls and women workers; and it is this kind of rough 'masculine' behaviour which effectively excludes most girls (and quite a number of boys) from youth clubs. But actual physical assault and the most violent threats experienced in the public sphere by the boys and girls I have talked to has come from within their own gender category. And because boys, in their expression of physical violence, do not transgress the boundaries of what constitutes acceptable gendered behaviour, as girls would, and are therefore violent more often, it is actually *boys* who are ironically most regularly vulnerable on the streets to attacks by other boys (and for similar reasons, to being picked up by the police). The dominance exercised by boys over girls is rooted rather in their ability to enforce the boundaries between femininity and masculinity, which in a context of violent physical engagement would be in danger of erosion. These boundaries are secured by them through harassment, through the policing of sexuality – to maintain a double standard – and through the branding of gender unorthodoxy (of activity, initiative and independence) as unfeminine and undesirable.[12]

These different forms of regulation which exist for boys and girls within the category of youth, which are lived out through their relationships with each other, have an immediacy that often structures the experience of youth quite as significantly as class does (McRobbie, 1982: 48). However it is not only that boys and girls are placed differently in relation to each other, they are also placed differently in relation to their adulthood. I would like to suggest that there are systematic differences which exist between the ways in which most males and females experience generational boundaries and the process of becoming adult. Given the present state of research this is a largely unsubstantiable claim, but one which I think is worth making in the context of this argument, since implications of political importance emerge from it. To return to the proposition, it is customary to conceptualize masculine youth as a temporal phenomenon. Manhood (defined in relation to women, to children, to labour) and its concomitant social power in this society, is significantly different from boyhood. It is marked off from it. One could speculate that the recognition by young men of the provisional nature of their subordination as youth is what prompts them to struggle against it and in this fashion to accelerate the process of their transition into adulthood. This accentuated differentiation between manhood and boyhood has a long history. It is apparent in traditional labour hierarchy (Cohen, 1982). A recurring phenomenon in many cultures, it echoes (to enter other levels of analysis and speculation) the distinctive infantile rupture between boys and mothers, the commonplace absence of fathers from the domestic domain, and may well signal a key aspect of masculinity as a problematic and ambivalent construct. The details of the distinct nature of boys' transition into manhood are beyond the scope of this discussion, but the process is certainly not unchanging and is currently being postponed and reconstituted by high rates of unemployment. (And of course one way for boys to occupy and mitigate this prolonged moment of youthful powerlessness, of joblessness, compulsory schooling and economic dependence, is to acquire practice in the relations of domination and exclusion *vis-à-vis* other groups – girls and immigrants for example.)

The situation for young women is different. Boundaries between girlhood and womanhood are far less accentuated, and the confined and permanent status of womanhood cannot be easily distinguished from girls' transient subordination as youth. The apparent inevitability of subordination is perhaps one of the factors responsible for girls' lesser propensity to resist the specific social constraints imposed upon them as young people. Where they do rebel against the confines of girlhood, this is likely to take the form of overt expression of sexuality and can include pregnancy and motherhood. In a context in which sexuality is considered appropriate for adults only, girls' expression of it amounts to a form of subversive behaviour which, unlike other forms of adolescent resistance, does not jeopardize femininity. However, as a strategy of resistance it is limited in its effectivity for precisely this reason. Although constituting a challenge to parental and school authority, it does not free girls from the regulation of boys (unless of course it is lesbian sexuality).[13] Ultimately and paradoxically, girls' most common form of rebellion serves only to bind them more tightly to their subordination as women. But on the whole girls appear less inclined than boys to struggle against their status as youth. Labouring in the home, pleasing and serving others, their girlhood merges into womanhood. This state of prolonged dependency and infantilization – of femininity – may be disturbed in early adulthood only to be recomposed at the moment of marriage. This may appear a bleak and pessimistic portrayal, and it is important not to underestimate the authority of women *within* the home, nevertheless both compared to men and because of their relations with men, most women never really acquire 'adult' status and the social power that accompanies it. Perhaps in compensation, though also because their lives more closely resemble those of the adults of their sex, girls are more likely to be awarded the social designation 'mature'.[14] This position of subordination which women and girls hold in common, and the distinctive nature of their relation to each other that results from it, suggests that generational difference does not contain the same meanings for them as it does for men and boys. These assertions remain largely speculative and a great deal of work would need to be done in order to give them proper substance. But however insubstantial they may be at this point, they seem worth making, since to question the commonsense assumption that the transition to adulthood is a process unmodified by sexual difference has political as well as theoretical consequences.

Also relevant to the discussion about girls and the youth service are those arguments which suggest that class boundaries, like generational boundaries, tend to be anomalous in the case of women. The location of women in class categories has never been a straightforward matter (Delphy, 1981) and differences between them have their own historical fluctuations which do not necessarily reflect the class position and relations of their husbands. For example, since the beginning of this century a number of factors have contributed to a diminution of difference in the experience of middle- and working-class women and girls. In the domestic sphere, the decline in the number of servants, the emphasis on the importance of mothering and household management for women of all classes (Davin, 1978) and the similarity of structural relations between women and their husbands, regardless of their standards of living, are among these.[15] The conventional focus on income differences between male 'heads' of families can obscure the social position held in common by women whose labour in the home is unremunerated. A further factor which has contributed to a levelling of difference between women of different class origins has been the rise in the rate of marriage breakdown and the concomitant increase in the number of women-headed households. Class differences in educational provision are no longer as acute as they once were, in spite of the fact that middle-class girls are still far more likely to continue to higher education. In the labour market discrimination against employed women does not operate in a predictable manner in class terms. Studies in recent years have shown that working-class women quite often have higher-status jobs than their husbands (Garnsey, 1978) (that is to say, according to the Registrar-General's classifications; however, these skilled non-manual women's jobs are not necessarily better paid) whereas middle-class women, with some exceptions, are likely to have less prestigious and less well paid jobs than the men of their class origin. They are under-represented in positions of power and responsibility, even in predominantly female areas like teaching and social work. So the work of women of all class origins tends to cluster round the low-status white-collar occupations, and here too it would be an error to assume that women were as polarized by class as men are. Heath has summed up his research on this issue in the following way: 'Womanhood is a leveller. The restrictions on women's job prospects mean that they are much less divided by their social origins than are men. Class discrimination divides men, but sexual discrimination brings women together' (1981: 135).

The politics and practice of youth work with girls

The proposition that class and generational distinctions are of less significance for women than for men has implications for youth work,[16] in that men and women youth workers are placed differently in relation to the young people that they work with. For example, the demand by women youth workers for better work conditions and opportunities for themselves is an integral part of the demand for an improvement in the general level of youth service provision for girl users. The lesser significance of class and generational difference is enhanced by the unstructured 'integrated'[17] and informal nature of the youth work context, as well as by the less 'professionalized' status of the youth worker (compared with the schoolteacher). A consequence of these particular combinations is that women and girls associated with the youth service have the potential to construct alliances and to provide for each other a degree of egalitarian support which might well not be available to men workers whose common terrain with working-class boys is far more circumscribed. Relations with boys are limited not only by the usual style of intervention employed by many male workers, but also because (whatever their origins and political affiliations) men employed in the youth service are more likely to be 'adult', 'middle class' and hold senior positions in the youth service.

These potential alliances have not always been recognized by radical women youth workers. Socialist analyses, which prioritize class, assume that class operates uniformly across gender divisions and conceptualize youth work as one form of class (and generational) control, have tended to predominate. Emphasis on class, and therefore on class and cultural *difference* have often been demoralizing and have also helped to obscure the degree of homogeneity which exists between women youth workers and working-class girls.

But over the last few years, things have started to change. An increasing number of women youth workers are organizing in order to create for themselves a stronger base, to improve both their own conditions of work and the quantity and quality of youth service provision for girls. *Working with Girls* newsletter has won permanent funding from the National Association of Youth Clubs, a step which, as the editorial points out, 'hopefully signals the recognition of work with girls and young women as a valued and validated central part of mainstream youth work' (*Working with Girls* newsletter, 15, 1983). Pressure has been put on training institutions to take the issue of work with girls more seriously, to provide more flexible conditions for 'mature' women students, and to increase the proportion of women teaching staff. The different emphases in these demands – on organization and better conditions for women workers on the one hand, and on improved provision for girls on the other – are linked and complement each other. As one worker in the Camden Report points out, 'It is . . . vital for girls to see alternative images of women, exercising authority and power in decision-making, dealing with difficult and . . . troublesome situations' (1982: 28). Although the presence of women in senior posts is no guarantee that the needs of girls will be attended to, the Camden study found that where this was the case, work with girls was indeed more likely (1982: 6). However the nature of these interventions in youth work and the political perspectives underlying them are not uniform and remain to be examined and evaluated.

The London Youth Committee Report on *Youth Service Provision for Girls* (ILEA, 1981), which was referred to earlier, is an interesting document in this respect in that it highlights some of the these different perspectives. Of course it must be remembered that the sometimes contradictory ways in which the arguments in it are couched reflect not only the general political context and the different positions of the individual authors, but also their common recognition of the need to convince the authority to increase its expenditure on facilities for girls. It is nevertheless worth looking at the theoretical differences which coexist within the report.

The perspective which predominates is liberal. It is declared that the main aims of youth work should be 'to enable each individual to fulfil his or her potential as an individual and as a member of society' (p. 5) and to provide 'choice' for girls as well as boys, both in the youth service and in the selection of adult roles.[18] In the conclusion it is stated that the main issue is one of unequal opportunities for girls; sex discrimination in the youth service is both illegal and unfair; appeals are made for a change of attitude among workers, management committees and youth officers. These kinds of statement fall into the social democratic 'equal access' tradition[19] and are fundamentally liberal in that, in spite of a relatively benevolent emphasis on choice and equal opportunities, they make no reference to the limitations of these, and slide over the existing power relations and resource distribution which underlie inequalities.

Simultaneously present in the report is a second, conservative strand, evident in that appeals for more provision are justified by referring to the ways in which girls are increasingly a *problem*:

> Because of the changing patterns in society – rising unemployment, increased crime rate among girls, the rise in the number of teenage and unsupported mothers, etc. – in the future – it will be even more important for the Youth Service to address itself to the needs of girls and young women. (p. 18)

This is one of the key statements in the concluding section and it expresses notions which, as we have seen, have recurred throughout the history of leisure provision for young people. Reference to them in this instance may have been considered an appropriate tactic in order to gain maximum resources for girls. Nevertheless, whether used with tongue in cheek or not, the insertion of such arguments into the report indicates a recognition of the appeal that ideas of this kind continue to possess, and clearly substantiates the kind of analysis which suggests that an important purpose of the youth service is to contribute to the control of young people. It is ironic that an examination of the way in which girls have been marginalized in the youth service and have on the whole not constituted a problem on the streets, is ultimately able to illuminate the way in which the youth service has operated as a regulating device for boys.

But the report also contains a third more radical perspective in which it calls for an increase in provision for girls *only*. It draws attention to the fact that 'mixed' clubs are in practice predominatly boys' clubs; that in such clubs, facilities are normally monopolized by boys and that boys frequently intimidate girls. It points to resistance from administrative levels, male workers and boys to positive discrimination and the expansion of provision for girls only. Implicit in the report are arguments which are more clearly articulated in subsequent publications (like *Working with Girls*). These suggest that separate provision enables girls to develop more independence, self-esteem and confidence; that it can provide a context for them to discuss their experiences and feelings; that it offers the opportunity to girls of acquiring expertise in activities and skills traditionally considered masculine. The report refers to a girls' project in which it is claimed that 'girls have broadened their understanding of their own situation *as girls*' (p. 57).

Sections of the report, then, clearly embody certain basic feminist principles about the need for the disruption of traditional patterns of masculinity and femininity, for 'consciousness raising', and for autonomous organization. The report thus implicitly recognizes the political and agitational potential of work with girls. This recognition marks a departure not only from traditional, hierarchically organized types of youth work, it is also to be distinguished from much socialist provision. The Labour Party of the postwar period has been criticized for not recognizing the political and agitational possibilities in education. Finn et al. (1977) have argued that the Labour Party's focus on access to secondary schooling and on opportunities was at the cost of attention to the content and form of education. In that it failed to develop a concept of socialist education it 'remained an educational *provider* for the popular classes, not an educational *agency of* and *within* them' (1977: 153). These arguments can be extended to youth service provision, and indeed Gillis has pointed out that during the 1930s the membership of the socialist youth movement in Britain was small in comparison with that of the various bourgeois organizations. 'The low overall enrolments reflected the fact that neither the Labour Party nor the powerful trade unions had taken much interest in youth mobilisations' (1974: 148). Feminism of recent years has been unique in this respect, in relation both to schooling and to youth work. One of its most significant contributions is that it has usually gone beyond the question of more provision and a broader curriculum, to a scrutiny of the content, quality and implementation of these. The kinds of change that have been demanded by feminists in the areas of knowledge, organization and participation demonstrate quite clearly a commitment to the agitational and recruiting potential of schooling and of youth work.

However, as is to be expected, views about what counts as a valid feminist intervention are not uniform. Differences of opinion and approach (which are only loosely related to the range of political positions within feminism) are not always clearly defined and their implications both for and beyond youth work are not always considered. I want to identify and draw out some of these contradictions and different styles in youth work practice with girls.

Youth work with girls only is not of course inherently feminist, as the ILEA report indicates (1981). There are large numbers of girls' church groups, friendly societies, brigades, Guides and such like, which had among their initial objectives the protection of girls from sexual contact with boys, and which continue to have the aim of preparing girls for their future roles as wives and mothers (Dyhouse, 1981: 104–14; ILEA, 1981: 46). These will not be considered here. In this section the focus will be upon the kind of provision which has developed over the past few years largely as a consequence of feminist pressure and persuasion. Although constituting a very small proportion of youth work nationally, it is all the same a sector which is expanding very rapidly and implies either an absolute increase in resources, or a reallocation of funds from boys to girls. There are various types of work with girls and girls' projects, and although differences between them are not clear-cut, it is possible all the same to distinguish three broad categories of provision. It is important to point out not only that a substantial overlap exists between categories, but also that individual feminists may well support aspects of each type. This does not obviate the need to draw attention to the differences and their implications.

First there is the type of work in which the focus is upon *access* and *interaction*. The priority here is to compensate girls for their marginalization in the youth service, to single them out, establish contact and value their interests, whatever these may be. Thus quite traditional feminine concerns like nutrition and beauty are considered appropriate by some feminists if they are popular among girls and increase their recruitment to the clubs.[20] Although activities of this kind, and some girls-only outings and camps, seem quite traditional in their apparent endorsement of femininity and domesticity, this type of provision is often defended by feminists on the grounds that what counts is to attract girls to the youth service and to provide them with resources and a context in which to develop confidence, become independent of the approval and control of boys,[21] and enhance their solidarity with other girls. The continuous and personal interaction between women youth workers and girls is an integral aspect of this process.

In the second type of provision, which occupies a centre ground between the other two, the focus goes beyond access and interaction. It includes providing a context for girls to explore and develop expertise in activities, such as motor cycling, football, music-making and pool, which are usually monopolized by boys. Since this type of provision constitutes an entrance into the domain of male activity it implies, and frequently entails, a challenge to traditional assumptions about the nature of masculinity and femininity, and thence to an understanding of gender as a social construct. However it must be kept in mind that it is not impossible to imagine an instance in which girls ride motorcycles, play football,[22] and have the run of all the facilities in a club, yet which fails to address the question of gender relations and women's subordinate status.

A systematic examination of gender relations is one of the principal objectives of the third category of provision. This type of project is likely to consist of a series of social and political education evenings which focus upon specific subjects (like employment and unemployment, sexuality and the family), include the use of resources (like film and visiting speakers) and involve girls in discussion as well as in more informal workshops and activities.[23] (In this respect they embody those principles articulated by youth service policy-makers which propose that youth work should offer not only leisure activities, but also a 'social and political education': Davies, 1981; HMSO, 1982.) Within such provision the quality of personal interaction among girls, and between girls and women workers, although important, is not as vital an aspect of the intervention. Indeed these projects rely least upon a girls-only context in order to be effective. It may very well be the case that this kind of provision in a single-sex environment proves a more productive and gratifying experience for girls; however, the focus upon content – upon knowledge and consciousness raising – means that it does not *depend* upon the exclusion of boys in order to be feminist. The characteristic which defines this type of project as feminist is not, as it is with the other two kinds, its compensatory nature (the provision of access) and its girls-only context (the quality of interaction). Instead it is the fact of understanding and challenging social inequalities based on gender.

It is essential to reiterate that these are crude delineations of the different feminist approaches to youth work. Although provision will vary in the extent to which the main emphasis is upon recruitment or upon questions of sexual politics, in reality most interventions contain aspects of each of the three models. It is, all the same, worth constructing these examples – or 'ideal types' – in order to identify some of their limitations. But first I want to draw attention to certain factors which distinguish youth work from formal education and which must be taken into consideration when evaluating the issues of access and single-sex provision. The most significant among these is the *compulsory* nature of schooling. It is this which inhibits the gross marginalization of girls from taking place in education in the way in which it does within the youth service. Obligatory attendance, and the institutionalization of the transmission of knowledge in schools, pre-empts the extreme discriminatory practices which are possible in the less structured context of youth work.[24] It is precisely the non-compulsory unstructured nature of the youth service which permits such an unequal distribution of resources and the effective exclusion of girls. But it is not only that boys monopolize facilities, that girls are uninterested in the available provision or are made to feel unwelcome; it is also that parents are able to forbid the attendance of their daughters at clubs and insist that they stay at home. The voluntary nature of youth service provision thus not only reveals discrimination against girls, paradoxically it actually produces and reinforces it. This structural difference between youth work and schooling, and the effects it has, helps to provide an explanation for the greater unanimity among women youth workers than among women teachers for separate and special provision for girls.[25]

Under the circumstances I have described it is not surprising that the question of expanding youth work access for girls (of affirmative action) should be given priority, and that feminists should argue for special and separate provision for girls in order to attract them to youth service premises and to achieve a more just distribution of resources. However it is important that these demands be kept in perspective. There is a danger that the question of access can supersede all others; that too great a focus upon it can lead (as it did in post-Second World War Labour Party policy) to a neglect of the *content* of education (whether at school or in a youth club) and of the agitational potential of *knowledge*. When the traditional activity orientation of much youth work is combined with a certain feminist celebration of experience,[26] it is not surprising that the kinds of pedagogic girls' projects which offer a systematic study of the position of women in society are a relatively infrequent phenomenon. Yet these have proved popular even with girls for whom school has ceased to provide anything of interest,[27] and to ignore this aspect of work with girls is to risk shearing it of its radical potential. Demands for a more equal distribution of youth service resources and for provision for girls only (for greater and separate access) are in themselves relatively modest. The fact that they are so vociferously – and indeed often violently – opposed, although extremely significant, must not blind us to their intrinsically liberal nature. I shall return to this point later.

There are also certain problems which arise from the feminist concentration upon single-sex provision in the youth service. Although, as is clear from what has already been written, girls-only nights and projects are often the only means of ensuring that girls get more than a merely nominal share of youth service resources, there are all the same certain dangers associated with the demand for separate provision. Implicit in the politics and practice of youth work with girls only, there is a definition of girls' needs as distinct from those of boys. One of the risks to which I refer lies therefore in the possible conceptual slippage which can occur between an analysis which perceives girls' needs and interests as different from boys' *now* (because of a range of historical and social factors) and one which asserts a more fundamental and essential difference between boys and girls and men and women. A consequence of an assertion such as the latter by feminists could be to reaffirm a separate feminine sphere within which women become confined – to confirm rather than to attenuate gender as an organizing social category.[28] Such a consolidation of gender difference is ultimately self-perpetuating in that it tends to construct masculinity not only as an attribute of all males and undesirable, but also as immutable. In addition, although a feminist approach of this kind may (inconsistently) not assume an essential femininity for girls to parallel its notion of masculinity, it does all the same serve to confirm girls as different, as in some sense victims and in need of protection.[29]

A second risk in the establishment of separate provision for girls is that girls-only nights and girls-only projects fail to challenge or to offer possibilities to boys and men, except in so far as they feel excluded by them. There is a danger that questions of gender become once again hived off, and sexual politics a matter of concern for women only. This kind of scenario could inhibit a consideration by boys of the way in which they are implicated in the perpetuation of gender difference and of the ways in which many of them are simultaneously disadvantaged by it. Masculinity and femininity as social constructs present problems for boys as well as girls. Yet the withdrawal of girls and women youth workers from mixed provision and their examination of these issues in a single-sex context relies upon a small number of committed men in the youth service to initiate discussion about sexual divisions with boys.[30] Although I consider that single-sex meetings are a vital aspect of the development of girls' confidence and consciousness, ultimately shifts in ideas and power relations can be accomplished only through dialogue and engagement *with* boys and men.

Nevertheless, it is extremely important not to minimize the political impact that work with girls only has already had. Paradoxically, it is precisely the fact of boys' exclusion and the association of girls on their own, regardless of the content of such gatherings, that has generated attention and contestation over questions of gender throughout the youth service. Opposition and resistance to separate provision for girls and to a redistribution of funding has been widespread and often very bitterly expressed, not only by boys but also by men at all levels of youth service staffing and administration. In some instances the hostility has been so intense and menacing that it has resulted in the closure of girls-only nights; this in itself has been a remarkably politicizing experience for the girls and women involved. There are numerous examples of aggression and prevarication which can be cited by women youth workers.[31] The conflict surrounding youth work with girls only is an obvious indicator of its contentiousness and of its ability to disturb existing relations, but care must be taken not to misrecognize the situation. Violent opposition to such interventions cannot *alone* be used as evidence of their radical nature and effectivity, nor can it be used to justify their existence.

We are witnessing during the present period an expansion of government expenditure on the youth sector, primarily of course on YTS, in spite of widespread cuts in most areas of the social services. This is comprehensible only when perceived as part of a broader strategy designed to cope with youth unemployment and the problem of social order. At such a time it is of course vital to ensure that girls receive their just share of new as well as existing youth service resources. Contact must be made with girls before they are swallowed up into the domestic sphere, facilities must be provided in order to attract them to clubs and to enable them to enhance their leisure time. But if youth work is ultimately to do more than cope with young people as a problem, if the object of work with girls is also to disturb existing relations between the sexes, then it will not be sufficient to focus on questions of access and on the provision of a female environment. It will not be sufficient that girls-only youth work has proved threatening to many boys and men merely as a consequence of their exclusion from it. Feminist youth work is uniquely placed to modify barriers between adults and young people and to nurture the formation of alliances between women and girls. Its unstructured and informal nature creates the ideal context in which to conduct a social and political education. If the radical potential of youth work is to be exploited, it must maintain at the forefront the question of sexual politics; and in the long term men and boys must be included in the debate.

Notes

1. In many instances girls have been completely ignored: see for example Wilmott (1966); Robins and Cohen (1978); Corrigan (1979). See also Goldthorpe's study of social mobility (1980) and Halsey et al. on educational opportunity (1980). For a critical discussion of the invisibility of girls in youth studies, with particular reference to Willis (1977) and Hebdige (1979), see McRobbie (1980).

2. Studies of the new government training schemes have on the whole failed to examine the impact that these are having upon family organization and budgeting.

3. Attention has been drawn to this by Simon Frith (1981).

4. Since the work of the Chicago School in the early part of this century. More contemporary examples include Willis (1977) and Hall and Jefferson (1976).

5. She goes on to describe these children as 'scruffily dressed', the 'mental dullards', the 'emotionally unstable', the 'undisciplined' and 'semi-criminal' who, she says, come from 'insecure' and 'cheerless' homes where no one bothers to do anything with any regularity (Jephcott, 1954: 110–1). It comes as a surprise to note that sexual precocity and immorality are not included among her colourful epithets.

6. However, in a more recent government report on the youth service (HMSO, 1982: 60–1), 'cultural diversity' and 'the needs of the community' are given greater weight than 'integration' most probably as a result of pressure from ethnic minority organizations.

7. Large numbers continue to exist and were described by John Cunningham in *The Guardian* (27 Oct. 1980) as still representing 'a big old-fashioned chunk of Victorian missionary zeal, based on Christian ethics and wholesome pursuits'; they claim today to 'offer sound leadership, a disciplined atmosphere' and are 'very much against the more trendy places'.

8. This was also the case in the early 1950s (Jephcott, 1954).

9. The recent peace movement is an honourable exception.

10. The sociology of education has of course recognized gender *differences* and the way in which these are reinforced by schooling, but has not usually focused on power relations between boys and girls, though see Shaw (1980). Julian Wood (1984) is an exception among male commentators in that both gender and power are central concerns in his study.

11. The domestic context is a different matter, as are romantic sexual relations; both are frequently considered a legitimate arena for inter-gender violence.

12. For graphic accounts of this process, see again Julian Wood (1984).

13. For a further discussion of these issues, see Chapter 3.

14. Single mothers, although usually materially the least well off, are likely to be the exception here. Responsible for themselves and for their children, they are perhaps the most 'adult'.

15. These points are made and developed in Christine Delphy and Diana Leonard's paper 'The family as an economic system' (1980).

16. A number of youth workers have told me that girls' nights are more likely to be racially mixed than 'mixed' nights. It is possible that women in Britain are also, on the whole, less divided by race than men are.

17. Basil Bernstein in his chapter 'On the classification and framing of educational knowledge' suggests that a shift from collection to integration codes in schooling is likely to weaken the 'boundary between staff, especially junior staff and students/pupils . . . and may well bring about a disturbance in the structure and distribution of power . . . and in existing educational identities . . . . It involves a change in what counts as . . . knowledge' (1977: 104). This is of particular interest here because, although not specified by Bernstein, junior staff are of course most likely to be women.

18. The work of Eileen Byrne is quoted in the report in this context. For a discussion of the limitations of her liberal analysis, see Nava (1980).

19. Exemplified by postwar Labour policy which argued for 'equal opportunity' both as a principle of social justice and in order to avoid 'human wastage', but tended to overlook fundamental inequalities of condition. This dualism in Labour Party policy, and its commitment to gradualism, are discussed in Finn et al. (1977).

20. See for example the activities included in the Cheshire and Wirral Federation of Youth Clubs Girls Work Project, reported in *Working with Girls* newsletter, 14 (1983).

21. A male youth worker with obvious reservations about girls-only work made the following astonishing comment to the author of the Camden Report (1982: 30), 'I am not happy at the idea of encouraging girls to see themselves capable of enjoying their leisure without being dependent on boys.'

22. Football is a popular sport among women in Mexico.

23. There is a more detailed description of one of these in Chapter 3. The Mode III CSE Women's Studies Course at Starcross School, described in *Schools Council Sex Role Differentiation Newsletter 3* in some respects also fits into this category.

24. The introduction of an obligatory core curriculum in schools, although apparently reducing choice, actually increases the likelihood of girls receiving the same education as their brothers.

25. Although there are differences between socialist and radical feminists over the issue of separate provision, this alone cannot explain why in ILEA (for example) a number of teachers, parents and girls are demanding *mixed* PE and games in schools at precisely the same moment that their counterparts in the youth service are demanding *separate* facilities, which, given the non-compulsory nature of the youth service, appears to be the only way of ensuring that girls get any sport at all. The defence of single-sex schooling for girls has been most persuasively put by Shaw (1980), but research by Bone (1983) indicates that such a defence cannot be made on academic grounds.

26. This sometimes goes hand in hand with an anti-intellectualism – a denial of the power and usefulness of analysis and research to the feminist project. For a discussion of this see McRobbie (1982). These issues are also raised in the correspondence published in *Feminist Review*, 13 (1983). See Chapter 3.

27. This was the case with Jo at the girls' project described in Chapter 3.

28. There are many instances of such occurrences in the past. Delamont (1978a) has identified two kinds of feminist educationalist in the nineteenth century, the 'separatists' and the 'uncompromising'. The 'separatists' argued for a serious education for girls composed of a curriculum which although demanding should suit their needs as future wives and mothers. The 'uncompromising', on the other hand, insisted that girls have exactly the same school curriculum, however inappropriate, since anything else could be construed as pandering to a softer, inferior intellect, and could be used as justification for the continued exclusion of women from other spheres. Similarly in the early part of the twentieth century, the focus on motherhood, and the new ideologies surrounding it, were on the one hand to benefit women (through the improvement of welfare services) and, on the other, to confine them within the domestic sphere, to define yet again the boundaries between men and women, between masculinity and femininity.

29. Differences within feminism on this matter are discussed in Gordon and Dubois (1983) and in Chapter 6 of the present volume.

30. This is being done with growing frequency. See for example Smith and Taylor (1983). Men and women staff at Hackney Downs Boys School (ILEA) have designed a course for junior boys entitled 'Skills for Living' of which a central component is the interrogation of sexism. See also p. 23 of the Camden Report (1982).

31. There are several instances of this in the Camden Report (1982) and *Working with Girls* newsletter. For example a male youth worker reports that 'Due to harassment by the boys during the girls' night provision, damage to premises was caused, so the whole thing was stopped' (Camden Report, 1982: 29). The report also shows evidence of resistance from male workers. Another instance of opposition is the resignation in 1980 of the chairman of the London Youth Committee from the working party on provision for girls because he considered their report (ILEA, 1981) insufficiently moderate. In addition, requests to area youth committees for the funding of work with girls are regularly subjected to more rigorous scrutiny, in spite of the fact that they are almost invariably for smaller sums, than similar requests from traditional boys-only organizations.

COMMENT

Youth Service Provision, Social Order and the Question of Girls

In the autumn of 1980 I was invited to be one of the editors of a special issue of the journal *Schooling and Culture* on youth and community (no. 9, 1981). The first version of the chapter included here was written for this special issue. Cumbersomely entitled '"Girls aren't really a problem . . ." So if "youth" is not a unitary category what are the implications for youth work?' it was designed to address theoretical questions that the editorial group considered had been neglected in most of the commissioned contributions. These included not only the marginality of girls in youth work but also the consequences of this for our understanding of the part played by the youth service in the policing of boys. The production of this piece was thus prompted in the first instance by a sense of engagement in a collective political project. It was expanded over the following years as I did more research, into the less schematic more historicized version included here.

The pattern of using a sense of obligation to a group in order to produce, and deadlines set by others as an incentive to complete, is not uncommon, particularly within feminism, and has over the years generated much interesting work. Yet when I look back at my own history, my responsiveness to the requests of others and justification in terms of a larger political purpose, although sometimes productive, must also be seen as a pretty abject form of cultural nervousness. This was not the whole story however, since the nervousness coexisted contradictorily with a boldness and provocativeness in the texts themselves. Once licensed to write by these invitations I enjoyed being challenging and contrary. The fears were, all the same, deeply rooted, even if uneven in their expression, and are I think associated with my early sense of marginality, un-Englishness and femininity, as I pointed out in the Introduction (Chapter 1).

'Youth Service Provision, Social Order and the Question of Girls' was a piece of writing that I was working on at the time Part I of the lesbian girls article was being excluded from the book for which it was written. Although engaging again with the politics of feminist youth work, it does so from the relative safety of a more analytical and historical perspective. The final section of the chapter in which I discuss the agitational potential of knowledge and evaluate quite critically different practices in feminist youth work, was written much later when I was feeling braver and ready once more to write 'against'. It not only draws attention to the political limitations of certain types of girls' work, and in this respect develops some of the points already made in embryonic form in my reply to the letters in *Feminist Review* 13, it also places these in broader context by making comparisons with the postwar Labour Party's failure to recognize that the expansion of access would not alone transform political consciousness.

My point about the radical potential of knowledge and the limitations of equal access policies are probably more pertinent today than they were a decade ago. If we look at the kind of youth work with girls which has survived the 1980s, it seems to fall most often into the first category of provision that I describe, the kind that focuses on interaction in a girls-only context. As Clara Connolly, commenting on developments in the last ten years, has recently put it: 'girls' nights . . . succumbed to the closet charms of the "bedsit". Teenagers . . . made cakes, did each others' nails and hair, and learned to inhale a cigarette . . . These sessions were justified in feminist terms by referring to the "fostering of female culture"' (1990: 58).

Connolly traces the connections between separatist provision of this kind, which is nevertheless diluted in feminist terms, and more recent developments in multicultural youth work with girls. In the latter, the fostering of cultural – and therefore sometimes religious – 'identity' is privileged at the cost of both feminist principles and a more political analysis of racism and fundamentalism. Connolly raises the same kinds of theoretical and political questions about youth work as I do in my chapter, but in her case they are focused on race and cultural difference. It is interesting to note that over the past decade multicultural provision has expanded and gained in importance while youth work provision for girls only has declined (Connolly, 1990). It looks as though girls may not have been very attracted by the 'female culture' on offer. Or perhaps funding authorities have discovered yet again that girls are not much of a problem.

When I look back at this chapter and reflect on the context of its writing and why I thought what I thought, I am aware of the more general features of my life, of convictions and experiences, which influenced in complex and not such complex ways the political positions I developed or defended. There are several which spring to my attention now as pertinent in relation to this piece of work. In my argument for the agitational potential of knowledge I suspect I drew on the experience, recounted in Chapter 1, of the transformative impact on my political outlook of Rochelle Wortis' critique of John Bowlby. My insistence on including men and boys in the debate – amazingly a rather contentious position within feminism at that time – reflected not only my consistently held position about the need for feminism to face outwards, but also my heterosexuality and the fact that I was then the mother of three teenage sons. Finally my resistance to all-girl environments may well have been a consequence of my persecution at the girls boarding-school which I referred to in the Introduction, though I was not aware of this at the time.

These factors operated also at a more formal theoretical level. For a while during the late 1970s and early 1980s I had wrestled, alongside many other feminists, with the debates about the relationship between capitalism and patriarchy,[1] and had been tempted by the simplicity of the concept of patriarchy as a new metanarrative or construct with its own clearly defined principles and operations within which men and women were distinct and often warring categories. Although the logic of this conceptualization did not necessarily lead to separatism – it implied as easily a politics of contestation and hence the occasional victory, as I argued at the time[2] – nevertheless, as totalizing theories must do, it obliterated ambiguity and simplified questions which did not fit neatly within its overarching structure. As time progressed therefore, I drew on the notion of patriarchy less and less. Apart from the fact that the unruly elements of my experience could not be easily compressed into such a schema, I was also aware of the more general intellectual movement towards specificity and contradiction and of the limitations of a universalizing concept like patriarchy for theoretical work. This was despite its polemical usefulness. 'Youth Service Provision, Social Order and the Question of Girls' reflects this moment of transition. Theoretical attempts to categorize and generalize are overlaid in this piece by more nuanced qualifying historical detail and textual analysis in which contradiction and incoherence are emphasized. This is part of the longer intellectual movement from certainty to uncertainty that I describe in the Introduction.

Notes

1. See Chapter 1 for a detailed review of the debate and a bibliography. See also Nava (1980).
2. For a fuller version of my analysis of separatism see Mica Nava, 'Feminism, culture and the intellectual process', Section I. PhD dissertation, University of London, 1990.

5

THE URBAN, THE DOMESTIC AND EDUCATION FOR GIRLS

The process of urbanization in Britain during the nineteenth century which accompanied the development of capitalism can be related to a particular crystallization of social divisions, not only between classes but also between men and women and between adults and children. In this chapter I want to look at some of the changes that took place during this period, and at their impact on the development of education for girls. My approach will be to isolate the broader outlines of certain phenomena and contradictions which can help illuminate specific educational outcomes and their connection to the city, rather than to trace the fine detail of the history. In doing so I shall draw on historical narratives which have hitherto remained relatively discrete. My object will be to try and knit these together in order to create a more comprehensive picture of the city and what it represented for women of different classes.

A number of writers have pointed out that in the earlier part of the nineteenth century working-class boys and girls had a broadly similar experience of schooling, with a curriculum that was only slightly differentiated (Silver and Silver, 1974; Delamont, 1978b; Marks, 1976). Both boys and girls received on the whole only a rudimentary education appropriate to their station in life, in schools in which the emphasis was overwhelmingly upon inurement into habits of obedience. Girls in addition often received some instruction in needlework. This relative parity between the sexes was in marked contrast to the educational experience of children from the wealthier classes. The predominant pattern among the upper middle class was for girls to be instructed by governesses in their own homes in a limited range of feminine accomplishments designed to enhance their marriageability, while their brothers received a far more rigorous education in schools staffed by university-educated masters. However, by the end of the nineteenth century middle-class women had in many instances won for themselves a secondary and university education in which the curriculum was identical to that provided for the men of their class (Delamont, 1978b), whereas for children of the working class, the curriculum had become increasingly differentiated. By the turn of the century the schoolday of working-class girls was heavily weighted with lessons in housewifery, cooking, laundrywork, needlework and childcare while their brothers' was occupied with the study of maths, science, drawing and 'manual' work (David, 1980).

This transformation in the curriculum for girls was not internal to education and can only be understood through an examination of the

wider social context in which the process of urbanization plays a crucial
part. A number of factors were to combine in the latter part of the nineteenth century which resulted in the consolidation and institutionalization
of this emphasis on the domestic in the curriculum of working-class girls;
some of the *same* factors simultaneously contributed to an expansion of
opportunities and a slight erosion, or a redrawing, of the hitherto sharp
divisions between the public and private spheres for the daughters of
bourgeois and professional families. This contradiction not only indicates
that there was no simple pattern of progress in the education of girls, it
also reveals a degree of interrelationship between the advances made by
middle-class women and the domestication of the poor. These advances
were not, however, to be wholly maintained: the early twentieth century
saw certain setbacks in the education of middle-class women which can
again be linked with phenomena associated with the city.

The urban and the domestic as symbols

During the nineteenth century enormous changes were wrought upon the
geographical and social map of Britain as a consequence of rural dislocation, and the expansion of industrial capitalism and urban trade. Not least
among the changes of the nineteenth century was the massive increase in
population which, in England and Wales, rose from 9 million in 1801 to
32 million by 1901. The population of the County of London grew from
less than 1 million at the beginning of the century to about 5 by the end
(Sennett, 1977). The proportion of rural to urban dwellers also changed
quite dramatically, so the increase in London's population was indicative
not only of the overall expansion but also of migration from the country
to the city. By the end of the century 75 per cent of England's population
lived in cities, and the proportion aged under fourteen was between 30
and 40 per cent (Walvin, 1982).[1] Although northern industrial cities also
grew very rapidly, by the middle of the century it was London in
particular that had come to epitomize the urban 'problem'. London, more
than any other city, was characterized by a geographical separation of
classes, an erosion of traditional rural relations of deference and pater-
nalism, great poverty, insanitary and overcrowded housing, and an enormous under-class or 'residuum' of casual workers, depicted as the morally
dissolute and criminal, who threatened to disrupt the social order (Stedman Jones, 1976).

The early nineteenth century also saw considerable change in the
organization of domestic life. The increasing (though uneven) separation
of the workplace from the home affected both the working and the
middle classes. The widescale involvement of working-class women and
children in paid labour outside the home called into question the forms
of paternal authority which had characterized eighteenth-century family
life in an economy based largely on domestic production. The absence of
large numbers of working-class women from the home was also to bring

to the foreground in an unparalleled fashion issues of housekeeping. For the expanding bourgeoisie, the separation of the home from the place of work was to contribute to the gradual ascendance of a new ideal of family life in which the public and private spheres were clearly demarcated and men and women had their proper and naturally ordained place. The notions of separate spheres for men and women and of the moral influence of the home were promoted principally at the turn of the eighteenth century by Evangelicals who feared the influence of popular radicalism and the early stirrings of feminism (Hall, 1979). Yet by the second half of the nineteenth century these particular bourgeois Christian moralist ideas about what constituted appropriate behaviour for men and women had become so firmly established that the employment of women outside the domestic sphere, even those of the working class, was frequently considered unnatural, immoral and deleterious not only to their families but to the whole of society. A woman's place was increasingly perceived as a crucial aspect of the nineteenth-century social crisis.

It is clear that in this context both the 'urban' and the 'domestic' took on an unprecedented symbolic resonance, particularly among the middle classes. As concepts they grew to possess meanings which transcended the complexity of regional, historical and class variation, and took no account of the pervasiveness of poverty and unrest in rural areas and of exploitation and conflict within the family. In this process the urban and the domestic became symbolic classifications of opposition and exclusion which attempted to impose a moral and cognitive order on a rapidly changing, volatile and incomprehensible world. As Mary Douglas has pointed out, 'It is only by exaggerating the difference between within and without, above and below, male and female, with and against, that a semblance of order is created' (1966: 4). The city in this schema represented chaos and pollution; the familial, harmony and purity.

Many authors have pointed to these symbolic associations, to the fact that 'the image of the human condition within urban and industrial capitalism . . . was [of] social dissolution in the very process of aggregation' (Williams, 1975: 260). Raymond Williams points out also that during this period it was commonplace to identify the city 'as a source of social danger: from the loss of customary human feelings to the building up of a massive, irrational explosive force' (1975: 261). For the poor, cities were grossly overcrowded and insanitary. Yet within the dominant nineteenth-century conceptual framework, these structural aspects of the urban condition were transformed into issues of individual will: the problem of the city was perceived as *moral*. 'The evil to be combatted was not poverty, but pauperism . . . with its attendant vices' (Stedman Jones, 1976: 11). London in particular came to exemplify the problem of the pauper without bonds to the social order. 'The category of pauper functioned as a metaphoric condensation of a series of forms of conduct whose common feature . . . was a refusal of socialisation: mobility, promiscuity, improvidence, ignorance, insubordination, immorality, in

short a rejection of all those relations which are so essential in the formation of the social' (Rose, 1979: 23). Within the category of pauper it was
prostitutes, 'literally and figuratively . . . the conduit of infection to
respectable society' (Walkowitz, 1980: 4) and destitute street children who
particularly offended Victorian sensibility and confirmed the city as a
pollutant and a symbol of social dislocation.

In opposition to this vision of the city were set both the rural and the
domestic. As Davidoff et al. (1976) have pointed out, these were not only
analogous concepts, they were interrelated – the ideal home was situated
in the rural village community. Both symbolically exercised the power to
resist the encroachment of disorder and evil. They represented traditional
relations of patronage and hierarchy, integration, regulation, peace and
innocence. They were havens in a menacing and mercenary world. In
contrast to the public sphere, the domestic was increasingly defined as
private, moral and personal.

> During the 19th century the family came to appear . . . an idealised refuge, a
> world of its own, with a higher moral value than the public realm. The
> bourgeois family was idealised as life wherein order and authority were
> unchallenged. . . . As the family became a refuge from the terrors of society,
> it gradually became also a moral yardstick with which to measure the public
> realm of the capital city. (Sennett, 1977: 20)

Furthermore, in order to resist the chaos, pollution and immorality of the
public sphere most effectively, the true home needed to be totally
separated from the world outside. In 1865 Ruskin expressed it thus:

> This is the true nature of the home – it is a place of peace; not only from all
> injury, but from all terror, doubt and division. In so far as it is not this, it is
> not home; so far as the anxieties of the outer life penetrate into it, and the
> inconsistently-minded, unknown, unloved or hostile society of the outer world
> is allowed by either husband or wife to cross the threshold it ceases to be home.
> (Ruskin, 1902: 144)

Family life within this framework was above all defined as natural – part
of the natural order of things. Women's role within this schema was not
only decreed by nature, it was also quite pivotal. The wife represented the
heart of the organic family,[2] it was in her persona that the superior
morality of family life was invested. By her sweet and patient nature she
was considered ideally suited to the task of upholding harmony and
defending virtue. For women to venture outside the home for purposes
other than social and charitable visiting was felt to be unnatural and
improper. As symbols the urban and the domestic demanded a moral
evaluation of physical space: thus women in the home were cast as angels,
women in the city streets had 'fallen'.

It must be pointed out that this celebration of the rural and the
domestic and the corresponding condemnation of the urban was, with
some exceptions and variations, a theme which pervaded intellectual,
social and literary commentaries of nineteenth-century authors of both the
Right and Left (and has continued well into the twentieth century:

Davidoff et al., 1976). In much of this writing the urban and the domestic were inextricably linked not merely because they were cast as symbolic counterpoints. Domestic virtue was not only contrasted with urban vice and chaos, it was in addition frequently (and naïvely) conceptualized as a *solution* to the social menace of the nineteenth-century city. That the bourgeois domestic ideal was both made possible by wealth generated in the public sphere and dependent for its continuing existence on the labour of the despised urban populace, that its 'purity' was maintained at the expense of the urban prostitute (Banks and Banks, 1965), were for the most part conveniently overlooked. The dualistic notions so often expressed in the discourse of the period tended to obscure these kinds of complex interrelation. Combined with other factors they also ultimately influenced – though in a contradictory and class-specific manner – the development of education for girls in the latter part of the century.

The domestic as a site of labour

The domestic sphere in the nineteenth century was of course a great deal more than its common representation as a symbol of harmony, tradition and womanly influence. During this period the middle-class household was also a context in which an unprecedented number of men, women and children were employed.

> Large domestic staffs had, of course, characterised the great houses of the nobility for centuries past; what was new in the nineteenth century was the burgeoning of those 'of moderate incomes' – the manufacturers and merchants, the bankers, brokers, lawyers, doctors and other professionals whose incomes depended, directly or indirectly, on industrialisation and the rapid growth of towns that accompanied it. The large family, the large and over-furnished house, the entertainment of guests at lavish dinner parties, and the economic ability to keep one's wife in genteel idleness, all of which were essential attributes of the institution of the Victorian middle-class family, required the employment of domestic servants on a vast scale. (Burnett, 1977: 136)

Servant keeping was not confined to the wealthier sections of the middle class. Lower middle-class families were also employers of domestic labour, though on a smaller scale, and contributed to the mid-century expansion of demand for servants which coincided with the decline of traditional rural occupations for both men and women. By 1851 a greater proportion of the population was employed in domestic service than in any other area except agriculture. One in four females in paid work was a full-time domestic servant. Although many of these came from the countryside, the jobs were concentrated in urban areas, so that in London at the time of the 1851 census one-third of the female population (of all classes) aged between fifteen and twenty was employed in domestic service. Over the following twenty years there was an even greater upsurge of middle-class prosperity and the number of female servants expanded by over 50 per cent (Burnett, 1977). At a time when the work of working-class women outside the home (most particularly in factories) was increasingly subjected to criticism, domestic service remained exempt. Servants, it was felt,

> do not follow an obligatory independent, and therefore, for their sex an unnatural career; – on the contrary, they are attached to others and are connected with other existences which they embellish, facilitate and serve. In a word, they fulfill both essentials of woman's being: *they are supported by and administer to men.* [author's emphasis] (Greg, 1862, quoted in Davidoff et al., 1976: 168)

The employment of servants as a feature of Victorian middle-class domestic establishments was in a number of different ways to bear upon the education and activities of both middle- and working-class women in the second part of the century. It was first of all to lead to pressure for a greater emphasis on domestic subjects in the education of working-class girls. As one advocate for such an initiative put it in the 1850s: 'our object is to improve the servants of the rich and the wives of the poor' (Austin, 1857, quoted in Alexander, 1976: 62). This pressure was to become more intense towards the end of the century as new, better paid and more prestigious jobs involving a lesser degree of personal scrutiny became available for unmarried women. The ensuing 'servant problem', which was more prevalent in city areas, and was compounded by the entry of younger girls into compulsory schooling, was to contribute to the focus on domestic science in the curriculum of girls after the 1880s.

The employment of large numbers of increasingly expensive servants as an essential feature of respectable Victorian homes was also to have indirect effects upon the education of middle-class girls. The growing cost for middle-class men of running a domestic establishment commensurate with their status, and their reluctance therefore to embark on marriage (Banks and Banks, 1965), was a factor which contributed to the pressure from unmarried middle-class women for an adequate education which would enable them to support themselves. (In 1851 it was estimated that there were one million unmarried adult women in the population. A causal factor as significant as the unwillingness of men to marry was the large-scale emigration of men to the United States and the colonies which had left half a million 'redundant' women of marriageable age in Britain, primarily from the 'upper and educated sections of society': Greg, 1862, quoted in Hollis, 1979: 38). Yet another consequence of the employment of large numbers of servants was that married women of the upper middle class were released from the more arduous aspects of domestic responsibility. Although the 'leisure' that this provided was often consumed in the intricate maintenance of social relations and social boundaries, it was also to allow many of these women to extend the frontiers of the private sphere beyond the confines of their own homes to a preoccupation with the domestic lives and education of the poor. This point will be returned to in the next section.

The domestic sphere was of course not only a site of paid employment for women of the working class. Large numbers of unmarried women from genteel families were employed as governesses,[3] virtually the only respectable form of paid occupation open to them. The employment of governesses, like that of domestic servants, enhanced the status of their middle-class employers; though within these households the social position of governess was anomalous and often humiliating. They were appallingly paid, and as destitute 'ladies' were neither one of the family nor one of the servants.

> What is the position of governess? she has none. While engaged in a family . . . she is infinitely less considered than the servants; she has no companionship whatsoever; . . . the governess is condemned to solitude . . . though her habits and manners are to *form* the habits and manners of the young, they are unfit for those already formed. (*English Woman's Journal*, 1860, quoted in Hollis, 1979: 90)

The social marginality and poverty of governesses were also factors which, when combined with a consciousness of their own limited training as teachers, were to contribute to the growing struggle of middle-class women to gain for themselves an education which would enable them to be financially self-sufficient and socially and intellectually respected.

However, as I have already indicated, in the middle of the century employment outside the domestic sphere was not only considered inappropriate for ladies of the middle class, it was increasingly thought of as immoral for women of the working class as well. The home, whether of their fathers, husbands or employers, was becoming enshrined as the proper place for all women to spend their time. Towards the end of the first half of the century the hitherto broad scope of paid labour for working-class women (and children) was gradually though unevenly being reduced, partially as a consequence of protective legislation. The separation of the workplace from the home, which prevented women from engaging in waged work at the same time as caring for the house and children, and the exclusion of women from many new areas of employment as they opened up, were further factors which contributed to the gradual curtailment of their work outside the home. Contemporary census returns are unreliable sources on women's participation in the labour market since so much remunerative work done by women was casual (particularly in London) and home-based (Alexander, 1976). Yet bearing these limitations in mind, official figures indicate a very substantial change in the pattern of women's paid work in the second half of the nineteenth century. According to these, one in four married women with husbands alive was in employment in 1851; by 1911, nine out of ten of such women were engaged solely in housewifery (Oakley, 1976: 44). This recomposition of the working-class family, which produced the working-class 'housewife', was further confirmed by the introduction of compulsory elementary education, which effectively withdrew the labour of older children from the domestic sphere. Many women probably welcomed a reduction of their strenuous and ill-paid labour outside the home and the

opportunity to concentrate on domestic tasks, but for others the curtailment of paid employment for themselves and their children entailed yet
greater hardship and was resisted.

What is evident overall is that in the context of concerns about unsupervised 'marauding' street children, infant mortality, insanitary housing,
inadequate domestic skills, neglect of husbands ('the employment of
married women . . . is undoubtedly an evil . . . because it disables them
from making their husbands' homes comfortable': Greg, 1862, quoted in
Hollis, 1979: 55), there was in the second half of the century an increasing
recognition of the contribution to social order which could be made by
working-class women in their capacity as homemaker. Women and girls
were in the course of those years to be selected both as a focal point and
as a point of access to their class for a series of philanthropic, medical
and educational initiatives designed in large part to improve the values,
health and behaviour of the poor (Donzelot, 1979).

Philanthropy, the urban and the domestic

During the eighteenth century charitable visiting to the homes of the poor
had begun to take on a new importance as a consequence of increasing
social dislocation. In that period it had become established as a means of
maintaining pastoral contact, alleviating distress and reinforcing traditional relations of hierarchy and obligation, and was particularly
prevalent among Evangelicals, who chose this as a way of practising
religious principles (Hall, 1979; Summers, 1979). Anne Summers (1979)
has argued that in the early part of the nineteenth century it became in
addition a way of recruiting domestic labour for the rapidly expanding
households of the middle class. The responsibility for visiting fell
predominantly upon women, who were considered uniquely suited to the
task. Interestingly, even the most vehement of the early Victorian
propagandists for the notion of separate spheres supported the idea that
ladies should engage in philanthropic visiting. It was hoped that through
the tactful deployment of their moral influence and domestic knowledge,
deferential social bonds between the classes could be maintained.

However, the expansion of the cities and the increasing physical
segregation of the rich from the poor within the mid-nineteenth-century
metropolis disrupted these traditional forms of personal contact. Fears
that the consequences of this social separation might be to increase the
'demoralization' of the urban poor, and thus the threat of insurrection,
provoked an upsurge in charitable handouts. Yet in the new context these
gifts no longer had the capacity to elicit obligation and co-operation
(Stedman Jones, 1976). Indeed, charity itself grew to be seen as part of
the problem and was held responsible for the perceived lack of thrift and
self-reliance of the poor: 'the mass misery of the great cities arose from
spasmodic, indiscriminate and unconditional doles' (B. Webb, 1926,
quoted in Hollis, 1979: 226). The underlying problem was understood in

terms of the moral deficiency of the individual and the family. Poverty was seen by most philanthropists 'not as a structural or economic problem for society, but a moral one. It was a function . . . of personal failure; as such it would . . . be solved through the reform and help of individuals' (Summers, 1979: 52). This analysis of urban 'demoralization' and the recognition of the inadequacy of traditional 'indiscriminate' charity precipitated new approaches within philanthropy. In 1869 the Charitable Organization Society (COS) was established in London with the objective of recreating personal contacts with the poor and co-ordinating the allocation of charitable funds to ensure that payments were made only to the 'deserving'. In this way virtues of thrift, self-sufficiency and industry would be promoted and further demands for payment would be less likely. Intrinsic to the new method of allocation and character-building was the classification of need and merit, and as a consequence the surveillance and rendering of advice to the individual within the domestic context.[4]

Women were absolutely central to these philanthropic initiatives, as both their objects and their perpetrators. Donzelot has pointed out that in the shift in philanthropic activity in France (which paralleled that of England) from charitable handouts to an emphasis on savings, autonomy and advice,

> it was necessary to change the criteria for granting aid; the order of priorities had to reflect this concern to reinforce family autonomy. Children came before the elderly, for 'beyond childhood there was the whole period of maturity . . .'. And women before men, for by aiding them one was also aiding their children. (1979: 66)

It was via women and children that the moral, hygienic and budgeting norms were to be diffused into the families of the working class.[5] A central component of this philanthropic intervention was subsequently to be the institutionalization of free compulsory education; this both withdrew children from the domain of 'deficient' parental influence while simultaneously feeding back into the family the new norms acquired in the context of the school. (I shall return to this in greater detail in the next section.) Donzelot goes on to suggest that the singling out of women and children in this way represented a curtailment of patriarchal authority in the working-class domestic sphere. This is an assertion which seems impossible to substantiate (and has been criticized as 'incipiently anti-feminist': Barrett and McIntosh, 1982: 104) in that it totally fails to take account of the growing economic power of working-class men compared to their wives within the family. During this period working-class women and children were gradually being excluded from the labour market and were being forced into financial dependency in increasing numbers, a phenomenon which received considerable support from many working-class men. As Henry Broadhurst stated at the 1877 Trades Union Congress:

> It was [the] duty [of] men and husbands to use their utmost efforts to bring
> about a condition of things, where their wives would be in their proper sphere
> at home, instead of being dragged into competition for livelihood against the
> great and strong men of the world. (Quoted in Weeks, 1981: 68)

However, it can be conceded that the imposition of compulsory education
did curtail paternal appropriation of child labour (though this was
compensated for among certain sectors of the working class by the secure-
ment of the family wage)[6] and that the focus of philanthropy on women
and girls (which of course preceded COS) *did* raise the status of both
middle- and working-class women by identifying them as potential carriers
of domestic expertise.

This was both recognized and exploited by many of the middle-class
women active in the philanthropic project. Although many men supported
their involvement there was also opposition, and contemporary comments
indicate that middle-class women found it necessary to justify their
activity first in terms of the centrality of working-class women to the
desired transformation of the 'morality' of the social order, and secondly
in terms of their own suitability as catalysts of this purpose. Thus:

> It is for woman, in her functions of mother, housewife and teacher, to effect
> those urgently needed changes in infant management, domestic economy,
> education and the general habits of her own sex. . . . It is for her to teach and
> apply the laws of health in her own sphere, where men cannot act. (Powers,
> 1859, quoted in Hollis, 1979: 239)

And:

> We care for the evils affecting women most of all because they react upon the
> whole of society, and abstract from the common good. (J. Butler, 1869, quoted
> in Hollis, 1979: 223)

And:

> I am convinced that *women* should have a greater share in it. No Boards of
> Guardians . . . can be expected to manage girls' schools as they ought to be,
> neither can male inspectors alone inspect them. Results would be far different
> if the influence of women of feeling were largely introduced. (L. Twining, 1880,
> quoted in Wilson, 1977: 53)

And:

> We might almost say that the welfare of the work girl is at the root of . . . the
> question. How are we to improve the lives of our working classes? . . . if we
> raise the work girl, if we can make her conscious of her own great respon-
> sibilities . . . we shall then give her an influence over her sweetheart, her
> husband and her sons. (M. Stanley, 1890, quoted in Dyhouse, 1981: 106)

It has been suggested that philanthropic activists, particularly those associated with COS who were drawn mainly from urban professional groups,
were able through their specific forms of charitable practice to elevate
themselves to the level of the 'urban gentry' in relation to the poor (Stedman Jones, 1976). However, this observation fails to take into account the
specific and contradictory position of the vast numbers of *women* who

were involved in philanthropic projects of one kind or another. It has been estimated that towards the end of the nineteenth century there were 20,000 women who were paid officials of charitable societies, and a further 500,000 who were voluntary workers; in addition there were 200 women on school boards and over 800 who were guardians of poor law unions (Hollis, 1979: 226–8). Although many of these women, fore-runners of today's social workers, may have exercised 'tremendous despotism' as Octavia Hill admitted having done (Malpass, 1982), their interests and concerns were not identical to those of the men of their class. It cannot be assumed that they were engaged *only* in dispensing middle-class morality and socializing the poor.

In the latter part of the nineteenth century philanthropy was a means for many women of the middle class of extending the terrain of the domestic sphere so that it grew to encompass domestic issues in the wider society. Although in some ways this affirmed the notion of their 'essen-tial' womanliness, it also fractured the Victorian domestic ideal by offer-ing women new areas of influence and power which required both time and commitment, and which must inevitably have resulted in withdrawing from their husbands some of the service and attention to which they had become accustomed. In addition, through the gradual professionalization of philanthropy, the establishment of training courses, the founding of girls' clubs (see Dyhouse, 1981) and of settlement houses in poor areas, the formation of a Union of Women Workers, and much more, women philanthropists acquired a new social visibility. As a contemporary partici-pant put it, 'the public has learnt a new respect for the capacity of women' (quoted in Hollis, 1979: 257). However it is essential to emphasize that the energy of these women was not directed only towards the enhancement of their own public status. Many were also completely dedicated to achieving social reforms which would improve the living circumstances of the poor, in spite of the fact that in some instances these reforms were not in their own interest as members of the middle class. The campaigns to improve and regulate the pay and conditions of domestic servants are an example of this, as the following indicates:

> There are many reasons for the great disinclination which girls have for domestic service . . . [it] is incessant hard work at all hours of the day and sometimes of the night also. It is at best but a kind of slavery. . . . One feasible suggestion of an improvement is a system . . . under which servants could go home at nights. Heads of household might then have to wait upon themselves a little more than they do now . . . but girls of the working class . . . are just as much entitled to freedom of choice as any other persons are and we must not try to 'bump' people, especially women, into what we think are their places. (Paterson, 1869, quoted in Hollis, 1979: 64)

The explicitly feminist note on which this excerpt ends is also an exam-ple of the commitment demonstrated by many women involved in philan-thropy to other women regardless of their social position. This was particularly exemplified in the 1870s and 1880s campaign to repeal the

Contagious Diseases Acts[7] within which Josephine Butler was particularly prominent. Butler, a member of the mid-nineteenth century Langham Circle of feminists which included many women active in philanthropy and education, criticized the Acts on the grounds that it was women whose lives were effectively circumscribed by them; it was women rather than men who were detained and subjected to humiliating personal physical examination, described by her as 'instrumental rape'. Butler insisted on placing the plight of prostitutes within a broader analysis of the political economy of women and in pointing to the similarity of the position of *all* women in relation to men regardless of their class. There is no doubt that many women of the middle class active in the campaign to repeal the Contagious Diseases Acts (as well as in other philanthropic projects) often 'expressed an identity of interest . . . with their "fallen sisters"' (Walkowitz, 1980: 7). They also formed alliances with working-class men (ibid.). These expressions of solidarity with the poor and the vociferous defence of prostitutes against their largely middle- and upper-class clientele simply cannot be understood as a manifestation of *class* interest or as part of the attempt of 'the new professional gentry . . . to place itself upon equal terms with the traditional aristocracy and to visit . . . its newfound status upon the poor' (Stedman Jones, 1976: 270).

Nevertheless, middle-class women's involvement in the philanthropic initiatives of the latter part of the nineteenth century was to have paradoxical consequences. In spite of the fact that many of the women were closely connected to the expanding feminist movement, that many were motivated by a humanitarian concern to alleviate suffering rather than a desire to assert the social values of their class, that some supported more liberal measures and the intervention of the state in order to solve the problems of unemployment rather than the policies advocated by COS, and that their influence on social policy was often progressive, ultimately philanthropy was probably to have more far-reaching and more positive effects upon its women activists of the middle class than upon the poor to whom they administered. The doctrine of 'separate spheres' – the ideological separation of private from public life – was towards the end of the century to have been subverted by philanthropy,[8] but in ways which were quite class specific. The employment of large numbers of servants by wealthier families and the explosive nature of the urban context enabled middle-class women to extend their sphere of influence beyond the confines of their own homes. They gained a measure of public visibility and authority precisely through their intervention into the 'private' sphere of working-class women and through their public exercise of domestic expertise, while all the time maintaining unimpaired their traditional authority within their own private spheres. In contrast, the elevation of the importance of the domestic resulted for working-class women in the gradual *curtailment* of their public activities while simultaneously *undermining* the 'privacy' of their domestic sphere.

Changes in the education of girls

Some of the earliest pressures for a broader and more serious education for middle-class women arose from a need to improve the training of governesses and teachers in small private schools for girls. This had proved to be so lamentably inadequate that many could not compete in formal examinations with working-class girls who were training to become elementary school teachers in the pupil-teacher apprenticeship scheme established in the 1840s. 'It was increasingly felt that working class education was better than that for the middle classes and it should not be' (David, 1980: 108). In spite of a number of developments in the mid-nineteenth century, this view of the general standard of education for middle-class girls was echoed by the Taunton Commission which in 1865 reported on girls' endowed schools and criticized 'the want of thoroughness and foundation; want of system; slovenliness and showy superficiality; . . . undue time given to accomplishments . . . very small amount of professional skill' (quoted in Hollis, 1979: 140–1).

But education for middle-class women did not simply signify a reassertion of social hierarchy or a more rigorous acquisition of knowledge. In a context in which over one-third of women were not married, in which many middle-class women were forced to suffer the indignity of financial dependence upon fathers and brothers, and in which the financial position of married women (prevented by law from owning property) was similarly circumscribed, education grew to be perceived by some women as the means of access to paid work in the public sphere and thus to the severance of economic dependence and inequality. It was argued that 'Women want work both for the health of their minds and their bodies. They want it often because . . . they will have children and others dependent on them – *for all the reasons men want work*' (Bodichon, 1857, quoted in Spender, 1982: 297).

Not only was the demand for education by middle-class women distinctly radical in that it was perceived as a vehicle for their emancipation and thus challenged prevailing assumptions about the appropriate behaviour for ladies, it was also linked through the individuals who participated in the campaign to a number of other radical causes of the mid- and late-nineteenth century.[9] The women and men (many from nonconformist professional families) who were active in the struggle to improve educational provision for girls were often personal friends of those involved in the promotion of social reform in other fields. Several were to participate in the campaign to change legislation regarding married women's property, the Contagious Diseases Acts repeal movement, attempts to open occupations to women, the movement for women's suffrage, as well as radical initiatives within philanthropy.

In the middle of the century, the discontent with existing standards of education provoked some women active in these circles to establish (with the support of some men and in the face of considerable opposition and scepticism from other members of their class) a few institutions at both secondary and university level which provided a more scholarly education for middle-class girls and young women. In these institutions few concessions were made to domesticity or accomplishments; girls were provided with a curriculum which was far more demanding than hitherto.[10] Within this new movement to improve the education of middle-class girls, there were significant differences of approach. Sarah Delamont (1978a) has identified two distinct strands: the 'uncompromising' and the 'separatists'.

Among the most important of the 'uncompromising' pioneers of girls' education were Frances Buss, founder of North London Collegiate School and Emily Davies, founder of Girton College, Cambridge. This strand was initially to be the more influential of the two in that a far larger number of schools were to be patterned according to the principles established by Buss and her followers in the Girls' Public Day School Company, providers of endowed high schools throughout the country for young ladies from the middle classes. These women argued, in the tradition of the enlightenment, that differences between men and women were a product of the environment[11] and not natural, that there must be 'but one true theory of education for men and women alike' (Tod, 1874, quoted in Dyhouse 1981: 141). Moreover, in order to be taken seriously, girls must have exactly the same curriculum and examinations as boys, regardless of the inappropriateness of the predominance of classics within these. Davies was a particularly unremitting opponent of modifications to the curriculum, which were proposed by some in order to take into account the specific experience and expectations of women. Her position was that 'Only by following to the letter the educational courses laid down for men could women claim to be measured with men. Any diversion from this iron rule . . . would be interpreted by a skeptical public . . . as a sop to women's inferior intellects' (McWilliams-Tullberg, 1980: 126).

The 'separatists', among whom were Dorothea Beale and Anne Clough, forerunners in the education of girls of the *upper* middle class at both public boarding-schools and university level, argued that the existing emphasis on classics in the curriculum and examinations of boys of that class were not the most apposite for girls, whose future would be different; they proposed a more varied curriculum and special examinations. Underlying their programme was the conviction that men and women were fundamentally different, and although they insisted that women should be well educated, this was to prepare them better for tasks suited to the exercise of womanly influence. However, to assume therefore that these women were not feminists is to simplify the issue and project upon it the criteria of late twentieth-century feminism. Walkowitz (1980)[12] and Banks (1981) among others have drawn attention to the range of positions (as well as their contradictory nature) which were taken up by feminists in the nineteenth century. Important among these, and one which undoubtedly contributed to the gains made by women during this period, was that which stressed the value and defended the autonomy of women's unique proficiency within 'their' sphere. Thus the expertise promoted by the separatists in education was precisely that which was exploited by many women philanthropists and which ironically enabled them to make inroads into public life.

During the latter part of the nineteenth century there was a very substantial expansion in the provision of secondary education for middle-class girls along the lines fought for by those feminists active in the 1850s, and endorsed by the Taunton Commission in 1865. Indeed in the 1890s the Bryce Commission concluded that 'there has probably been more change in the condition of Secondary Education for girls than in any other department of education' (quoted in Lawson and Silver, 1973: 343). At the same time increasing numbers of places were made available to women in higher education. Nevertheless, although there is no doubt that in terms of educational standards women had by the end of the century made enormous progress and had in many instances achieved for middle-class young girls a curriculum and examinations which were virtually identical to those of their brothers, the long-term gains are harder to assess. Opposition to their objectives was widespread and took a variety of forms. Educational institutions were constantly under pressure to compromise by demonstrating their respectability and suitability for young ladies in order to maintain the financial, political and moral support of the public (Delamont, 1978a). Conventional femininity and modesty were placed at a premium within these institutions. It was felt that too great a visibility of 'strong-minded' women and too open an alliance with the women's suffrage movement might jeopardize the educational cause, and for this reason Emily Davies withdrew her active support from the suffrage campaign (McWilliams-Tullberg, 1980). Tremendous opposition was also manifested in the numbers of astonishing medical theories which were developed during that period and which purported to demonstrate significant physiological and mental differences between men and women. It was alleged that too much intellectual work could have dangerous consequences for the health of adolescent girls and young women; indeed in extreme cases cerebral exercise could lead to sterility, inability to breastfeed and even death (Dyhouse, 1981; Duffin, 1978; Griffiths and Saraga, 1979). (Unsurprisingly no such concerns were expressed about the frail constitutions of young women of the working class.) Resistance to women's participation in higher education was often particularly strong. In 1897 Cambridge undergraduates celebrated the university's continuing refusal to grant women the title of their degrees with 'a night of riotous bonfires, fire-works and fun' (McWilliams-Tullberg, 1980: 141).[13]

Overall, the attempts to create educational opportunities for middle-class women were opposed far more virulently than was the involvement of middle-class women in philanthropy. It is possible that the relation of education to domesticity appeared more tenuous and thus placed in question the femininity and respectability of women educators in a way in which charitable visiting and the deployment of domestic advice did not. Equal education for women represented an encroachment upon a male terrain; its object was to prepare women to compete for jobs and become financially independent of men rather than to minister to the poor on a voluntary basis. As Barbara Bodichon pointed out in 1857, 'there is a prejudice against women accepting money for work' (quoted in Spender, 1982: 297). So it is ironic, yet not surprising in such a context, that women's achievements in the field of education managed to open to them on the whole one paid occupation only – that of teaching (McWilliams-Tullberg, 1980). Education was not then the vehicle for emancipation for middle-class women that it was hoped and feared it would be, in that it usually led directly back into the confines of the secondary school classroom. However teaching did offer the possibility of financial independence and, as with philanthropy, the involvement of middle-class women in it helped to expand the conceptual boundaries of the bourgeois domestic domain. The school can be considered to occupy a midway point – the interface – between the private and the public spheres; as such teaching cannot be considered *merely* an extension of women's traditional sphere of influence. Like philanthropy, it also constituted a point of entry into public life.

The education of working-class girls

The education of working-class girls was quite different. An expansion of educational provision for children of poor families was not only demanded from within their class – by its recipients – it was also imposed as part of a wider response to the social dislocation of the nineteenth century. As with the philanthropic enterprise, the concern with the education of the poor was not uniform in nature. Undoubtedly much was motivated by a benevolent determination to eradicate ignorance and improve the quality of working-class life. However, after the middle of the century, compulsory education (as well as being considered a necessary sequel to the 1867 Franchise Act: Simon, 1974) also grew to be perceived as a solution to the urban problem: to demoralization and the threat of insurrection. Compulsory schooling was to be a means of clearing the streets of the many thousands of vagrant and rebellious children neither at school nor at work whose growing numbers increasingly preoccupied the Victorian imagination. Simultaneously it was to be a means of socializing them (with iron discipline) into habits of obedience and thrift and of disseminating through them moral order into the homes of the poor.

As was pointed out in the section on philanthropy, girls were considered quite crucial to this enterprise of diffusing bourgeois norms. In the early part of the century the education of working-class girls, where it existed, was not a vehicle for the transmission of domestic skills to the degree it was to become after the introduction of compulsory schooling. Although provision had varied from school to school and region to region, on the whole boys and girls in schools for the poor had received a similar education, with an emphasis on obedience, piety, the three Rs, and with extra needlework for girls.[14] As the curriculum for working-class children in general broadened and became more vocational, as domesticity became equated with moral order, and as the demand for trained servants expanded, so domestic economy became a central component in the education of urban working-class girls. Carol Dyhouse (1981) has documented the impact of Education Department legislation on the curriculum of Board schools after the 1870 Education Act. Under pressure from such groups as the National Association for the Promotion of Housewifery, domestic economy for girls was made into one of the compulsory 'specific subjects' for which government grants were paid. As a consequence the numbers of girls studying domestic economy rose between 1874 and 1882 from 844 to 59,812. Similar massive increases took place over the following years as a result of the payment of grants for cookery and laundry work (Dyhouse, 1981: 89). By 1900 the London School Board had set up 168 'cookery centres' designed to train girls from 470 local schools (Dyhouse, 1981: 90). However, this emphasis on domestic subjects was not accepted without a considerable amount of resistance, both from a few middle-class feminists (Dyhouse, 1981: 170) and in particular from women who felt that their daughters' time would be more fruitfully employed assisting in the home. One of the London School Board women superintendents complained that 'prejudice against [cookery instruction] was almost insuperable, parents put every possible obstacle in the way of their children attending classes' (quoted in Dyhouse, 1981: 90).

On the front line of this educational enterprise to domesticate the children of the urban poor were the elementary school teachers. It was they who were responsible for imparting the requisite moral values and maintaining discipline on a day-to-day basis. As Gerald Grace (1978) has pointed out, their position was crucial and contradictory. Before the middle of the century teachers of the poor were on the whole drawn from the working class. In order to ensure that they became effective civilizers rather than inciters of discontent, it was essential that their training be rigorous in the transmission of appropriate moral values as well as closely monitored. To guard against the employment of individuals who might have an improper influence, attempts were made to recruit more members of the 'respectable' middle classes.

> The education of trained masters and mistresses is very superficial . . . they are very often . . . full of airs and have no moral influences over their scholars. I think this is not so much the fault of the training colleges. . . . Pupil teachers being taken generally from the very lowest class of society, they are destitute of that mass of information which children of respectable parents imbibe without knowing it. . . . It seems to me very desirable that young people of a

higher grade should be encouraged to enter on the work of popular education. (Evidence to the Newcastle Commission, 1861, quoted in Hollis, 1979: 92)

Although this kind of appeal coincided with the growing demand of women from the middle class for paid employment, it was eventually girls from the *lower* middle class, as Frances Widdowson (1980) has pointed out, who entered elementary teaching in increasing numbers (and who were to contribute to the enhancement of its professional status). With the advent of compulsory education and the expansion of demand for teachers, recruitment was increasingly directed at women from this class, both because as women they were cheaper than men, and (as the above quote shows) because they came from a respectable background and thus already possessed the required moral attributes suited to what Grace has described as the 'missionary' enterprise. By the end of the century, women constituted 60 per cent of teachers in elementary schools (Lawson and Silver 1973).[15] Interestingly, Widdowson has noted that during this period ladies from more genteel backgrounds were advised to enter elementary teaching (if at all) in rural areas, in that this more closely 'corresponded with the accepted conventions of the solid middle-class domestic ideology of the 19th century' (1980: 31), and the domestic–urban dualism to which I referred earlier. On the whole, however, late nineteenth-century attempts to recruit 'ladies' into elementary teaching were unsuccessful both because these women were unattracted by the low status of the work and because their more protected and liberal educational experience in middle-class schools was considered as unsuitable preparation for it (1980: 31).

It was thus women from the artisan and lower middle class who came increasingly to dominate the occupational group. One consequence of this was that modifications were made in the courses offered by training colleges. The heavy concentration on domestic skills, the emphasis on moral instruction and surveillance, and the extremely narrow academic preparation of the early years, considered appropriate for girls from the working class, were slowly abandoned in favour of a rather more liberal education which began to resemble that of girls from a higher social standing (1980: 31). In spite of these changes, it was still women from the lower middle class whose arduous task it most often was to discipline working-class children and to administer the regime designed to improve their morals, manners and domestic skills (though in this capacity they were supervised by male headteachers and a male inspectorate). The personal contact between women of the more prosperous middle class and the poor was on the whole confined to philanthropic activities and social work (which were likely to be voluntary). Yet in both instances it was overwhelmingly *women* who were agents in the project of disseminating bourgeois moral values and household skills to the wives and children of the urban working class. As I have already pointed out, paradoxically it was precisely the process of domesticating the poor which enabled women of the middle class to extend their own spheres of influence. It was also these activities, rather than the pursuit of better education for themselves, which appear to have received least opposition from the men of their class.

Motherhood, physical deterioration and setbacks

I have drawn attention to some of the changes which took place in women's education and the domestic sphere during the latter part of the nineteenth century and to the complex relationship between the advances which occurred for middle-class women and the consolidation of domesticity for women of the working class. But it is important to point out that the gains made by middle-class women were in many instances short lived. As Carol Dyhouse has argued, 'the history of the women's movement since the late nineteenth century serves in many ways to demonstrate the resilience and ideological resourcefulness of a society or culture threatened by feminism: there is no simple tale of steady progress' (1981: 61). The early twentieth century saw the introduction of a special emphasis on mothering. The new ideology of motherhood was to encompass *all* women. Although in its expression it was to take forms which varied according to the social position of the women concerned, its overall effect was to transcend class and to contribute to a narrowing of the gap between the domestic experience and education of both poor and rich women.

Anna Davin has pointed to the growing importance of population as a national resource at the turn of the century. This was a period in which imperialist objectives appeared to be threatened by the diminishing vitality of the British race. Concerns were exacerbated in 1900 when one-third of men recruited to fight the Boer War were found physically 'deficient' for this purpose. At the same time Britain's industrial superiority in the world was being challenged by the United States, Germany and Japan. It was this context which provoked a wave of anxiety about high rates of infant mortality, the extremely poor health of large sectors of the population, and the decline of the birth rate, particularly among the middle classes (Davin, 1978). Urbanization was again to be a crucial component in the crisis. It was the city environment which was held largely responsible for the decline in the nation's fitness and for the production of the 'physical degenerate'. 'The casual residuum once more became the topic of anxious debate, provoked this time not by fears of revolution but by intimations of impending imperial decline' (Stedman Jones, 1976: 330). As a consequence, state intervention into matters of social reform was considered increasingly warranted. Yet although the urban maintained its symbolic resonance as a causal factor in contemporary understandings of the issue, the *solution* to the problem of public health and declining national power was perceived to reside in the quality of mothering and in the family. Again it was the private sphere upon which attention was to be focused. However in contrast to the nineteenth century, when moral inadequacy and the paid work of wives outside the home tended to be blamed for domestic incompetence, the problem of the early twentieth century was defined in terms of 'fecklessness' and of ignorance among poor women in the skills of mothering (Davin, 1978). Once again the issues of poverty, bad housing and insanitary conditions so pervasive in the urban environment, were relegated to second place.

Eugenicist ideas about the degeneration of the race and the importance of heredity and selective breeding, although initiated in the latter part of the nineteenth century, were given a new impetus in this context. It was these theories which fuelled the opposition to middle-class women's increasing participation in the public sphere. So those women who pursued higher education, who chose to restrict the number of children they gave birth to, or worse still, who chose to remain unmarried, were accused of 'shirking' their responsibilities to the nation. As women from 'superior stock' they were considered particularly crucial to the promotion of racial progress and national efficiency. Since it was argued that intellectual work impaired women's reproductive processes, higher education for women was indeed a danger to 'Britain's proud position among the nations of the world' (quoted ibid.: 20): 'Many of the most cultivated and able families of the English speaking race will have become extinct, through the prime error of supposing that an education which is good for men must also be good for women' (quoted in Duffin, 1978: 82).

Unsurprisingly, these concerns for Britain's international position were to find expression in contemporary proposals for education. A parliamentary committee set up in order to investigate the 'physical deterioration' of the nation, pointed in its report in 1904 to the appalling conditions of urban living for the working class, and proposed '"Some great scheme of social education" which would aim "to raise the standards of domestic competence" and would underline the importance of proper ideals of home life among young girls destined to become wives and mothers of future generations' (Dyhouse, 1981: 92). In this it was typical of a number of publications and official reports of the period. The consensus was that elementary schooling for girls had hitherto concentrated too much on reading and writing, and insufficiently on nutrition, hygiene and in particular on preparation for maternity; this was in spite of the developments in the teaching of domestic economy which had taken place in the last decades of the nineteenth century. The next few years saw a tremendous expansion in the provision of training for motherhood and domesticity for working-class girls, in the belief that this would improve the health of the nation. It was recommended that domestic subjects should take precedence over others in the school curriculum which were considered irrelevant – like maths – and that such instruction should not be confined to girls in elementary schools but should be provided for all ages. Helena Bosanquet, active in philanthropy from the days of COS, wrote in 1904 on the subject of physical degeneration:

Begin with the girls in school, and give them systematic and compulsory instruction in the elementary laws of health and feeding, and care of children, and the wise spending of money. Go on with the young women in evening classes and girls' clubs; and continue with the mothers wherever you can get at them. (Quoted in Davin, 1978: 26)

Overall these developments in the education of working-class girls in the first years of the twentieth century represented a consolidation and institutionalization of what had gone before, rather than a reorientation. The ideology of motherhood confirmed and entrenched the key position of women and girls as the points of access to the working-class family, and as the relayers of the standards of behaviour which were considered necessary in order to combat the problems of the urban environment.[16]

The impact of the new emphasis on motherhood on the education of middle-class girls was more complex. Among the advocates of a good education for middle-class girls during the latter part of the nineteenth century, it had been those who were uncompromising in their demands for a curriculum identical to that of middle-class boys who had been able to achieve most success through their capture of large numbers of girls' day schools. However, in the context of the early twentieth-century focus on motherhood, the views of these educationalists became far more contentious and divisions between them arose. A number of headmistresses of previously 'uncompromising' schools became supporters of eugenicist principles, and they endorsed the notion that many educated women were evading their responsibilities to the nation and acting selfishly in their pursuit of intellectual work (Dyhouse, 1981). It was increasingly felt that 'the old "blue stocking" type, who prided herself on not knowing how to sew or mend, and who thought cooking menial and beneath her, no longer appeals to anyone' (Gilliland, 1911, quoted in Dyhouse, 1981: 163); domestic 'science' and 'arts' should be elevated to be a compulsory feature of the curriculum for all secondary school girls, and should if necessary replace traditional science, maths and classics. It was argued that a serious and 'scientific' study of domestic economy was not demeaning; on the contrary, it would raise the status of the housewife and mother.[17]

Yet there was also considerable opposition to this line, particularly from the Girls' Public Day School Trust which was willing to forgo government grants rather than submit to pressure from the Board of Education to introduce housewifery into the curriculum. Its members argued that to do so would be to undermine the educational objectives of the schools (Dyhouse, 1981). (None the less, concessions were made later by the introduction of household management for girls over seventeen [David, 1980] and as educational provision grew increasingly to be linked to adult occupations over the following years, so further concessions were made.) Claims that domestic training constituted a science worthy of university study were ridiculed by some contemporary feminists and dismissed as 'pretentious', 'a travesty of science' and 'a degradation of university standards and an insult to women' (quoted in Dyhouse, 1981: 168).

It must not be assumed that positive and negative responses to the issue of domestic education in the secondary school curriculum of middle-class girls signalled in a simple fashion a division between feminists and anti-feminists.[18] Within feminism of the late nineteenth and early twentieth centuries there was, as today, a range of political and theoretical positions. It has already been pointed out that the 'uncompromising' believed that differences between men and women were largely environmental in origin and that the school curriculum for boys and girls should therefore be identical; this position can easily be located within the framework of late twentieth-century feminism. Less easy to reconcile with the ideas of today (though not impossible)[19] are the views of the 'separatists'; often rooted in religious and, in some instances, eugenicist principles (Gordon, 1977), these claimed that women were essentially different from men – indeed even superior – and that their special attributes should be exercised in order to improve the city and society at large. So, for example, women engaged in urban settlement work had 'not only a right, but a duty, to bring [their] womanly qualities to bear upon the city and ultimately upon the world so that it too, like the 19th century home, would become clean and orderly, and pure' (Banks, 1981: 94). It was this second strand which enabled some feminists to make their mark upon the public sphere; this they accomplished through exploiting their 'natural' propensity to be morally superior, to mother and to understand the intricacies of domestic management during periods of national anxiety about the city and the nation's health. By stressing the 'naturalness' of women's domain this approach was in many ways successful; it proved less threatening and therefore defused opposition at a time when the support of men was particularly crucial if women were to be granted the vote. It was also on occasion quite radical. A substantial number of women of this conviction, who were also socialists, were involved both in Britain and the United States in the rapidly expanding urban settlement movement of this period which was concerned to ameliorate the conditions of working-class women and children in their communities.[20] The new valuation of motherhood was also to be used some years later to justify demands for improved maternity and infant welfare.

Ultimately, however, the discourse of motherhood and scientific housekeeping, although permitting certain gains, constituted a new form of regulation which served to define more narrowly than for some time the special sphere of women. It was in a most particular way to affect those women of the middle class for whom mothering and housework had scarcely been an occupation in the latter part of the nineteenth century. The early twentieth-century invocation of motherhood and housewifery served to inhibit the relegation of child-care and domestic supervision to servants who it was felt would in all probability be ignorant of the requisite scientific knowledge. As motherhood grew in social importance, so child-rearing became defined as a more exacting task which required the expertise of the initiated. Another extremely important factor in this reconstitution of the private sphere for middle-class women was the marked decline in the availability of servants at the turn of the century. Overall, this period saw a reduction in the gap between education and domestic experience of women of different classes. The ideology of motherhood, of 'natural' differences between the sexes, and the emergence of scientific theories to support these, exalted as part of a response both to the crisis of the city and to the demand of women for the vote, were effectively to narrow the sphere of *both* middle- and working-class women.

By drawing attention to the increasing similarity in the pattern of middle-class and working-class women's confinement to the home, it is important not to minimize the significance of material differences in standards of living. However, differences between women do not in a simple fashion reflect the class positions and relations to their husbands. Distinctions between women have their own historical fluctuations, which are related to the degree of opposition to their participation in the world of men as well as to factors of the kind I have discussed, such as the threat of disorder and ill-health, the availability of employment and servants, and demographic change, all aspects of the development of capitalism and the urban context of the nineteenth and early twentieth centuries. Deeply implicated in this complex positioning and in the specific consolidation of the role of housewife/mother during the twentieth century are notions of natural difference and the importance of good mothering to social order. These have continued – as indeed have many of the symbolic meanings of the urban and the domestic – to hold a central place in family discourse right up to the present time.

Notes

1. More than twice as large as the proportion of children in the population today.

2. In which the husband represented the head (Davidoff et al., 1976).

3. In 1851 there were an estimated 250,000 (Delamont, 1978a).

4. See Donzelot (1979) for a further discussion of the shift in philanthropy from the gift of charity to the rendering of advice.

5. This period saw an increasing number of state interventions into the lives of the poor on medical and sanitary grounds. Walkowitz (1980: 71) points out that 'the mid-century sanitary movement . . . created a close identification of public order and public health'.

6. For a discussion of the family wage, see Land (1980). The economic dependence of wives upon their husbands could in practice only be realized within the labour aristocracy; nevertheless as an ideal it was widespread and percolated down to all but the most destitute.

7. The Contagious Diseases Acts were sanitary measures introduced during the 1860s in an attempt to control prostitutes, who were perceived by many as the source of venereal disease as well as of a more general moral and physical pollution.

8. This point has been emphasized by Paul Hirst (1981) in his discussion of Donzelot (1979).

9. Several were members of the Langham Circle (see p. 108).

10. In the view of one recent historian who was critical of this educational development, 'The curriculum and organisation of these schools . . . undoubtedly suffered from their connection with the feminist movement' (Peterson, 1971: 159)!

11. As did for example Harriet Taylor and John Stuart Mill (Mill, 1869). For a discussion of Taylor's influence on Mill, see Spender (1982).

12. See also Wood (1982).

13. Full degrees and university membership were not awarded to women until 1948.

14. Working-class schools were frequently mixed, unlike those of the middle classes, and older girls were often recruited to help care for younger children.

15. By 1914 the figures had risen to 75 per cent (Widdowson, 1980).

16. The part played by boys as well as girls in this capacity was commented upon by the London School Board inspectors in 1903: 'The results achieved by the Board have not been confined to the children. The influence of the schools has had a very wholesome and civilizing effect upon parents in the poorer quarters of London' (quoted in Rubinstein, 1977: 257).

17. In the United States at this time home economics was similarly becoming a subject which both confined women and established them as experts in a field of national importance. In fact Ehrenreich and English (1979) have pointed out that the alleged salience of the study of home economics was used during this period by some feminists to justify their access to higher education.

18. See Banks (1981) for a further discussion of this.

19. The views of many of the women involved in the Greenham Common peace movement in the 1980s can be compared with those of the nineteenth- and early twentieth-century 'separatists' in that they believe women to be essentially less violent than men, and thus better placed to fight for peace.

20. See for example the work of Jane Addams (1910) in Chicago.

COMMENT

The Urban, the Domestic and Education for Girls

This chapter is based on a lecture first given in the early 1980s as part of a sociology of urban education course at Homerton College, Cambridge, where I was teaching part-time. During a review of the course I drew the attention of my (male) colleagues to the absence of questions of gender on the syllabus, to which they responded by suggesting that I do a lecture. I went away and searched out in the University libraries all the relevant literature. There was not much. As yet this was an area relatively uninfluenced by feminist thought and I found it challenging to imagine how to recast the dominant paradigms in order to take account of gender. The solution I came up with was to understand the urban as a peculiarly gendered symbol. This is what gave me an entrance to the material. I used secondary sources and drew them together in order to explore the symbolic resonance not only of the urban but also the domestic. As I investigated the nineteenth-century context of philanthropy, domestic service and schooling I was struck by how the material would not sit easily within a theoretical framework which gave a simple priority to sexual difference. Class was a more important theoretical-political division between women, particularly in the nineteenth century, than I had predicted. This piece then confirms the break with the formulaic and limiting nature of 'patriarchy' as a concept.

As a piece of writing it confirms another break as well. Although rooted in feminist commitment, it was primarily an academic intervention, removed from the turbulence of feminist polemic and activism. The political and theoretical front line of engagement with other feminists was often more than I could bear. Confronting men was proving more straightforward and in many ways more fruitful. It was also consistent with my conviction that feminism should face outwards and address issues and constituencies not already immersed in feminist debate.

Theoretical analysis of the relationship between women and urban life has begun to develop in interesting ways over the last few years. The city in this body of work is both a symbolic and a material territory, as indeed it also is in the previous chapter. While some of the contributions to this expanding debate assert women's exclusion from the city, and hence from the experience of modernity (Wolff, 1985) others stress women's occupation of urban spaces, even in the latter part of the nineteenth century, and the freedom and excitement that city life has been able to offer.[1] Today, as the twentieth century draws to a close, the city remains mythologized, its symbolic register peculiarly resistant to transformation. Now, as before, it signifies danger, incitement, chaos, pollution and decay. As before, it is posed against the rural which continues even now to signify purity, tranquillity, family life, neighbourliness and nature. The persistence of these mythologies and their presence across the spectrum of political opinion is not easily made sense of. One could speculate that they are best understood as a denial of the ways in which women are increasingly making the city their own.

Note

1. See, for example, papers by Lynne Walker 'Vistas of pleasure: Victorian urban spaces' and Elizabeth Wilson 'Women in the city' both presented at 'Cracks in the Pavement: Gender/Fashion/Architecture', a Design Museum symposium April 1991. See also Elizabeth Wilson (1991) The Sphinx in the City and Mica Nava (forthcoming) 'Shopping around: women, modernity and consumerism'.

6

DRAWING THE LINE: A FEMINIST RESPONSE TO ADULT–CHILD SEXUAL RELATIONS

The contemporary feminist movement in the United States and Britain and feminist ideas about sexuality developed in large part both out of, and in reaction to, the libertarian and liberation politics of the 1960s. Within the libertarian theoretical framework, sexuality was understood as an energy and source of pleasure which needed to be freed from societal constraint.[1] Sexual repression was perceived as intimately linked to political authoritarianism: it was both a consequence of it and contributed to its persistence. One of the tasks of socialists was to undermine the prevailing sexual codes, to explore hedonism both for its own sake and for what were considered to be its inevitably progressive political ramifications. Important among the targets of these libertarian critiques were monogamous marriage, the age of consent, legislation relating to homosexuality and abortion, and almost any other sexual taboo which placed limits upon the 'free' sexual expression to which every individual was entitled.[2]

Rooted as it was in this tradition, the women's liberation movement in the early days insisted upon the sexual liberation of women, and mounted a critique of the double sexual standard – of the way in which the constraints of the puritan ethic and monogamy operated most particularly for women. The campaign for free abortion on demand was (in part) an aspect of this general struggle to centre-stage women's sexual freedom and pleasure, as was the focus on the clitoris as the source of female orgasm. This in turn suggested, at least theoretically, the potential dispensability of men and contributed to a gradual assertion of the radical nature of lesbianism. At the same time the early women's liberation movement formed alliances with the emerging gay movement because it was considered that homosexuals, both female *and* male, were also constrained by the existing rigid 'gender system' and its ideology (located somewhere 'out there').[3] However, alongside these liberationist-feminist celebrations and explorations of sexual possibility in which women were cast as active, initiating and powerful, there developed during the course of the 1970s a new sensitivity among feminists to the ways in which sex and sexual relations could be as oppressive as the more conventional targets of feminist attack. In this more sceptical analysis, sex ceased to be perceived as a fundamental drive which needed to be liberated. Instead the nature of sexuality was increasingly understood as socially constructed, as shaped by a range of historical factors among which the differential in social power between men and women was quite central.

This shift away from libertarianism can be seen with hindsight to be associated with a diversity of theoretical and political developments. On the one hand it signalled a (minority) theoretical interest in what, for instance, Freud and Foucault could contribute to a feminist understanding of the production of sexuality. On the other hand, and this was both the dominant and the more directly political response, it ushered in a revival of emphasis on *differences* in sexuality between men and women, and upon women as *victims* of male power and sexual desire. This kind of perspective underlies the notion of sexual harassment, and draws attention to the way in which unwanted sexual attention from men towards women in, for example, the context of work, constitutes an exercise of power and a form of exploitation. The idea of women as victims of male lust has contributed to the focus of some feminists upon pornography as one of the key supports of male supremacy.[4] It is also evident in the withdrawal of some women into political celibacy and political lesbianism,[5] and in the division of the gay movement along gender lines. There are of course important differences both between and within these more recent concerns of feminism, but what they have in common is the underlying idea of women as often powerless (despite the fact that feminist organization over these issues amounts to a counterattack), and sexuality, particularly heterosexuality, as often menacing and exploitative. The predominantly liberationist view, with which these more recent analyses are in conflict, cannot however be simply relegated to the past; here too the debate has continued and developed. Over sexual matters in general feminist positions are best understood as distributed along a continuum which (to extrapolate from Gordon and Dubois, 1983)[6] has at one pole the notion of sexuality as danger and women as victims of male power, and at the other, sexuality as pleasure and women as increasingly self-actualizing and powerful in relation to men.

This is not the only polarization to occur within the women's movement in recent years. There are a number of cross-cutting continua along which feminist theory and politics have been ranged,[7] and it is interesting to note that in these divisions individuals have not always found themselves aligned in any predictable fashion with others. However, this lack of consistency does not necessarily detract from the usefulness of the specific concepts, and in order to make sense of the issue under scrutiny in this chapter, that of sexual relations between adults and children, it is the sex-as-danger/sex-as-pleasure continuum which has seemed the most fruitful and apposite. Cross-generational sex pushes to the fore the contradictions between the libertarian and protectionist feminist perspectives. It also introduces interesting theoretical questions about gender and generational difference. In this chapter the discussion of these issues will use as a point of departure a specific instance: it will be based on a case study of a sexual relationship between Phil, a boy of fourteen, and Mr Smith, a forty-year-old teacher at his school.[8] Although perhaps not immediately obvious, this peripheral and stigmatized sexual encounter between two males *is* a matter for feminists and feminist theory in that it has at its centre the question of sexual power.[9] It also challenges the idea of men and women as unambiguous social categories which stand in immutable opposition to each other, because in sexual relation to adult men, gender divisions within the category of youth are attenuated. In the context of cross-generational relations, boys may be as powerless as girls. Another purpose in examining such relationships is that they can cast some light upon the multifaceted nature of masculinity, a problematic often neglected by feminists, who have in some instances been guilty of retaining notions of essential (and disagreeable) masculinity while simultaneously refusing any notion of essential or natural femininity. Finally, and of particular importance in this instance, the question of sexual relations between adults and children is a relevant one for feminists in that it is most often women who have responsibility for the care and protection of young people.

This last point is crucial, because this chapter is not only about the struggle to achieve a coherent theoretical evaluation of sexual relations between adults and children in spite of the apparently irreconcilable positions taken up by feminists. It is also about the dilemmas posed for feminists by the moral principles which reside within these theoretical critiques. Feminist contributions to social analysis have always been characterized, either explicitly or implicitly, by the formulation of a range of moral-political prescriptions about ways of being in our everyday lives.[10] The essence of these feminist moral imperatives is that they require more than a merely abstract response to the terms of reference of any particular argument; in addition they frequently demand assessments of real-life episodes (which in all probability cannot be compressed into any specific theoretical framework) and also a material response – a course of action. This chapter then concerns itself as well with the response (the course of action) of Mary, an individual feminist whose responsibility it was to care for Phil.

Although this is a particular narrative, it raises a number of general points about cross-generational sex and about the often incompatible nature of the moral precepts which emerge from the sex-as-danger/sex-as-pleasure discourse. In addition it raises questions about the viability of individual feminist interventions in contexts which are already overdetermined by legal and bureaucratic factors and which therefore permit only the most limited of initiatives. It thus draws attention to the inadequacy of existing methods of dealing with such issues, yet at the same time this specific case is able to indicate to us what a more satisfactory procedure could look like. There is another point which must be stressed: it must not be assumed that the presentation in this chapter of a particular narrative amounts to evidence of the uniqueness of such an occurrence. Sexual encounters between teachers and pupils in secondary schools are commonplace. Since Mary communicated to me the details of the incident in which she and Phil were involved, numerous other such relationships all over the country have come to my attention.[11] The majority of these have occurred between male teachers and girl pupils, but as I shall argue here, this fact does not radically alter the way in which such events are to be understood. In describing Phil's case I have occasionally incorporated aspects of these other incidents. What I recount here then consists of a composite of a number of stories. I have chosen to present my arguments in this format, that is to say to use as a central feature a single constructed instance, since this is most effectively able to illustrate the complex and contradictory nature of real experiences which almost invariably defy easy categorization. Finally, a case history – a particular rather than a general account – is able to prompt readers into considering what their own responses might be in such a situation; if it is able to accomplish this, then the use of a particular story amounts also to the construction of a practical political exercise.

The story

At the time of the incident Phil was homeless. He was an intelligent and independent boy who got on badly with his parents, and over the previous few years had a number of times been told by them to leave the house and find somewhere else to live. When this happened he would spend several months away from home; on this occasion he had already spent about ten weeks circulating between the houses of three or four of his schoolfriends, his girlfriend Polly, and Mr Smith, a teacher at his school who had a daughter of about Phil's age. On the whole Phil seemed to like this itinerant existence, though sometimes he was obviously upset and would talk to his friends about the difficulties with his parents and the problem of having nowhere permanent to live. Then at one point, for one reason or another, most of his temporary accommodation options collapsed. Eventually he ended up living on a long-term basis with his schoolfriends Mike and Anna Green and their mother Mary. After he moved into the Green household he told Mary about his friendship with Mr Smith. Mary had known that Phil and Mr Smith, who was an interesting and agreeable man, had always got on well together, that they enjoyed spending time together discussing ideas, and that Phil valued the way he had been singled out by Mr Smith for his special attention. However it became clear that Phil now wanted to talk in greater depth about the friendship. It emerged that Mr Smith had also declared his romantic and sexual feelings for Phil, and that Phil had found these unwelcome. Phil told Mary that Mr Smith had nevertheless persuaded him to have sex on two occasions. Although Phil cared for Mr Smith and was grateful to him for his support and interest, especially when he was having problems with his parents, he insisted that he had not wanted to have sex. However, he had agreed to it finally because he had not wanted to jeopardize the friendship, which he valued very much. But the sex had disgusted him, Phil said, and his strategy for coping with it was to pretend it was not happening. After the first time, which had taken place one weekend when Mr Smith's wife and daughter had been away and Mr Smith and Phil had got quite drunk together, Mr Smith had declared his remorse and concern and vowed it would not happen again. Phil had felt reassured by Mr Smith's promises and had continued to visit his house to show he still trusted him. Then one night a few weeks later Phil was feeling very depressed: he and Polly had had a row and split up; he had phoned his parents' house in an attempt to contact his older brother whom he had not seen for several months; when he left the message his mother had apparently not recognized his voice; his brother failed to return the call. So in the end, in despair he went to see Mr Smith, who took him out to a restaurant for a meal.

In the restaurant they chatted about different things, drank quite a lot of wine, and gradually Phil started to cheer up. Then Mr Smith apparently told Phil that he had recently had sex with Jeremy, another boy in Phil's year at school. Mr Smith told Phil that Jeremy had vomited after the incident, and that Jeremy's parents had told Mr Smith that they were worried about their son because he was looking unwell and behaving strangely. The story outraged Phil, who felt both that Jeremy had been exploited and, at the same time, that Mr Smith's protestations of love to himself could not have meant very much. He felt that his own position as the object of Mr Smith's affection and attention was being threatened, and he got quite drunk. After the meal he asked Mr Smith to drive him to Polly's house, but when he got there he felt unable to ring the bell because of his recent row with her. He said he felt too drunk and depressed to go to anybody else's place, and finally agreed to spend the night at Mr Smith's house. When they got there, Phil and Mr Smith went straight upstairs to Mr Smith's study. They had sex. Phil said he knew it was going to happen yet felt too miserable to say no. He said he felt that in some way Mr Smith was urging him to pay back all the kindness he had shown him, and that he owed it to Mr Smith to respond. But he said that the experience was a nightmare, and the memory of it continued to be a nightmare. Afterwards he felt sick and ran out of the house in tears; he sat sobbing on the pavement for about fifteen minutes, not knowing where to go. Finally Mr Smith came out looking for him and took him back to the house. Phil fell asleep almost immediately on the sofa and left the next morning without seeing anyone.

As she listened to Phil's story Mary was struck by the way in which he held himself responsible for what had happened; he stressed that he had allowed the sex with Mr Smith to take place. At the same time she was aware that in spite of the irony with which he recounted the events, Phil was upset and confused. This combination did not have the seamless quality of fantasy; indeed because of its contradictory nature, Mary was from the beginning convinced of the truth of Phil's story (as were most people who subsequently heard it and knew both characters in it). She told me that it was clear to her that Phil wanted help in making sense of what had happened. He had apparently already told the mothers of two of his friends: one had assumed that Phil had wanted the relationship and was mature enough to make up his own mind; the other was shocked because she considered that all sexual activity for fourteen-year-olds was wrong. Neither approach had seemed satisfactory to him. Mary sensed that Phil wanted a different interpretation from her; he knew she was liberal over sexual matters, he also knew she was a feminist, and in addition, an advisory teacher for the education authority. What kind of help was he asking for?

Mary told me she reflected for some time before telling Phil that in her opinion Mr Smith seemed to have been insensitive to Phil's feelings and taken advantage of his trust and need for friendship during a particularly insecure period in his life. She pointed out that young people might sometimes appear quite seductive to adults, they might want physical affection, but that did not give adults the right to impose sexual contact. Adults, and particularly teachers, had a responsibility not to abuse their positions of power. The consent offered by Phil in the situation which he had described seemed pretty meaningless, since not to consent could well have threatened the friendship. Besides, in a legal sense consent was not at issue; even if a young boy or girl desired and enjoyed sex with an adult, which was apparently not so in this case, it remained that such relations constituted a criminal offence. Mary made it clear that she considered sex between fourteen-year-olds a different matter, even though that was illegal too, because two fourteen-year-olds were much more likely to be equal. She also made it clear that her reservations about what had happened had nothing to do with the fact that this was a homosexual encounter. Phil said it was a great relief to talk about everything, and that although he felt betrayed and used, he could probably cope with what had happened. But he still felt very angry on Jeremy's behalf; Phil had noticed how miserable and solitary Jeremy often seemed and thought that Jeremy had probably not been able to talk to anybody about what had happened.

Over the following days Mary struggled with the contradictory thoughts and feelings that Phil's story had provoked in her. At stake was whether the matter could be left or whether she had a moral obligation to do something about it beyond helping Phil to make sense of it and deal with it. How many other children had Mr Smith seduced? She needed to sort out in her mind the difference between this event and a relationship she knew of between a sixteen-year-old boy and his twenty-two-year-old woman teacher, to which she could find no serious objection. Did she find that more acceptable because there was less discrepancy in age, and the relationship therefore created fewer incestuous echoes? Or because the woman's power as a teacher was balanced by her pupil's maleness?[12] Or because the pupil had shown no ambivalence about his desire, and no emotional pressure seemed to have been involved? Or because that particular boy at sixteen was definitely no longer a child? Probably all of those things. What difference did the heterosexual nature of that relationship make to her response to it? Mary said the questions presented themselves ceaselessly. Her own biography was rooted in the libertarianism of the 1960s, yet feminism in the 1970s had made her far more aware of the exploitative nature of many sexual relationships, of how aggressive, indulgent and damaging they could be. Then again, was what Mr Smith had done more damaging than the punitive and undermining behaviour which was legal and quite routine among sections of the teaching profession?[13] Perhaps not. In evaluating the issue it was important to distinguish between the moral-political and the legal. Legally this was an offence, yet so were certain other things that Mary condoned. So that was not decisive. Nevertheless it was an issue which would undoubtedly be significant if the matter were to be taken further. Should she take it further? What would happen to Mr Smith, to his wife and child? What did Phil want? By presenting her with the problem so soon after his arrival, was he in some unconscious way testing out the strength of her commitment to him as his new surrogate parent – playing the new mother off against the old father? To what extent was she responding to that test rather than to the issue itself?

Mary felt that if she decided to take it further, Phil must be consulted, but at the same time it was imperative that he should not feel responsible for the consequences of any action taken by her. In what manner should she take if further? Phil had obviously cared for Mr Smith; how much had he wanted the sexual encounter to take place (in spite of what he had said) and was that in any sense relevant? Legally it was irrelevant. Professionally it was irrelevant. As a teacher Mr Smith had a responsibility not to take advantage of children in his care, however infatuated they might be. And Phil had insisted all along that he valued the friendship, the attention, the caring that Mr Smith had offered but that he had not wanted sex. He had not welcomed the metamorphosis of father figure into lover. Morally, in terms of the moral principles constructed by feminism and socialism, it seemed untenable for a man of forty to take advantage of a child who was excruciatingly vulnerable by virtue of his homelessness and the rejection he had experienced from his parents. Besides, Mr Smith was a teacher of the subject at which Phil most excelled and would undoubtedly wish to pursue through to A level. What impact would the relationship have upon Phil's academic work if nothing were done? And then there was always Jeremy to consider, and any other children in the past and future.

Mary pondered upon the matter and discussed it at length with friends over a period of days. She considered the implications for Phil, for Mr Smith and his wife and daughter, and for the other children at the school. She concluded finally that there seemed to be three options open to her: to do nothing; to approach Mr Smith; to approach the headteacher. To do nothing, she eventually decided, would constitute a form of collusion; it would also be a denial of Phil's request for help. She reminded herself that whatever the consequences of some form of action, the ultimate responsibility would not lie with her, but with Mr Smith who had failed to consider the personal and professional implications of his own actions. *The issue had been initiated by him.* To approach Mr Smith directly would be to offer him the opportunity of presenting his version of the events. But Mary felt that the likelihood in such an instance was that Mr Smith would simply deny everything and the matter would turn into a personal confrontation between the two of them in which she would have insufficient authority to achieve a satisfactory outcome. Alternatively, Mr Smith might admit to the relationship and Mary might be able to extract a declaration of intent about the future, but what value could such apologies and avowals have? By that time the most appropriate resolution seemed to Mary to be that Mr Smith should leave the school quietly with a reference which would indicate that he was not a suitable candidate for teaching in primary or secondary schools. The option of approaching Mr Smith directly would not accomplish this. Mary also felt that if at a later date Mr Smith repeated this kind of behaviour – perhaps with serious repercussions for the child – and it emerged that she had been in a position to prevent it, she would not be able to justify her course of action to the school – or indeed to herself. During the period of these reflections Phil was becoming as indignant on his own behalf as he had been on behalf of Jeremy. He was also angered by the fact that Mr Smith had ignored him totally since the second incident; it confirmed his growing sense that Mr Smith's attention and concern were evidence of a sexual interest only. He was absolutely willing for the matter to be taken to the headteacher and uncharacteristically asserted that he did not mind if in consequence he was seen as a child in need of protection. To approach the headteacher directly was the course most often advocated by the many friends Mary had consulted, so finally this was what she decided she would do.

The head was sympathetic, sensitive and, predictably, disturbed about the matter. She too saw such incidents in terms of an unacceptable abuse of power, and stated categorically that the homosexual nature of the event did not enter into it. As Mary had expected, the head agreed that if Phil's story were true, then Mr Smith should not be allowed to remain in the school. However, what Mary had not anticipated was that the matter could not be dealt with at the head's discretion. The local education authority had devised a set procedure for such questions and it was incumbent upon the head to report the incident to her superiors. The procedure was set in motion and the matter was suddenly out of Mary's control. Phil was instructed to write down in detail what had happened to him – not an easy task. The following day the head presented Mr Smith with a copy of this statement and suspended him pending an investigation of the issue. Mr Smith apparently made no comment and was understood to have left his home immediately. The procedure also demanded that Phil's mother report the matter to the police. The head, Mary, Phil and Phil's mother (whom Phil had not seen at all for almost three months and who knew nothing about the incident) were all extremely unwilling to involve the police, but the education authority insisted that as this was a criminal offence it was obligatory to do so. They said that their own internal inquiry could not proceed if the police were not informed and pointed out that no other method existed for dealing with the issue. Phil's mother therefore reluctantly took Phil to the police station to make a statement, and he accompanied her reluctantly. Phil spent three harrowing hours there, arguing with his mother and with the police, who acted in the style for which they are notorious in cases of rape by subjecting him to an aggressive and humiliating investigation that included probing for intimate details about the sexual encounter. The police also insisted on raising the issue of consent by referring to a recent case of an eleven-year-old girl who had had sexual intercourse with an adult man and who had, according to the police, 'acted provocatively'. At this Phil quite properly told them that consent was not at issue and walked out of the police station in tears, abandoning the uncompleted statement and determined, both for his own sake and for the sake of Mr Smith, not to return.

However, the education authority procedure was apparently too inflexible to allow for this. Once Mary had reported the matter to the head, it seemed that Phil was obliged to pursue it according to the rules regardless of the personal cost to all concerned. It was suddenly revealed by the authority that if Phil failed to continue with his statement to the police, this would amount to an admission that he had made 'a malicious allegation'. The consequences could well be that Mr Smith would return to the school, and that Phil would have to leave it, would leave his friends, and would have upon his record a statement to the effect that he had made a serious and untrue accusation against a teacher. Yet to pursue the matter with the police seemed as bad if not worse. It entailed the continuation of the traumatic and degrading interrogation at the police station, as well as a court case in which Phil would undoubtedly undergo a rigorous cross-examination in order to establish in minute and sordid detail the precise nature of the physical contact he had had with Mr Smith, for which in any case there was no substantiating evidence. Furthermore, in such a context Phil's unstable background would in all likelihood be exposed and held against him by Mr Smith's legal representatives. There was certainly no guarantee that the veracity of Phil's statement would be accepted in a court of law. Though if it were, the consequences would also be appalling. In that case there was a real possibility that Mr Smith would receive a gaol sentence (probably in isolation since that is the lot of sexual offenders), a punishment which neither Mary nor Phil felt was at all commensurate with the initial 'crime'. The matter was out of their hands and in the hands of a government bureaucracy and legal system with which, over this question, they could not agree.

The dilemma was acute, indeed overwhelming. Mary had never before experienced such moral turmoil. Phil insisted that the prospect of the court case as well as the responsibility for Mr Smith's possible conviction and sentence, and the effects of these upon his family, were all much worse than the original experience. He could not go through with it. Yet the education authority had warned that the consequences of withdrawing his allegation at this point would be extremely severe. Why should Phil have to suffer twice over for Mr Smith's indulgence and lack of responsibility? There no longer appeared to be an acceptable way out of the situation. Mary regretted that she had not researched the likely repercussions of her intervention more thoroughly; all she had ever intended was for Mr Smith to leave schoolteaching. She felt no more able to tolerate responsibility for a gaol sentence than Phil could. But then neither could she stand by and tolerate Phil's exclusion from the school for being unwilling to go through with an allegation which had in the first instance been presented to the authorities by *her*. No alternative options seemed available.

In despair, Mary sought legal advice. The lawyer whom she consulted made it clear that a refusal by Phil to testify against Mr Smith in court did not legally amount to a withdrawal of his allegations. Phil and Mary felt enormously relieved. However, a few days later the head phoned Mary to tell her that Mr Smith had returned home. He had contacted his union solicitors and was categorically denying the whole episode. Apparently the education authority had decided that as the police felt they had no case (since Phil refused to testify) then they could not proceed with their own internal inquiry. According to the head, the consequences of this would definitely be that Mr Smith would be free to return to the school and that Phil must leave it. Because Phil was unwilling to pursue the matter with the police, the assumption continued to be that his allegations must be malicious. It appeared that there were two standards of justice in operation here: Mr Smith could not be made to leave the school because there was insufficient evidence that the accusations were true, yet Phil could be thrown out in spite of the fact that there was no evidence that his statement was false. The implications were both paradoxical and extremely disturbing: it looked as though the result of Mary's attempt to protect the child was that he was going to be more damaged and victimized than ever. This would be the ultimate irony.

Since the education authority appeared to have no power either to proceed with an internal inquiry or to prevent the return of Mr Smith to the school unless there was a criminal conviction, Mary felt that the most that she could salvage from the imbroglio at that point was an agreement that Phil would not be expelled. Phil himself agreed that under the circumstances to stay at the school and coexist with Mr Smith was the remaining option most worth fighting for. So Mary phoned the authority again; stated unequivocally that Phil's refusal to testify was not the legal equivalent of a withdrawal of his allegation; reiterated her support for

Phil's decision not to proceed, since that seemed the least traumatic course of action for him personally; made it clear that she would vigorously oppose any attempt to exclude Phil from the school; and demanded to know on what grounds this was being proposed. It was then that she discovered that the 'set procedure', to which the authority had often referred, was not nearly as immutable as had been implied. At that point it emerged that in spite of the threats, there was no statutory obligation to exclude Phil from the school in such a case. His continuing attendance at the school would only be in question if Mr Smith insisted upon his expulsion from it, and was in addition able to convince his fellow trade unionists to support such a demand with industrial action – an extremely improbable event given the particularities of the context.

So it came to pass that Mr Smith also opted for coexistence, and although he neither demanded Phil's expulsion nor minded being seen chatting to him in the corridor, most of the time he continued (when asked) to deny the accusation which had been levelled against him. By then a number of people attached to the school in various ways (staff, students, parents) knew about the incident, and as far as Mary could tell, found the substance of Phil's story quite credible. However, on the whole the return of Mr Smith to the school appeared to have received an extremely low-key response. To all intents and purposes then, the closing scenario of the drama looked remarkably like the opening one.

What can be concluded?

One of the things this case history does is to draw attention to some of the complexities of those occurrences in real life which demand from feminists both a form of moral political assessment and also a decision about a course of action. Mary, in her attempt to evaluate the events recounted in this story, referred to a number of principles deriving from feminist theory and politics, yet these proved insufficient to enable her to develop a consistent and unambivalent response. At the crux of her dilemma lay a number of contradictions. The first of these was rooted in the diversity of feminist theory and its inability to offer a coherent analysis or set of principles which could act as guidelines for instances of this kind. The second was rooted in the dissonant and frayed nature of the circumstances themselves; the particularities of this case were not easily categorized. Finally the whole matter of Mary's response was made more complex by the inadequacy of existing official methods for dealing with such issues. What would a more satisfactory procedure look like? These are some of the questions and contradictions which will be addressed in greater detail in this final section.

I shall start by examining some of the arguments which have been put forward both for and against sexual relations between adults and children. But before doing so I shall focus briefly upon a terminological point. In this chapter the phrase 'sexual relations between adults and children' has on the whole been used in preference to 'paedophilia' because the very expression paedophilia appears to foreclose certain debates. Its use serves to reaffirm the category of 'the paedophile',[14] who is thus cast as an aberrant personality – a total identity – defined by the fact of sexual attraction to pre-adolescent and early adolescent children. To refer instead to 'sexual relations between adults and children', though more unwieldy, may help to avoid the pitfalls of definitions which pre-empt certain readings, and may perhaps offer the possibility of a less partisan interpretation of the issues.

The defence of such sexual relations has been most forcefully put by a certain (very small) section of the gay libertarian Left (predominantly by men, but also by a few women who identify themselves as part of the feminist movement and who tend to cluster at the extreme end of the sex-as-pleasure continuum).[15] Although in principle the debate has included heterosexual relations, it has focused primarily on what has been termed by its advocates as 'man–boy love' (statistically a tiny minority – estimated at 10 per cent [Wilson, 1983a: 121] – of cross-generational sexual relations). This has partly been because, among libertarians, men lovers of girls have been less outspoken in their own defence. It has also been a consequence of the inordinately heavy gaol sentences meted out to men found guilty of homosexual relations with children in the United States during the 1970s compared with those guilty of heterosexual (including incestuous) relations with girls under the age of consent. Quite properly it has been pointed out that this is evidence of the massive prejudice that exists against gay relationships rather than of the concern to protect underage children. This is also borne out by the status in popular (male?) mythology of sexual relations between adult women and boys, which although a largely undocumented and unverified phenomenon, retains a romantic and quite distinct image from that of the archetypal man-in-raincoat-molester-of-boys. Sex between women and girls also remains relatively undocumented and uncommented upon, though Pat Califia (1981) in her discussion of man–boy sexual relations, argues in its defence.

Although differences exist between those who defend cross-generational sexual relations, on the whole the most interesting arguments have tended to make the following points. Childhood must be understood historically as a relatively recent social construction, children in advanced capitalist and patriarchal societies are oppressed within the family; they are financially dependent and have no right of political or sexual expression. The relations of domination and subordination between adults and children are not dissimilar to those between men and women. 'The language of "protection" and "innocence" is precisely that used to subordinate women in the nineteenth century' (Presland, 1981: 76). In fact, the argument goes, children are no more sexually 'innocent' than women have been presumed to be. Children experience sexual desire and pleasure from a very early age, as psychoanalysis has revealed, and sometimes the objects of their desire are adults. Children must have the right, as adults do, to initiate, consent and derive pleasure from sexual encounters, 'to define their own sensual relationships with adults' (Moody, 1981: 153). Califia has stressed the importance of distinguishing between a 'consensual sex act which takes place between two people of different social status and a sexual assault (which can easily take place between people of equal social status)' (1981: 138). A child's consent must not be taken less seriously than that of an adult; children are capable of and regularly do both consent and refuse to do many things required of them by adults. It must not be assumed that such sexual relationships are imposed upon children or that they are necessarily distressful for them.[16] Proponents of man–boy love have pointed out that their critics – who have drawn attention to the power disparities between adults and children – have focused on sexuality (and primarily upon gay sexuality) to the exclusion of other spheres in which power disparities exist, such as the family, education and the economy. Gayle Rubin (1981) has emphasized the need to avoid playing into the hands of the Moral Right, who deny the very existence of childhood and early adolescent sexual feelings, both gay and straight. However, although defending the 'diversity of human sexuality' and the rights of 'stigmatized sexual minorities', she does concede that young people can be abused and exploited in such relationships. Finally Moody (1980) draws attention to the frequently aggressive and bigoted police interrogations of the victims of sexual assault which he argues are very likely to be more traumatic for the child than the initial sexual encounter. On the whole the literature about sexual relationships between men and boys, by those who are advocates of it, tends to concern itself with the task of justifying such relationships, with attempting to dispel prejudice, emphasizing the sexual desires of children, claiming for cross-generational sex an innocence and purity,[17] and readdressing the issue of consent. Although drawing attention to the social construction of childhood, that is to say to the way in which definitions of childhood and modes of protecting children have varied historically, the category of paedophile itself appears rarely to be problematized. I have come across no attempts to deconstruct sexual relationships between adults and children. The paedophile is, he exists.[18] The why and how his desire is constructed remains unexamined.[19]

The principal arguments against cross-generational sexual relations, which also emanate from within the feminist and gay movements, probably represent the overwhelming majority of individuals and occupy an enormously wide range of positions along the sex-as-danger/sex-as-pleasure continuum. Divisions between positions (and most certainly between the poles) are particularly acute and acrimonious in the United States. But in Britain also there are significant differences between those who take up a kind of latter-day 'social purity' position of extreme protectionism (more often in relation to girls than to boys), and those who locate themselves somewhere between the midway point and the libertarian sex-as-pleasure extreme, but who nevertheless oppose sexual relations between adults and children.[20] The arguments outlined here do not represent a specific position in this spectrum; they are intended to convey the main points made by most of the feminist critics of cross-generational sex. These start by questioning the *nature* of childhood sexuality advanced by the defenders of man–boy love. Although agreeing that children have sexual feelings and desires, the opponents of cross-generational sex argue that it should not therefore be supposed that what children want is to engage in sexual *acts* (that is to say in mutual mastur-bation, fellatio, penetration); theirs might be a far more diffuse desire for physical contact and affection. As Elizabeth Wilson has said in relation to incest between adults and children:

> Because we believe that children do have sexual desires, it does not follow that adults should engage in sexual relations with them; nor does it follow that, because a child may have *unconscious* incestuous impulses of a vague nature towards a parent, it consciously desires the adult expression of them. (1983a: 123)

The recognition of childhood sexual feeling does not mean that children's sexuality can be unproblematically equated with adult sexuality. There are likely to be disparities not only in the nature and object of desire, but also in 'experience . . . physical potentialities, emotional resources, sense of responsibility, awareness of the consequences of one's actions, and above all, power between adults and children' (Gay Left Collective, 1981: 60). It is this issue of disparities of power which has been most focused upon by feminist and gay opponents of cross-generational sex. In a social context in which inequalities of power between adults and children are the norm, 'consent' cannot maintain the meanings that it might have between adults with similar social positions and perceptions, or between adults and children in some utopian world. As Angela Hamblin and Romi Bowen have argued:

> To consent a person must know what it is she is consenting to and she must be free to say yes or no. We argue that a child does not have the power to say yes or no. Children do not have the knowledge or independence to make a deci-sion about sex with an adult. They have been brought up to obey adults. They depend upon adults for the resources to live. (Hamblin and Bowen, 1981: 8)

In a social context in which adult men can give or withhold gifts, money, affection, approval, even a home, the notion of consent merges impercep-tibly into coercion. Robin Morgan, one of the more vehement feminist opponents of cross-generational sex, has stated that she thinks that 'boy-love is a euphemism for rape, regardless of whether the victim seems to invite it. . . . When somebody powerless is getting fucked, literally and figuratively, by somebody who is powerful, that is a rape situation' (quoted in Califia, 1981: 137).

If consent and coercion cannot be properly separated out in cases of cross-generational sexual relations, then it is irrelevant to point to the greater social power of boys compared to girls. What is at stake is boys' relationship to adult men, in which they are relatively powerless, not to girls. (Indeed boys as victims may experience an added anxiety and shame because of the particular taboos associated with gay sexuality; however they may also possess an added strength in that they can use those taboos against their assailants by threatening to expose them.) Since such sexual relations so frequently occur between children and the adults who are responsible for their care and with whom they have an emotional relationship (like relatives and teachers), the issue is not merely one of a confusing and possibly unpleasant sexual experience which can afterwards be easily forgotten. Although such events are not invariably traumatic, they very often are and many victims of such relationships have only in adulthood been able to reveal how they continued to experience a sense of horror, betrayal and self-blame for many years. As children the possibility of refusing to consent had not seemed available to them. Of course most proponents of paedophilia insist that consent is essential and they argue that it can easily be distinguished from coercion in that sexual relations are often initiated by the child and enjoyed by him or her. One critical response to this assertion has been to draw attention to the fact that, ironically, the principal spokespeople on behalf of cross-generational sex have been adult men, not boys or girls (e.g. Millett and Blasius, 1981: 81), and that until recently the argument was posed in terms of the rights of men to have sex with children rather than the rights of children to have sex with adults. It is important to stress that many feminists and gays who oppose adult–child sexual relations because of disparities of power and the likelihood of exploitation, support the right of boys and girls to have sexual relations, gay or straight, with each other, and oppose recourse to consent legislation in order to inhibit these. Where some feminists have argued to maintain the legal age of consent this has been primarily in order to protect abused young people (mainly girls) from the ordeal of having to prove, as happens in the case of rape, that they did *not* consent to sex with adults. It has also been to provide young girls with a legal prohibition to refer to if they feel under pressure to have sex, whether from adults or their peers. However this protectionist feminist position has by no means been uniformly accepted by young people themselves on the grounds that it can reinforce the sexual double standard, limit sexual activity and be used to justify the non-dissemination of contraceptive advice to those most in need.[21]

This discussion has only marginally addressed the more common manifestation of adult–child sexuality in schools, that is to say the covert (sometimes overt) sexualizing of certain teacher–pupil relations in the pedagogic context, in spite of the fact that Phil and Mr Smith's relationship represents an extreme expression of this process. The subject demands a chapter to itself. I would like to point out, however, that as an issue it is encumbered by similar sorts of sex-as-positive/sex-as-negative contradictions to those encountered in an examination of cross-generational sex. For example, does the sexualizing of teacher–pupil relations in the classroom amount to a form of sexual harassment, and disadvantage those who are singled out in this way? Or alternatively, could the essence of successful learning precisely lie in the investiture of certain subjects and pedagogic relationships with a covert form of sexual desire? Perhaps a bit of both, but all this represents a divergence from the principal topic under scrutiny in this chapter – the seduction of Phil by Mr Smith – that is to say *the actualization* of the fantasy and innuendo (both conscious and unconscious) which permeate the social context of schooling, yet usually remain unrecognized.

Mary's reaction to this 'actualization' of what most often remains fixed at the level of fantasy indicated that she had referred to aspects of both sets of arguments – to those opposing and those defending sexual relations between adults and children – in order to make sense of the event.[22] Part of the difficulty in arriving at a coherent evaluation stemmed from the contradictory nature of the circumstances themselves. Phil at fourteen could not easily be categorized as a child. He was streetwise, well informed, and astute both about his own feelings and the complexities of family life. Yet he was *also* sensitive, innocent and vulnerable. Physically not out of puberty, he could not, either, be categorized as an adult. What ultimately seemed to define him as a boy rather than a man in this particular context was his immaturity *in relation* to Mr Smith. If Mr Smith had been twenty instead of forty, the power disparity and incest symbolism could not have had the same significance. If Mr Smith had been a woman of twenty, the power disparity would have been even less. Thus both masculinity and youth as social constructs possess meaning in so far as they are counterposed to and interrelated with on the one hand, femininity and on the other, age. Phil in relation to his fourteen-year-old girlfriend was situated in a different discourse. But in terms of his power relations to Mr Smith (though obviously not in terms of his sexual desirability) his masculinity made very little difference.

The issue of consent in Phil's story seems to present fewer problems. Although he formally consented, the nature of his consent was hardly free from those features, like indebtedness and the fear of withdrawal of affection, which suggest that consent cannot be easily distinguished from coercion in very many instances. Yet the fact that the sexual act itself was not pleasurable for Phil should not on its own be used as evidence to convince us that the consent was in fact coerced. For of course many sexual encounters to which adults consent, which they desire, turn out to be disappointingly unpleasurable. On the other hand, the fact that the experience of sex with Mr Smith was such a 'nightmare' for Phil might precisely be evidence of the specific and distinct nature of pubescent sexuality. One could speculate that what Phil found exciting was the discovery of his own power as the object of Mr Smith's desire. But being aroused by the power to arouse is not at all the same as enjoying the sweaty and focused urgency that the real-life adult thing too often is – as many women are well aware.

Then there was the question of Jeremy who had apparently vomited, and all the other children for whom Mr Smith was responsible in his capacity as teacher – with whom he went on school trips, to whom he gave extra lessons after school, and whom he might invite to his home in the future in order to become better friends with his own daughter. There was also the unpalatable fact that Mr Smith might well have referred deliberately to his encounter with Jeremy as part of a strategy to seduce Phil again. Phil was, after all, homeless and drunk, he had recently broken up with his girlfriend and not been recognized by his mother; he was therefore particularly likely to feel displaced and open to persuasion. There is no doubt that Phil had felt deeply betrayed and disturbed by the transformation of Mr Smith from attentive and attractive father figure into sexual assailant.

On balance, having considered the full range of debates and having taken into account the details of the particular instance, Mary continued to feel that Mr Smith's behaviour had been indulgent, exploitative and indefensible. He should not have done what he did and should not be in a position, such as teaching in secondary schools, where he could do it again. Nevertheless, in spite of this, she was not sure that her course of action in going to the head was something she would repeat were the same circumstances to recur. What had been clearly revealed to her by the incident was the inadequacy of the existing procedure for dealing with such matters. For a start, the 'set procedure' devised by the disciplinary department was opaque in the extreme. No information was given to Mary about the scenario that was likely to unfold, about the possible nature of the police and court interrogations, about the likelihood of a criminal conviction for indecent assault and the range of possible prison sentences. No formal statement was provided about the authority's policy and past practices in such instances, nor about the principles which determined the establishment of an internal inquiry. No explanation was given for the fact that an internal inquiry could be conducted only if the police considered that there was sufficient evidence to proceed with a criminal prosecution. Why, if an obligation of the education authority was to act *in loco parentis*, did it insist that Phil undergo a harrowing police investigation and cross-examination in court in which the most intimate of details would be publicly inspected? The demand seemed particularly misplaced since, given Phil's 'unstable background' and because there was no substantiating evidence for his allegation, whether Mr Smith would be found guilty remained in question. The determination of the authority to involve the police at all costs as part of the set procedure was of course a consequence of the criminal nature of the occurrence. Yet it seemed remarkably unconducive to the promotion of trust and good relations as well as unlikely to encourage the co-operation of young people in similar instances in the future, since for many of them the experience of the police and courts might well be more painful than the original sexual encounter.

But not only was the education authority procedure opaque, and open to criticism on the grounds that both its refusal to conduct an internal investigation and its insistence upon the introduction of criminal proceedings could be counterproductive – as in this instance they were – it also appeared to Mary that its representatives had acted in a calculatedly dishonest manner in suggesting that Phil would have to leave the school if he did not go through with the police inquiry. Since it had been hinted to Mary that Phil's story was considered extremely plausible, it seemed that the threats to expel him could only be understood (with hindsight) as part of a strategy designed to persuade and pressure him to continue with the police statement and to testify in court. This was the only chance of obtaining the legal conviction required in order for the education authority to prevent the return of Mr Smith to teaching. Yet, to put it bluntly, this would be to sacrifice Phil for the sake of the school and other children who might be at risk in the future. It was this contradiction which most starkly exposed the weaknesses of the institutional procedure. Theoretically designed to protect the child, in practice it appeared to offer two options only: Phil should either have said nothing, or be prepared to endure the whole mortifying business from the beginning to the very end – *on his own*. Forced into being the isolated representative of all other victims in the past and future, Phil himself would have been victimized several times over.

It was precisely the crude nature of the procedure which rendered it ineffectual, or at least at first glance appeared to do so. Because it so thoroughly bludgeoned the fine gradations of Phil and Mary's judgement, they withdrew from it. Yet paradoxically the very limitations of the procedure were ultimately to contribute to a more subtle and satisfactory solution than anyone could have anticipated. The fact that a complaint was embarked upon but not pursued, that Mr Smith finally went back to school, did not simply return the matter to square one. On the contrary, a considerable amount was accomplished through this aborted attempt to do something about the matter. For a start, when it was finally all over, Phil felt pretty good. He had demonstrated unequivocally to Mr Smith that he would not be taken advantage of. At the same time he had gained from Mary substantial evidence of her commitment to protect and care for him. In addition Phil had largely managed to avoid the traumas of the police and court. His friends had been extremely supportive and loyal. Although he felt not entirely approved of by the headteacher of the school because he had not seen the matter through, this was compensated for by Mr Smith's understandable appreciation. Under these circumstances, the prospect of co-existing in the school with Mr Smith was not unpalatable.

The procedure embarked upon but not completed had other positive effects as well. Mr Smith had received a warning. It was not unreasonable to assume that he was a great deal less likely to repeat such incidents than if nothing had been done, so children in the future would be less at risk than Phil himself had been. One other consequence of having taken the matter a little way along the route of the set procedure and then abandoning it was that it allowed the subject to emerge from its traditional regime of silence. Since the issue was raised, but not judged, it provoked Mr Smith's friends and colleagues to make assessments for themselves. And interestingly, the response of the other teachers suggested that they too believed the gist of Phil's story in that none demanded his exclusion from the school, *yet* neither did they instantly demand the dismissal of Mr Smith (though they would henceforth be alert to a possible repetition of such conduct). Thus it appears that, haphazardly, by dint of the failure of the set procedure, an opportunity arose for the members of the community of the school – those most familiar with and sensitive to the personal circumstances of both Phil and Mr Smith – to begin to address the matter. Through attempting to avoid the harshest consequences of legal intervention, a way was fortuitously found which provided local surveillance and some measure of protection, which in principle (and in this instance) was more appropriate to the particular than the institutionalized procedures of the law and education authorities are capable of being.

One could argue then, that the option arrived at by Phil and Mary, that of going halfway and then stopping, could be recommended as an example of how to deal with such issues under present circumstances. As a method it could undoubtedly be refined. An imaginative and detailed strategy lies beyond the scope of this chapter, but, for example, ways could be devised within schools of convening committees (of which students would also be members) in order to alert the whole school community to the problem of sexual harassment and to insist that it receives the attention it deserves. The focus in this chapter on the relatively uncommon phenomenon of a sexual relationship between a male teacher and a male pupil must not be allowed to obscure the fact that it is overwhelmingly *girls* in schools who, on a daily basis, are the victims of unwelcome attention from both male teachers and male pupils. It must also be stressed that a proposal for an alternative procedure of this kind is not an argument for abolishing the age of consent, since this legislation continues to provide a form of protection for young people and continues to define the issue as one that is serious.[23] What the proposal does represent is the possibility of recourse to additional and distinctive forms of regulation. This itself is indicative of the more general contemporary shift in the location of illicit and taboo sexual practices away from the realm of the law and penalty (Foucault, 1979). However, this shift must not be interpreted simply as a more subtle and sophisticated form of surveillance. Nor should it be interpreted merely as a relaxation of regulation, part of the more general liberalization of attitudes and law towards sexual behaviour. The proposal constitutes a distinct but continuing and emphatic form of vigilance which is fuelled by the feminist insistence upon the centrality of the exercise of power in many sexual relations, whether between men and women or between men and boys. The focus on power may ultimately be able to transform our understanding of the substance of these relationships. Instead of locating and analysing them within a paradigm of sexual behaviour – in terms of sexual freedom or sexual variation – they must be decoded and read as practices which are above all manifestations of *domination*, and are profoundly intertwined with the social and historical contexts in which children and adults, male and female, are positioned.

Notes

1. See for example the work of Wilhelm Reich and Herbert Marcuse. Lynne Segal (1983b) discusses this background in ' "Smash the family?" Recalling the 1960s'.

2. For example David Cooper said in *Death of the Family* (1971): 'Making love is good in itself and the more it happens in any way possible or conceivable between as many people as possible more and more of the time, so much the better' (quoted in Segal, 1983b: 53). See also *The Little Red Schoolbook* (Hansen and Jensen, 1971).

3. The argument is elaborated by Fernbach (1980).

4. Much has been written about this issue. See for example Rosalind Coward and WAVAW (1982); Paula Webster (1981); Andrea Dworkin (1981); for a very useful overview see Chapter 7 in Elizabeth Wilson (1983a).

5. See discussion by Hilary Allen (1982).

6. Linda Gordon and Ellen Dubois (1983) in their article: 'Seeking ecstasy on the battlefield: danger and pleasure in nineteenth-century feminist sexual thought' examine theoretical and political differences between nineteenth-century 'social purity' feminists and early twentieth-century women sexual radicals. They suggest that aspects of these different traditions are echoed in today's divisions between feminists. Elizabeth Wilson (1983b), in her introduction to the Gordon and Dubois article in *Feminist Review* 13, situates these observations in the context of the American debate, though they are clearly relevant to discussion in Britain as well.

7. The capitalism–patriarchy debate has provided another. For a discussion of these differences see Anne Phillips (1981).

8. These are of course pseudonyms.

9. It is vital to keep in mind that the overwhelming proportion of adult–child sexual encounters take place between men and girls.

10. This argument is developed in Chapter 2.

11. I know of no systematic research in this area. Information is difficult to obtain since incidents of this kind are often only known about locally; details of them tend to be hushed up and frequently do not even reach the administrative levels of the education authority.

12. Valerie Walkerdine (1981) has drawn attention to a remarkable instance of this process.

13. At the time of these events an astonishing 90 per cent of education authorities in this country had not banned corporal punishment; a high proportion of schools continue to use it on a regular basis.

14. A historically specific category constructed in relation to legal and psychiatric discourses of the nineteenth and twentieth centuries, though details of this process are hard to come by.

15. For example Pat Califia and Gayle Rubin (both contributors to Daniel Tsang [ed.] [1981] *The Age Taboo*, a collection of articles which examines the issue of sexual relations between men and boys) are known among feminists in the United States for their libertarian defence of sado-masochism.

16. PIE (Paedophile Information Exchange) in its pamphlet *Paedophilia* (1978) quotes a study by Lauretta Bender and Abraham Blau: 'The reaction of children to sexual relations with adults' *American Journal of Orthopsychiatry*, (1937), in which it is claimed that: 'The emotional placidity of most of the children would seem to indicate that they derived some fundamental satisfaction from the relationship. The children rarely acted as injured parties and often did not show any evidence of guilt, anxiety or shame. Any emotional disturbance they presented could be attributed to external restraint rather than internal guilt.'

17. In fact there are (at least) a few known cases where individuals associated with those groups which defend, theorize and attempt to cleanse paedophilia, have deceived and taken advantage of boys in council care and other difficult personal circumstances.

18. The paedophile is almost never a she.

19. Elizabeth Wilson (1983b: 38) has made this point in relation to sado-masochism and Gayle Rubin's libertarian defence of it.

20. Of course virulent criticism has also been articulated by right-wing moral crusaders, such as Mary Whitehouse, who oppose all forms of sexual behaviour unsanctioned by marriage, most particularly those which are homosexual. These views are not considered in this chapter since they did not enter into Mary's deliberations when evaluating the issues.

21. Underage sex has also frequently been used as a pretext for taking young girls into council care; see for example Deirdre Wilson (1978). A number of astute and persuasive criticisms of the age of consent legislation are made by young women in 'Sex under sixteen' in *Spare Rib* (1981).

22. How individuals end up 'selecting' a particular set of views is a very complex business and cannot be understood without also taking into account unconscious mental processes.

23. The age of consent is a complex issue which is only superficially addressed in this chapter. An argument could be made for abolishing it and putting in its place a professional code of practice in which sexual relationships between teachers and pupils, although not illegal, would be grounds for dismissal (as they are between client and practitioner in the medical profession). This would be likely to improve the rate at which such offences get reported, since the police and courts would not be involved, and might therefore be more effective than existing procedure. However a reform of this kind would fail to protect those children assaulted outside educational institutions. A very high proportion of child abusers are family friends and relatives who are not covered by incest legislation either.

COMMENT

Drawing the Line: A Feminist Response to Adult–Child Sexual Relations

Mary in this chapter is a thinly disguised version of myself. Phil was a friend of one of my sons and lived with us as a foster child. The events described here took place in 1983. 'Drawing the Line' was written out of an urgent need to document and make sense of the events as they occurred. 'Local intellectuals,' to refer again to Foucault's observation, are characterized by their engagement 'at the precise points at which their own conditions of life or work situate them' (1980). This piece was one more such a project; in this case the 'precise point' was sexual relations in the local school.

'Adult–child sexual relations' as I called the phenomenon I observed, was understood at the time as a predominantly gay male question and was not much discussed outside the literature on or by paedophiles and advocates of 'man–boy love' (Tsang, 1981). It was not until later in the decade – partly as a consequence of feminist agitation – that the heterosexual and familial nature of the phenomenon gained widespread recognition. As this happened 'child sexual abuse' became not only the dominant term and concept but also a much debated public issue (see *Feminist Review*, 28). However, in 1983, on the cusp of the libertarian/sex-as-danger divide, sex between adults and children had a much more ambiguous position. It was mostly taboo and disavowed, and was not yet considered an appropriate subject for a volume of essays aimed at the expanding feminist market. In this sense my account was ahead of its time.

Paradoxically, in the climate of today, after eight years of AIDS, after more than a decade of Conservative rule and associated attacks on the 'permissive' society, and with the ascendancy of sex-as-danger convictions within feminism as elsewhere, the piece now appears to have a rather dated quality in relation to sexuality. It also seems slightly dated in its advocacy of the 'collective' and 'community' solution. These were strategies which seemed more plausible before the demise of the Greater London Council (GLC) and the more general undermining of municipal socialism and idealism during the late 1980s. To acknowledge this datedness is not to disparage the piece of work; on the contrary, there seems much to regret in the fading of these left libertarian principles. In fact the strength of the chapter probably lies in its rootedness in this political tradition which, combined with the specificity of case history, resulted in a refusal to foreclose on what might be the *meaning* of Phil's sexual encounter, unlike more recent work on child sexual abuse. Thus it was not immediately assumed that the experience was wholly evil and destructive, as became the tendency within feminism a few years later when the extent of incestuous abuse against even very young children was exposed.

Overall there are many thematic and theoretical continuities between 'Drawing the Line' and the earlier chapters in this book. These emerge in the delineation of differences between feminists, in the (re)investigation of feminism as moral code, and in the insistence that boys too can be exploited. In terms of my own theoretical and political development, the chapter reveals a continuing search for moral justice and certainty, yet at the same time, in working through the intricacies and contradictions of a specific instance, it also exposes the limitations of such a pursuit and indeed the impossibility of moral absolutes more generally. In this respect it represents another step along the intellectual route outlined in the Introduction.

7

OUTRAGE AND ANXIETY IN THE REPORTING OF CHILD SEXUAL ABUSE: CLEVELAND AND THE PRESS

The phenomenon of child sexual abuse erupted on to the front pages of Britain's newspapers when it was discovered, in June 1987, that an unprecedented number of children in Cleveland, an area of high unemployment in the north-east of England, had been made subjects of place of safety orders and removed from their homes because it was suspected that they were victims of sexual abuse by adults. Over the following weeks the Cleveland story retained its status as important news and, indeed, continues to do so as I write and the official inquiry into the events there proceeds.

This chapter is not an attempt to establish the 'truth' of what happened in Cleveland, even if this were possible. What I want to do here is to explore the way the press tried to make sense of a phenomenon which had hitherto been kept a family secret, tabooed and disavowed, and which, as a consequence of media attention, grew over a period of weeks to occupy a position of prominence in public discourse and popular consciousness.

What conceptual apparatus – if any – did the press rely on in order to understand the issues on which it focused so much attention and anxiety? In what way – if any – did the shaping and selection of news contribute, not only to the way child sexual abuse was popularly understood, but also to the formulation and consolidation of a viewpoint which might be identified as belonging either to the Left or to the Right? To what extent were debates within feminism taken into account in this process?

In addition to addressing these questions, I want to look at the explosion of media preoccupation itself. Similar escalations of media concern have in the past been usefully illuminated by applying to them the notion of 'moral panic'.[1] These are likely to occur at particular moments of social crisis when people fear that traditional values and institutions are under attack. The media play a key part in sensationalizing the situation and, importantly – particularly in relation to the singling out of paediatrician Marietta Higgs in the Cleveland case – in identifying and legitimizing the folk devils who become the targets for popular persecution. This process also includes the orchestration of 'expert' opinion which can contribute to increased demands for state intervention and the (re)formation of popular consent to a more conservative social order.

In certain important respects the Cleveland affair can be defined as a moral panic; and though it may not fit this definition in a predictable fashion, the way it does so is pertinent for feminists as well as for a study of the media. An investigation into how certain coded meanings were produced, and how Marietta Higgs was posed in opposition to Labour MP Stuart Bell, the other major figure in the controversy, can also offer an insight into the way the newspapers tried to establish for themselves a reasonably coherent position which would be consistent with their more general editorial policy. This was not an easy project, as we shall see. In fact, one of the most interesting things to emerge from an examination of the press coverage over this period is that despite the vilification of the tabloids – accusatory headlines and photos of Marietta Higgs dominated many front pages in late June and early July – a great deal of the reporting both in the popular press and in the qualities was characterized by confusion and contradiction.

This is not surprising if one considers the deeply disturbing, opaque and unprecedented nature of the Cleveland events. Few other issues in recent years have provoked such acute dilemmas. The peculiarly complex combination of elements and circumstances in the Cleveland case has undermined previously reliable moral and conceptual schema, and it is not only the media that has been confused in its response. This has also been the case for feminists, for those involved professionally in the area and, not least, for the general public.

In order to formulate its stance in relation to Cleveland and make sense of the phenomenon of child sexual abuse, the press has had to evaluate the discourse and interventions of disparate medical, legal, social work, charity and psychoanalytical orthodoxies and practices. The 'experts' from these fields, upon whom the media rely in order to define and explain events, have themselves been deeply divided. Their conflicting interpretations have, in this emotionally charged instance, exacerbated the confusion of the press and made the task of 'orchestrating' and classifying expert opinion extremely difficult. Few other issues in recent times have done as much to reveal the way in which expert knowledge is politically inflected. To compound matters, the press has also had to take into account the views of politicians and of its readers. Politicians have not been a great deal of help. Tory and Labour MPs have not taken up consistent positions and new cross-party alliances have been formed (*The Times*, 29 June). Readers are not an easy constituency either: though they may be parents, they are also sons and daughters, and are as likely to identify with the survivors as with the abusers.

In many newspapers, the uncertainty that this lack of closure has produced has been manifest in the contradictory messages conveyed in different articles on the same page, and even within articles, as well as in editorials of different and sometimes consecutive days. The selection of objects of adulation and persecution – the targeting of goodies and baddies – has likewise not been straightforward. However, this attempt by newspapers to find and settle into interpretations with which they feel comfortable, this continual jostling of position, should not be read as evidence of infinite openness. It is important to recognize that the questions repeatedly posed, the solutions offered and the stories returned to, have all fallen within a narrow range. Moreover, they have been singularly neglectful of feminist argument.

Yet the paradox is that despite this, feminism has not been absent from the Cleveland affair. On the contrary, it has had an extraordinarily powerful symbolic presence in the person of Marietta Higgs. Whether this semi-conscious attribution by the press has been in the form of accolade or desecration, it has been there; and it has frequently taken the place of feminist critique. Certain clusters of meaning which have been evoked in references to her are evidence of this displacement. As the formation of a chain between Marietta Higgs and feminism begins to become apparent, we are reminded of the other more glaring association by which feminism, via Marietta Higgs, is linked to and even identified with the target of moral panic. In this way the spectre of feminism becomes folk devil.

How these chains of association and processes of displacement occur, and how, in conjunction with other associations connected with Stuart Bell, they might have affected the construction and appropriation by the newspapers of particular viewpoints on the Cleveland affair, I hope to uncover by looking in greater detail at some of the key moments and features of the narrative.

The narrative

By the final weeks of June 1987 the issue is firmly on the front page. The number of place of safety orders on children suspected of being victims of sexual abuse in the general area of Cleveland has risen to 200 over the preceding few months, compared with 30 during the whole of the previous year. The orders appear to have been based only on physical diagnosis of sexual abuse (the reflex anal dilation test) made by two paediatricians at Middlesbrough General Hospital, Drs Marietta Higgs and Geoffrey Wyatt. It subsequently emerges, however, that many of the cases were referred by social workers and GPs. The abuse is assumed to have taken place in the home. The scale of the issue is brought to light when existing social service facilities are no longer able to cope with the number of children taken into care, and when parents of allegedly abused children demand second opinions and contact their local Labour MP, Stuart Bell.

By 24 June an 'independent panel of child-health specialists', which includes woman police surgeon Dr Raine Roberts, has been established to review the cases of suspected child abuse and concludes that there have been serious errors of diagnosis in seventeen cases; Roberts refers to 'the flimsiest of flimsy evidence'. This is the signal for a number of newspapers to begin to call in other 'experts' to evaluate the conflicting theories. What counts as evidence, social service policies and appeals procedures all begin to come under scrutiny, and there is a plethora of human interest stories, most of which focus on the anxieties of the parents whose children have been removed.

The disputed diagnoses also become the signal for Stuart Bell to begin to develop his public profile as the defender of misjudged parents. At the same time we witness an entrenchment of denials that incestuous child abuse has occurred. The response of the press in this instance must be contrasted with earlier reporting of phenomena like ChildLine, a help line for physically and sexually abused children, and the death of Kimberly Carlisle.[2] In these instances the press defended the interests of the children and called for more vigorous intervention by social workers. Now many of the popular newspapers, following the lead of Bell, who has claimed that *parents* have suffered many miscarriages of justice, turn around and call for the dismissal of Marietta Higgs and Geoffrey Wyatt on the grounds of their alleged incompetence.

However, it is soon clear that Wyatt is going to be a less significant personage in the evolving scenario than Higgs. It is her photograph that starts to act as a coded reference for the events of Cleveland, and her private and professional life that is examined in the daily press, not his. The Cleveland Social Services Department, with its policies of immediately removing the child from the family even where there is no evidence that the alleged abuse has been committed by the father,[3] also takes a back seat. It is Higgs who is attributed with the power and misguided dedication which then construct her as the causative agent in the crisis.

Over the following weeks Cleveland maintains an extremely high profile as newspapers respond to Bell's accusation in the House of Commons that Marietta Higgs and Sue Richardson, consultant social worker for Cleveland Social Services in charge of child abuse, have 'conspired and colluded' to exclude police surgeon Alistair Irvine from examining children suspected of having been abused. Media attention is bolstered yet again when Bell accuses Cleveland Social Services Department of exaggerating its child sexual abuse figures in order to increase its funding and 'empire build'. The story starts to diminish in importance, though does not disappear, once an official inquiry is conceded.

Denial and acknowledgement

Throughout this period many newspapers remain inconsistent in their reporting of the 'scandal' that they are themselves responsible for promoting. What then are the contradictions which seem to have provoked such a crisis of irresolution?

Even for those not disposed to minimize the extent and the gravity of child sexual abuse, many of the Cleveland procedures have been deeply disturbing. Considerable anxiety has been expressed about the fact that, partly as a consequence of disputed – possibly exaggerated – estimates of the incidence of child sexual abuse, a number of children appear to have been arbitrarily subjected to a disagreeable type of clinical examination, the validity of which is contested. Social services have responded to this disputed and apparently uncorroborated evidence of sexual abuse in quite inappropriate ways: children have been taken away, sometimes in the middle of the night, from their families, schools and communities. Parents appear to be refused access and have minimal rights of appeal. All this has caused suffering and it is not unreasonable to assume that the damage will be long term both for children and for parents.

Yet it is important to recognize that, although these worries have a rational and persuasive kernel, they constitute only a relatively modest part of a much broader position which is overwhelmingly characterized by denial and traditionalism. In this version, the seriousness, the extent, and sometimes even the existence of child sexual abuse are denied. The mythical 'traditional' family, and by implication the role of the father within this – the father as patriarch – is defended.

Thus, for example, in the *Daily Mirror* and in *The Sun* of 26 June it is defiantly reported that the children have suffered no other sexual abuse than that inflicted by the doctors who examined them. Michael Toner, in the *Sunday Express* of 28 June, asserts, without offering any evidence, that he simply does not 'believe in the avalanche of child abuse suggested by the Cleveland figures'. He also refers to 'fashionable' (that is, not traditional) 'zeal'. A number of papers make comments of this order. Lesley Garner in her article in *The Daily Telegraph* of 1 July, entitled 'Overboard on child abuse', prefaces an interview with Valerie Howarth, new director of ChildLine, by voicing 'the suspicion that we are encouraging, even inventing, a newly fashionable problem'. Awareness of child sexual abuse is being 'zealously encouraged', she says, and concludes by warning us that: 'Few people know what forces are unleashed once society begins to tamper with the mechanics of the family.' It must be noted, however, that Garner's succinct expression of denial and traditionalism is contradictorily placed at the beginning and end of a piece which, in the middle, gives serious attention to the views of Howarth.

Despite this kind of reporting, many newspapers do at the same time accept that children *are* sexually abused. This acknowledgement is what constitutes the core of the second, conflicting approach to the question. Thus although the press may express anxieties about aspects of the Cleveland Social Services response, it simultaneously gives a public platform to other professionals in the field whose arguments undermine the public denial of the seriousness of the problem. So from some newspapers it emerges that the rate of reported incidence of sexual abuse is growing all the time, particularly among children aged between three and five, and that abusers, who are overwhelmingly men and of whom a significant proportion are fathers and stepfathers, often intimidate children to such an extent that it becomes necessary to remove them to an environment where they will feel confident enough to reveal the details of their experience. In this view the family is not always a safe place; fathers (and sometimes mothers) can exploit the power they have over their children in astonishingly brutal ways. Survivors of incest and sexual abuse report harrowing stories of manipulation, threats of violence, long-term trauma and denial.

A number of newspapers express support for this general perspective. Among the most consistent is the now defunct *London Daily News*, which must be honoured for publishing early on one of the very few pieces clearly informed by feminism. Entitled 'The sins of the fathers', it argues that 'sexual abuse is the consequence of the way [boys] have learnt to be "men"' (Rutherford, 1987). Other papers are both less sophisticated and less consistent. *The Sun*, for example, after running abusive headlines like 'SACK THE DOCS' (26 June), suddenly changes tack and acknowledges the existence of abuse in Cleveland in a front-page article entitled 'THANK GOD FOR DR HIGGS' (30 June) which is about a woman whose children were 'saved' by Marietta Higgs. 'Dr Higgs was marvellous. I'm very grateful', the woman is reported as saying. The accompanying photograph shows Higgs with a wry smile. Inside, however, *The Sun* reverts to its old self with an article entitled 'DOC IN "HUSH-UP PLOT"', which continues: 'Woman doctor plots with social worker' (30 June).

The *Daily Mirror* also moves backwards and forwards from an abrasively anti-Higgs position which denies the occurrence of abuse (this is the dominant approach: see for example 26 and 30 June) to one which acknowledges its existence (28 June) and, echoing Esther Rantzen and Michele Elliott who are interviewed in the same issue, argues in its editorial that: 'Helpless children must not suffer simply because we cannot bear to face the facts.' The *Star*, surprisingly, given its reputation as one of the most scurrilous of all the tabloids, carries a rather progressive and comprehensive analysis (see Alix Palmer, 31 July). Palmer's position is that current child sexual abuse figures are probably an underestimate and that 'Cleveland is not alone'; she is critical of government cuts in social services and the impact of these on social workers' morale; she acknowledges the violence of many abusing fathers yet is also anti-imprisonment, since this is likely to drive the problem underground, and argues for a programme 'in which abusers can take responsibility for their actions'.

The *Daily Mail* coverage of the Cleveland events has also been extremely interesting. The paper is often accused of producing the worst of tabloid writing (and is referred to in this way during the course of the Cleveland events by several of the 'quality' papers; see for example *The Daily Telegraph*, 1 July and the *Observer*, 28 June). During the crisis it ran a daily cover line announcing itself as the paper which 'revealed the scandal to the nation', and had regularly sensationalist headlines. Yet at the same time it often devoted space to the views of Higgs' supporters, and oscillated in the position it took up. Perhaps more than any other newspaper, it presented us with contradictory messages – with both approaches simultaneously. Thus the portrait of Marietta Higgs (Shears, 1987) is sympathetic – it describes her devotion, expertise and integrity –

even though in the title she is referred to as a 'crusader' and Adelaide, the city she trained in, as 'the abuse capital of the world' (ibid.). Roger Scott (1987), in a thoughtful piece, though with predictably inflammatory headlines, acknowledges the problems of Cleveland and weighs up the issues surrounding child sexual abuse as carefully as journalists in the liberal or 'quality' press. At the same time, however, there are many pieces which use the crudest conventions of gutter journalism like, for example, the lead article on 30 June which is headlined 'THE CONSPIRACY'.

The Guardian and *The Independent* are among the 'quality' papers which, particularly in the early days, acknowledge increases in child sexual abuse. 'We must not recoil from the implications', argues *The Guardian* (25 June) while *The Independent*, though quite critical of Dr Higgs, states in its editorial: 'Talk of balancing parents' and children's rights is completely mistaken in this context. Children are not their parents' personal property' (25 June). (This position will not be adhered to consistently, however, as I will demonstrate later.) A number of papers carry letters critical of their own traditionalist stance; see, for example, the letter page in *Today* (27 June) which is headed 'Why criticise the child watchers?' The *News on Sunday*, a left paper which claims to have uncovered the Cleveland affair in the first place and has always taken the side of the parents, carries similar critical letters.

What we begin to see then as we open the newspapers each day through late June and early July is the emergence of two quite sharply differentiated sets of assumptions and emphases, even though these are often not yet clearly identified either with a party political position or with a newspaper's general viewpoint. It is an indication of the absence of a coherent sexual politics both on the Left and on the Right that this confusion over Cleveland occurred and persisted. So given this lack of a politically informed guidance, how did the public and the press make sense of the events and make up their minds about where to offer their moral support?

Higgs and Bell

Very early on in the crisis over the Cleveland events, Stuart Bell becomes identified as the central representative of the first position outlined above, that of denial or reluctant acknowledgement, while Marietta Higgs is identified with the second. As the principal antagonists in this symbolic war of position, these two individuals will go on to become critical forces in the formation of national ideas about child sexual abuse.

Bell opens the battle with a salvo in defence of the beleaguered parents, and in doing so singles out and targets Higgs as his main opponent. It takes only a few days before Alistair Irvine, Cleveland police surgeon, recruits himself as Bell's second-in-command and further polarizes the situation. He contributes to the consolidation of Higgs as representative of a particular viewpoint when he publicly attacks her professional judgement and claims he has been prevented by her from examining suspected cases of child sexual abuse. Irvine is reported as saying, 'these doctors are seeing things that are not there . . . Dr Higgs' methods seem almost to be an obsession' (*The Sunday Telegraph*, 28 June). The other main recruits to Bell's army are the Revd Michael Wright, local priest and architect of parents' support groups, who writes a poignant article for *The Guardian* (29 June) entitled 'When fear stalks the innocent', and local Tory MPs Richard Holt and Tim Devlin who join Bell in making political capital by calling vociferously for the suspension of Dr Higgs.

As the courts start to return children one by one to their parents (though they remain wards of court) because there is insufficient evidence of sexual abuse, and it becomes even more difficult to evaluate the situation, a number of figures step forward to declare their support for Marietta Higgs. The *Observer*, itself consistently sympathetic to her, reports on a statement of support from a group of twenty-five women doctors from Northumbria who provide a service to the police in cases of child sexual abuse and who claim that Dr Higgs has 'lifted the lid on the horrifying scale of sexual abuse from which we have averted our eyes for too long' (*Observer*, 28 June). However it is Sue Richardson, Middlesbrough consultant social worker in charge of child sexual abuse, who is appointed to the role of Marietta Higgs' chief second by Stuart Bell himself when he accuses both under parliamentary privilege of 'colluding and conspiring' to deny access to the police in sexual abuse cases (all papers report this on 30 June; *The Guardian* reports Sue Richardson's denial on 1 July).

Stuart Bell escalates the crisis yet again, and adds new recruits to Marietta Higgs' team, when he points the finger once more, this time at Dr Jane Wynne, Leeds University paediatrician responsible for developing the use of the diagnostic methods employed by Higgs and Wyatt. Bell objects to her presence on the panel of child sexual abuse professionals established to assess Middlesbrough Hospital practice, because, he argues, her presence might threaten its impartiality. Another recruit to Marietta's side, this time more of a volunteer than a victim of Bell's conscription methods, is Esther Rantzen. Well known as a TV personality and for her involvement in ChildLine, her voice is heard in a number of articles and interviews (see *Sunday Mirror*, 28 June and *The Sunday Times*, 5 July), as are those of Valerie Howarth, director of ChildLine (*The Daily Telegraph*, 1 July, and the *Star*, 9 July) and Michele Elliott, author of *Kidscape*. Rantzen focuses on the distress of the survivors, Howarth on policy and Elliott on educational projects with children. All three express general support for Higgs. In the House of Commons it is Labour MP Clare Short who is most outspoken in her defence. Marietta Higgs and Clare Short are together accused in an astonishingly sloppy article by Ferdinand Mount (*The Daily Telegraph*, 3 July) of being 'panic-stirrers' who have *caused* the moral panic by 'ventilating the extraordinary claim' that 10 per cent of children in Britain are sexually abused. Although Cleveland Social Services spokespeople also publicly support Higgs, as do a substantial number of medical, psychiatric and social work professionals, these individuals are not personalized in the press in the way that the women are. And they rarely have their photographs printed.

Gradually, then, two opposing positions begin to emerge in the coverage of Cleveland, though neither fits neatly into existing political frameworks or is easy to evaluate. What we see instead is the formation of opposing teams of individuals whose public image we feel able to assess quite easily. Over this critical period the public images of these two teams become inextricably identified with two opposing positions on child sexual abuse. Indeed, it is the team personality, rather than the issues, which appears to influence the press, and therefore the public, in their response to the Cleveland affair.

If this is the case, we must examine the crucial components of these public images. What do the different people represent? How do these images operate to produce and convey particular meanings? The most striking feature of the teams as I have set them out above is that one is composed almost entirely of men and the other almost entirely of women. It is rare that professional women are singled out for public attention to this extent and in this fashion. The very clear division made between men and women in the Cleveland case points to a possible explanation of how the papers came to make sense, whether consciously or not, of what went on.

In addition to gender, each of the chief protagonists occupies other positions of symbolic significance. The meanings associated with these different positions need to be drawn out. Let us look first at Stuart Bell and his team. What does he stand for and support? What coded messages about him and his supporters are transmitted by the newspapers? How is his persona contrasted with that of Marietta Higgs? The first thing to note is that he is indigenous: a northerner, local, son of a Durham miner; salt of the earth, populist. The parents he defends are 'his' people, he claims; his own five-year-old son, recently admitted to Middlesbrough Hospital after an accident, could have been one of the luckless children taken into care. He himself could have been one of the parents. For him and for his supporters, parents are an undifferentiated unit: fathers, almost always the perpetrators of abuse, are not distinguished from mothers; power relations are never made visible. Bell is a right-wing Labour MP: 'This is Middlesbrough not Russia', he is reported as saying in disbelief when he first heard of children being taken from their homes (*Daily Mail*, 15 July 1987). Politically situated at the point where right-wing labourism merges into Thatcherite populism, he is against the growing influence of the Left in local government and social services, and accuses his opponents of 'empire building'. I have already pointed out that his principal allies in the campaign to defend innocent parents (read fathers) are Tory MPs Richard Holt and Tim Devlin, the Revd Michael

Wright and police surgeon Dr Alistair Irvine. As Beatrix Campbell has said: 'These are the *traditional authorities*' (*New Statesman*, 31 July).

A number of quite different associations and prejudices are mobilized by the persona of Marietta Higgs. To start with, apart from being a woman, she is foreign and middle class – an outsider in Cleveland. We hear from the *Daily Mail* (27 June) that her German mother and Yugoslav father separated when she was two and that she was brought up by her mother and stepfather in a 'splendid' house in Australia. She is herself a working mother of five children and is unconventional in her domestic arrangements – her husband looks after the home and children. A number of commentators have hinted that these factors may have played a part in her diagnostic decisions (*Daily Mail*, 27 June and *Daily Express*, 28 June). No allusions of this nature are ever made in order to explain the behaviour of Stuart Bell. Marietta Higgs is a modern career woman. She is personally neat, dignified, determined and professionally highly respected by colleagues for her dedication, integrity and clinical expertise. Many of the newspapers refer to this, yet it is almost as though these are coded references which simultaneously suggest that she is *too* conscientious and rather *too* clever – neither very English nor very feminine.

Worse than that, she is also identified with a group of younger 'committed' professional women and men in social services, with connotations here of the inner city, left radicalism and anti-police sentiment (see *The Guardian* editorial, 1 July 1987). Left intellectuals are also drawn into this network of associations when a couple of newspapers report that Sue Richardson is married to a lecturer in Humanities at Teeside Polytechnic. Oh horrors! Marietta Higgs' concern for the interests of children and her determination to uncover sexual abuse – described by *Today* (26 June) as her 'one-woman crusade' – construct her not only as anti-father, but possibly anti-men, possibly a feminist. This image produces another set of associations, and when these are in turn combined with her reputation as a conscientious worker, what emerges are numerous anxious references in newspapers across the political spectrum to zeal: excessive zeal; fanaticism; obsession; fashionable zeal; fashionable prejudice, and so on. It is worth quoting *The Independent* editorial of 30 June at length in this respect:

> Social changes have made both sexual abuse, and the inclination to discover such abuse where it does not exist, more likely. Divorce, remarriage and the increasing acceptance of illegitimacy means that growing numbers of children live with a step-parent . . . forms of sexual activity which were, until recently, considered deviant have become commonplace. Lesbianism and homosexuality are now socially acceptable. . . . Further, militant feminists are inclined to consider all men sexually aggressive and rapacious until proved innocent. The nuclear family, once the highest ideal, is now too often regarded as unnatural and unattractive. . . . There is a danger that fashionable prejudice . . . [will] label parents guilty until proved innocent and break up families before rather than after abuse has been confirmed.

So here we have encapsulated the cluster of anxieties and associations triggered off by the persona and practice of Marietta Higgs. Modern fashionable ideas about sexual abuse are linked with unorthodox, dangerous ideas about sexual politics, with militant feminism, homosexuality and lesbianism, with the break-up of the traditional family and with anti-family sentiment. Other newspapers make connections with the Left and with hostility to the police. The chain of meanings established here implies that ideas associated with Marietta Higgs should be treated with suspicion. In this conceptual manoeuvre the interests of the child, and her exploitation, are made invisible.

Conclusion?

I have tried to trace the way in which Marietta Higgs was transformed, through her media representations, into a symbol – a standard-bearer – of feminism, and by association, of municipal socialism. It is important that we recognize this and understand the way in which newspapers have used her symbolic existence as a yardstick against which to work out their own positions. We must be aware of the way the press has mapped out the field and controlled the parameters of the meanings that have been produced. If we are not, we run the risk of being pushed by the media construction of Marietta Higgs as the representative of feminism and anti-traditionalism into uncritically offering her our approval.

It is tempting to do this, because we have seen her become the target of a massive and violent seizure of misogyny. This public convulsion has been fuelled not so much by dislike as by fear: fear of the woman doctor, the professional woman, the woman with knowledge and public power. We have also witnessed an astonishing attempt by many of the newspapers, following Bell's lead, to displace the guilt for the sexual abuse of children from the perpetrators on to Marietta Higgs. Responsibility for causing the moral panic has similarly, by a remarkable sleight of hand, been removed from Stuart Bell and the press, and projected once again on to the unfortunate Marietta Higgs (Mount, 1987).

Yet it is vital that we do not allow this powerful expression of misogyny to blind us to the problems in Higgs' diagnostic practice. Nor should Higgs' symbolic feminist presence be allowed to obscure the narrowness of the range of issues which were debated in the press. The marginalization of feminist critique is particularly disappointing given the body of feminist theoretical work on child sexual exploitation already in existence. Few newspapers asked questions about power in the family or ideals of masculinity and femininity when they attempted to explain child sexual abuse. Similarly, although the press made token references to the 'rights' of children, there was very little discussion of what this might mean, or of how the obedience and sexual ignorance in children might increase their vulnerability to sexual exploitation. With a few exceptions (for example, Weir, 1987) newspapers did not address the complex question of what Cleveland might represent in terms of the growing legitimation granted to the state to regulate and intervene in our domestic lives.[4]

Although it may be pleasing that feminism was so massively present in the reporting of the Cleveland affair in the symbolic form of Marietta Higgs, its vilification cannot give us much satisfaction. Although the issue of child sexual abuse emerged from its regime of silence and many papers engaged seriously with some of the progressive arguments, their continuous oscillation and the limited base of the debate do not amount to much of an achievement. As Roger Scott said in the *Daily Mail* (13 July 1987): 'There is no black and white in this story. It is too complex . . . . There are no winners. The children have lost the most.'

Notes

1. See, for example, Cohen (1972), Hall et al. (1978) and Fitzpatrick and Milligan (1987).

2. Kimberly Carlisle was murdered by her stepfather and the inquiry into her death ended just before the Cleveland affair hit the headlines. This was one of the cases in which the press criticized social workers for not being vigilant enough in their protection of children.

3. See the statement made by Cleveland Director of Social Services Michael Bishop and quoted in the press on 26 June 1987.

4. Although state intervention and the gathering of information about families is sometimes progressive and can benefit women, we cannot assume that this will always be the case.

COMMENT

Outrage and Anxiety in the Reporting of Child Sexual Abuse: Cleveland and the Press

This chapter was written in 1987, four years after 'Drawing the Line'. I was by then a member of the editorial collective of *Feminist Review* and was part of an issue group which in the wake of Esther Rantzen's ChildLine and in the midst of the Cleveland crisis was responsible for commissioning articles for a special issue on child sexual abuse (*Family Secrets, Feminist Review* 28, 1988). Among the many aspects we wanted to have investigated were media representations. I took on the task and decided to focus specifically on the press response to Cleveland. I was interested in exploring the different versions of this extraordinarily complex crisis about which it was so difficult to form a clear opinion. How were the different newspapers making sense of it? What differences would emerge between the 'quality' and the tabloid press, between the Left and Right, feminists and non-feminists?

It is interesting and pertinent to note that at the time there were few differences *within* feminism about this question. Child sexual abuse seemed to have the effect of drawing together and homogenizing feminist opinion, a surprising accomplishment given the long history of divisions between feminists. In this spirit *Feminist Review* included in the special issue the work of radical feminists and acknowledged their contribution in exposing and theorizing what was clearly a very brutal phenomenon. Nevertheless during the period of my involvement on this editorial issue group I was also experiencing some unease. There were a number of ways in which I could not accept the feminist orthodoxy. Yet in the face of widespread public denial, or at best a crude understanding of the issues, it seemed politically inappropriate to break ranks and qualify the feminist critique. My focus on newspaper reporting enabled me to sidestep these differences with other members of the issue group, to avoid speaking – or writing – what seemed in that context unspeakable. What then was the substances of my disagreement?

It was mainly about *meaning*. It seemed to me that the feminist orthodoxy inhibited even tentative explorations of gradation, interpretation, ambiguity, of the way in which context, sexual knowledge, fantasy and the intricacies of personal relationships might inflect how sexual abuse was lived. It seemed to assume that this was an irrelevant issue, that encounters of this kind were uniformly bad and traumatic in their effect. Diana Russell (1984) whose work was widely drawn on, was one of the worst in this respect. Concerned to establish the widespread incidence of sexual contacts between adults and children (mainly men and girls) and the source of the most pessimistic estimates,[1] she discusses nowhere in her book what might be the *significance* of the experience. This amounts to a 'fetishism of the event' as Ann Scott said of Jeffrey Masson (1988: 97).[2] Ann Scott is in fact one of the few contributors to *Family Secrets* who hangs on to the openness of meaning when, in her examination of psychoanalysis, the unconscious and child sexual abuse, she returns to the equivocal and multilayered notions of seduction and childhood agency.

Liz Kelly, another contributor to *Family Secrets*, also retains some sense of the disjuncture between events and how they are understood, but her political thrust as a radical feminist is to maximize the damage of what are usually thought of as relatively minor events rather than maintain open the question of meaning (1988). Paradoxically she therefore denies the logic of her own argument. If interpretation is what is relevant, not the nature of the event, then there is no reason to suppose that all instances of abuse will be seriously damaging, that sexual encounters will always victimize girls and women. Many could be experienced as quite trivial.

To make this point is not to minimize the gravity of child sexual abuse but to insist that all instances are not equal in their gravity. How they are experienced and re-experienced depends on many factors which include expectations, knowledge, fear, unconscious fantasy, guilt about sexual desire and experience, the chance to talk through the different facets of the occurrence(s) and so forth. As cultural studies has taught us, experiences and texts are polysemic; meanings are not absolute or fixed. Because in our culture sex is the privileged site on which the truth of our (gendered) selves is to be found (Foucault, 1979; Weeks, 1981) it is assumed that the damage inflicted by sexual abuse and rape will be more serious than other kinds. On what grounds do we make these assumptions? Will this always be the case? Here I want to expand on how biography and personal experience inform and shape our theoretical and political positions. The way in which this happens is not predictable and there are undoubtedly many unconscious factors at work which intervene between our experiences and the positions we adopt. All the same, since this commentary is about the complexities of the intellectual process and the political nature of personal experience, it is worth describing briefly two personal experiences which might have influenced – or which I use *post facto* as confirmation for – my present analysis.

When I was twenty I was raped. I was travelling through Mexico at the time, on my own, on buses, exploring the world, confronting danger, experiencing life. One night when I was staying with friends in the countryside I awoke to find a man trying to rape me. It was too dark to make out who it was, but I assumed it was someone I knew slightly who had been pursuing me sexually over the previous few days. I was angry and told him to go away. He hit me, pinned me down and forced his way into me. I had my period so the possibility of pregnancy, the greatest danger as far as I was concerned, was not at issue. When he finished he left and I fell asleep. The next day I realized that my assailant had been a stranger who had broken into the compound and done other damage to the small community I was staying in. If I had known this maybe my response would have been different. As it was, this seemed to me a trivial event, something to be expected and dealt with – rather like an insect sting – in the context of my travels.

Contrast this with a far more scarring experience of my adolescence: I was about thirteen, at a mixed public school, in the A stream. I wrote a story for creative composition which was long, fluent, passionate and probably influenced more by colonial adventure stories and the romantic fiction I had read in *Woman's Own* than by texts from the literary canon. My teacher hated it. He slammed it against his desk, shouted that he expected more of me, and picked out phrases and episodes to read to the class and ridicule. I flush with anger and shame to this day as I remember how the class tittered to see me, a bright and bold pupil, humiliated and exposed as an ignorant vulgar salacious and banal writer, unable to grasp the standards required for English (or perhaps Englishness). It was awful. There is no doubt that this experience damaged me far more than did the rape. The rape was simply unwanted sex. And sex, I was brought up, unusually, to believe by my free-thinking mother was part of life – it was often enjoyable but it could be disappointing – and I should pay no attention to conventional prohibitions. Perhaps as a consequence, it has never been much of a problem. Writing, on the other hand (like becoming English) has always seemed a dangerous exercise. Sometimes exciting, often painful, it has at once been permeated and deformed by anxious fantasies of omnipotence and fraudulence.[3]

It would be a contentious claim if I were to argue that a neat connection could be made between childhood experience and current crises, as perhaps the above anecdotes imply. It is of course not possible to establish a clear aetiology of particular problems. The unconscious works in mysterious ways and undoubtedly my difficulties with writing are overdetermined. All the same I offer these examples about myself both to illuminate my own theoretical position and to indicate the limits of the feminist orthodoxy on the subject. It is interesting to speculate what might be the link in my case between my writing problems and child sexual abuse, because without doubt 'Cleveland and the Press' was, of all the articles included here, the most painful and demanding to write. Could it have been that my adolescent writing trauma – *my* experience of abuse – was in the climate of editing the special issue of *Feminist Review*, unconsciously sexualized and thus conflated with child sexual abuse more generally? But then 'Drawing the Line' was one of the easiest and fastest to write, and that too was about sexual abuse. No, I think that the anxiety which encumbered the writing of 'Cleveland and the Press' had more to do with the intellectual and moral context of the editorial process which exposed me to the judgement of my peers and inhibited the voicing of the criticisms included here.

A more practical methodological reason for the writing difficulties (and perhaps a mark of academic maturity) was that I started out on this project without a clear argument in mind. Throughout the summer, as the Cleveland saga unfolded, I accumulated a mass of data and detail which confused me in its contradictoriness, until I realized that it was contradiction that I needed to explain. Finally, despite my doubts at the time about the feminist orthodoxy, it is interesting to observe how present feminism is in this chapter. I remember that it took me by surprise as I was writing to note how divided along gender lines were the supporters of Bell and Higgs, and how the symbolic power of Higgs could not be understood other than in feminist terms. It was gratifying to recognize this.

Notes

1. Diana Russell's definitions are extremely broad. For instance she includes in her category of incestuous child abuse: 'Any kind of exploitative contact or attempted sexual contact, that occurred between relatives, no matter how distant the relationship, before the victim turned 18 years old' (1984: 181).

2. Jeffrey Masson (1984) generated a notorious dispute within the psychoanalytic community as a consequence of his insistence that Freud had in bad faith suppressed the seduction theory and the importance of 'real events'. For an interesting account of the controversy see Malcolm (1984).

3. Valerie Walkerdine examines the fears of being fraudulent in relation to class as well as gender in her film *Didn't She Do Well?* (1990).

8

CONSUMERISM AND ITS CONTRADICTIONS

Over the last year or two a number of articles about the dilemmas raised by the buying of things, by style, self-adornment and the consumption of images, have appeared in the pages of magazines like *Marxism Today*, *New Socialist* and *Women's Review*, as well as in a range of less well-known academic journals and anthologies. Broadly, the debates have been concerned to establish whether an acknowledgement of the stubborn and complex pleasures afforded by these phenomena is evidence of a more sensitive and progressive analysis than hitherto – capable ultimately of providing the groundwork for a more popular political appeal to both men and women – or whether, as has also been argued, these preoccupations are diversionary, evidence merely of a mid-1980s capitulation to the Right, an obfuscation of the stark reality of capitalism's uncompromising hunger for new markets.

These questions clearly have political as well as theoretical implications; indeed, they combine in quite a unique fashion some of the major concerns of socialists and feminists. What I intend to do in this brief chapter is to clarify some of the substantive issues at stake here by placing them in their historical context. In this way we may be able to put into perspective and refine evaluations of some of the more recent developments in the debate.

It was the intellectual and political climate of the United States during the 1950s which provided the conditions for the emergence of some of the most virulent critiques of consumerism in the postwar period. This was the moment of the expansion of domestic markets, of the suburban housewife, 'consensus' and McCarthyism. It was a period of political conservatism in which the 'free choice' of goods came to symbolize the 'freedom' of the free world. The consumer society, as a distinctive form of advanced capitalism, relies to an unprecedented degree for its perpetuation upon the media, advertising spectacle, fashion and the image. Although a critical analysis of these aspects of mass culture was initiated by the Frankfurt School in the 1930s, it was not until the 1950s and 1960s that it really gained momentum. Herbert Marcuse, European Marxist and author of the seminal counter-culture text *One Dimensional Man* (1964), and Betty Friedan, author of *The Feminine Mystique* (1965), were two of the most influential contributors to the radical critique in the United States. Both operated with the conviction that cultural forms have the power to construct 'false needs', to indoctrinate and manipulate men and women into social conformity and subordination. Friedan, one of the first to focus on the significance of consumerism in perpetuating the particularities of women's oppression in postwar America, quotes an executive of the hidden-persuasion business: 'Properly manipulated . . . American housewives can be given the sense of identity, purpose, creativity, the self-realization, even the sexual joy they lack – by the buying of things' (1965: 181). The notion expressed here of the individual as passive victim is also reflected in other more mainstream discourses of that moment. The plausibility of the idea of 'brainwashing' – by communists and advertisers alike – gained considerable ground in the course of the 1950s and 1960s, and continues to have purchase to this day.

It is in the context of this conservative climate that we must understand the emergence in the late 1960s of the new feminist, socialist and black politics of style. Patched and second-hand clothes represented a rejection of the dominant ethos of consumerism and propriety. Peasant garments marked a display of solidarity with the poor and the Third World. Afro haircuts were a symbol of black American political consciousness; and the feminist appropriation of male workclothes has its own coherence when placed historically as a sequel to the excesses of early 1960s sartorial imagery in which woman was cast as helpless yet seductive child, doll, bird, baby, and so on. Thus what we begin to see, as the postwar era pans out behind us, is a period of intense struggle and engagement played out on the terrain of cultural forms and signs. Stuart and Elizabeth Ewen put it thus: 'In a society predicated upon the marketing of images, images become a weapon of resistance' (1982: 244; see also Hebdige, 1979 and Carter, 1984).

However, many of these new images, imagined in the first instance in the explosive climate of 1968 – the politicizing conjuncture for an international generation of young dissidents: war veterans, women, blacks and students – and developed during the 1970s, have over the last fifteen years in turn become current socialist and feminist orthodoxies. And with the emergence of municipal socialism in Britain in the 1980s, these orthodoxies have acquired a new power base to add to the influence already exercised through other cultural and political forms. Thus we see the consolidation – indeed, the institutionalization in some instances – of some of the moral and stylistic precepts formed by the generation of 1968, the 'old youth' as Frank Mort has recently dubbed them (1986). And, as this new left-feminist consensus gains ground, so it in turn produces its own resistances both within and beyond its immediate sphere of influence. These critical resistances take a range of forms and cannot be understood merely as a kind of inevitable generational revolt. They have been partially, and very importantly, fuelled by a keen sense of the failure of the Left and feminism, despite considerable gains, to capture popular consciousness as effectively as the Right.

All the same, it does seem to be the case that the specificity and significance of a cultural form or cultural analysis is substantially determined by the historical context of its production and reception – by

prevailing discourses. This implies that we can attribute no inherent meanings to fashions or to particular styles of masculinity and femininity.
Codes are immensely plastic and are constantly being reworked. Whether
make-up renders women respectable or deviant, whether muscular bodies
are in or out, whether streamlining is good or bad design (Hebdige, 1981),
indeed whether form is considered relevant at all – and here I am talking
not only about appearances and commodities but also about fashions in
language, ideas and morality – is to a large extent consequent upon
combinations of existing meanings and the historical moment in which
they come into being.

This is not to suggest that epiphenomena of this order are therefore
politically unimportant. On the contrary, they clearly manage to address
– and hence (potentially) to mobilize – popular imagination and desires
in a more profound and all-encompassing way than do some of the
classical material issues. Yet we must ask how far the different theoretical
and political positions taken up in relation to consumerism have been able
to advance the terms of the debate. It could be argued that by continuing
to allocate such a central place to the issues involved – to images and
commodities – we are not only interrogating but also contributing to the
explosion of discourses on consumerism as a late twentieth-century
phenomenon.

Zygmunt Bauman, in an important article on the genealogy of
consumerism, has argued that the contemporary focus on the body – on
adornment, food, fitness and sport – represents a popular struggle for the
reassertion of control, a response to the historical deployment of
individualizing techniques of power:

> Disciplinary power . . . was first and foremost about bodily control. It was the
> human body which for the first time in history was made, on such a massive
> scale, an object of drill and regimentation. Later consumerism was a product
> of failed resistance to such drill and regimentation. But what was negated could
> not but determine the substance and the form of its negation. (Bauman, 1983:
> 40)

The negation – the refutation – of bodily control and regulation is fought
out on a predetermined battleground: the body itself. But in Bauman's
account the chances of subversion are limited, in that, historically,
consumerism has constituted a form of compensation gained in a trade-
off against the encroachment of disciplinary power. Consumerism is
theorized here as, at most, a form of displaced resistance, and not, as I
would argue, as an ever-expanding discursive apparatus. In addition,
despite taking on aspects of Michel Foucault's method, and in the process
offering some riveting insights, Bauman seems ultimately to deny the
implications of Foucault's own insistence that where there is power,
however diffuse or pervasive, there is the potential for its resistance.

In my opinion Foucault's theoretical framework can be pushed further
and made to yield more productive questions and observations; its potential remains relatively unexplored. Thus, drawing on Foucault's model of

sexuality (1979) which is neither reductive nor celebratory, consumerism can be argued to exercise control through the incitement and proliferation of increasingly detailed and comprehensive discourses. Yet because of the diffuse nature of this control, because it operates from such a multiplicity of points and is not unitary, it is also vulnerable. If this is the case, then contemporary preoccupations with imagery and the buying of things can be understood not only as part of this new technology of power, but as, variably (sometimes simultaneously), both a form of subjection to it and a form of resistance. They are not inherently one thing or the other, since, if consuming objects and images is potentially subversive, this potential is countered always by its potential reappropriation and transformation into yet another model of regulation.

Our task, then, must be to detect those developments in consumer discourses (that is to say, modes of thinking as well as modes of operating) which constitute more than mere resistances to previous orthodoxies. Are there contemporary phenomena in the sphere of consumption which could be defined as an advance, as capable of acting upon vulnerable points and hence pushing back the networks of disciplinary power? There are two broad contemporary theoretical and political developments which I think may fall into this category and which are worth exploring to see whether or not they can be made to reveal progressive possibilities.

The first of these is the new, more nuanced understanding of subjectivity. This appears also in recent critical refutations of the notion that the media and advertising have the power to manipulate in a coherent and unfractured fashion and represent a move away from the notion of mass man and woman as duped and passive recipients of conspiratorial messages designed to inhibit true consciousness (see, for example, Root, 1986; Myers, 1986; Steedman, 1986). Interestingly, in symbiotic relation to this position – the daughter of it, as it were – is the apparently progressive polemical pursuit of 'positive images', a still widely current feminist and socialist convention, which, in addition to embodying rather simple notions of the good and the true, recalls and confirms the idea that images are able to persuade (to brainwash) in an unproblematic manner. The theoretical challenge to this kind of 'old youth' orthodoxy has come from an analysis which insists that the way in which any particular message is interpreted cannot be simply deduced from the intentions of its author/producer or from an examination of the product itself – or even from its context. Individual responses and criteria of assessment are forged out of and mediated by a range of experiences which pre-empt easy conclusions about meaning and appropriation and which are simultaneously rational and irrational. Current theories of culture and subjectivity take much more seriously notions of personal agency, discrimination and resistance, as well as (drawing on psychoanalysis) the contradictory and fragmented nature of fantasy and desire. Feminists in the 1980s have argued, for example, that women can read glossy magazines critically and selectively yet not disavow more traditional feminine identities and pleasures. In this respect, Suzanne Moore (1986) emphasizes the need to 'separate pleasure from the text and commitment to the text'; while Douglas Kellner (1983), from a different perspective, has argued forcefully that the desire for commodities is not in itself evidence of duping and indoctrination. Mass man and woman are treated here more respectfully than they used to be.

The second aspect of contemporary consumer discourse which seems to represent a radical break, yet which in terms of its political implications is also open to conflicting interpretations, is played out variously in the arena of sexual politics. Conventionally consumerism has been seen to confirm women in their subordination. A good deal of feminist intellectual work has documented the ways in which women have both been targeted as consumers and done a major part of the labour involved (approximately 80 per cent of purchasing power in the Western world is wielded by women: Scott, 1976). Another body of work has focused on the crucial part played in this process by advertising and women's magazines. Rather less attention has been paid to the contradictory way in which the relative status and power of women has paradoxically been enhanced by consumer society. Consumption (as a feature of modern capitalism) has offered women new areas of authority and expertise, new sources of income, a new sense of consumer rights; and one of the consequences of these developments has been a heightened awareness of entitlement outside the sphere of consumption (which may well have contributed to the conditions for the emergence of modern feminism: Winship, 1981). Jacques Donzelot (1979) identifies a similar contradictory singling out of women as experts in relation to the family. Thus the buying of commodities and images can be understood both as a source of power and pleasure for women (it has indeed given them a 'sense of identity, purpose and creativity') and simultaneously as an instrument which secures their subordination.

Consumerism as gendered practice has, however, shifted somewhat since the postwar decades examined by Janice Winship (1981). More recently there has been a blurring of the conventional distinctions in the advertising address to men and women; constructions of masculinity and femininity are less fixed; shopping and self-adornment have become less gendered – less specifically female – activities (Mort, 1986). A cruising of the text of *Arena*, the new fashion magazine for men ('for the Porsche driver with the designer stubble'), reveals men represented in many of the erotic and frivolous ways that feminists have traditionally found so objectionable when deployed in representations of women. What we begin to observe then, is not only a shift in practice, but also a destabilization of the positioning of men and women in fantasy. At the same time, girls' and women's magazines today, like *Mizz* and *Seventeen* (Winship, 1985), *Cosmopolitan*, even *Vogue*, and television programmes like *Brookside*, have increasingly become vehicles for the dissemination of ideas and the popularization of issues (among both men and women) placed initially on the political agenda by feminism.

So what are we to make of these developments? How are we to evaluate their significance? I think it is possible to argue that these disparate theories and practices constitute an advance on the cruder certainties of the immediate past precisely because of their more nuanced, complex and contradictory nature. Consumerism is here spilt from its historic one-to-one relation with production. And, of course, these theorizations have themselves had practical experiential consequences in that they have acted as a form of permission entitling members of today's left intelligentsia (Barnett, 1986) to enjoy consuming images and commodities (which of course does not necessarily mean spending lots of money) without having to feel anxious about whether these activities are good and correct. The optimists might argue in addition that, by reacting against the insularity and moralism of much left-feminist thought over recent years, these conceptual and behavioural changes amount to progress in that they are able to lay the groundwork for a less guilt-ridden, more popular politics of resistance which effectively seeks out vulnerable points. But the cynics would respond by insisting on a sharper distinction between what is oppositional and innovative and what is progressive. Judith Williamson (1986) has argued forcefully that popular culture must not be exempted from political criticism and exonerated merely because it is new and fun. The cynics might continue by claiming that the optimists' theories are a rationalization of their desires; an accommodative response to the new generation; a way of keeping up; in sum, a cop-out which, particularly during this period of recession, most brutally ignores the material injuries of class.

Which brings us to consumerism as economic activity. Although I have hardly touched on the relationship of consumption to production in this short piece, the crucial existence of such a relationship is largely responsible for shaping commonsense socialist and feminist understanding of the issues involved. Marx himself paid little attention to consumption, but his materialist method has provided the framework for those analyses which focus on the financial and motivational investment of capital (controlled predominantly by men) in the expansion of markets for its commodities – in popular consumption. Capitalism's pursuit of profit means that consumers as well as producers are exploited. It is this kind of approach which underlies so much condemnation of consumerism as practice. Without denying the significance of this, it is at the same time important to recognize the limitations of a neo-Marxist analysis which is not capable of offering us all we need to know about the question. Consumerism does not simply mirror production. Cultural forms and meanings are not reducible to class and the economic. Consumerism is far more than just economic activity: it is also about dreams and consolation, communication and confrontation, image and identity. Like sexuality, it consists of a multiplicity of fragmented and contradictory discourses. Bauman, like

Foucault, has argued that production is not a privileged force but merely one site on which the surveillance of populations is carried out; likewise with consumption. If this is indeed the case, then the implications of any particular consumer practice or argument cannot be deduced in advance. Consumerism is a discourse through which disciplinary power is both exercised and contested. While not negating its relation to capitalism, we must refuse to return it always to questions of production.

COMMENT

Consumerism and its Contradictions

'Consumerism and its Contradictions' was written after I had moved to the Department of Cultural Studies at the Polytechnic of East London. This was not only a geographical move, it also constituted a shift from sociology and education into a developing discipline whose roots lay as much in literary, historical and media studies, in philosophy, psychoanalysis and cultural practice as in sociology. Consumerism was an area I was focusing on increasingly in the course of my teaching. Linked to questions of style and subjectivity, the centrality of the body in modern discourse and the intricacy of symbolic meaning, it was proving a rewarding yet relatively uncharted field of study.

However, despite the shift into new territory, this chapter continues the interrogation of political and theoretical debates within feminism and the Left as well as the placing of texts and analyses in relation to more general historical developments. Where 'Consumerism and its Contradictions' marks a break, is in its subject matter and its theoretical approach. The earlier chapters of this book show an ambivalent relation to moral absolutes; we can trace a passage from a belief in the possibility of their existence to a growing acknowledgement of cultural relativism and the insistence here that meanings are contingent upon other meanings. In its rejection of certainties and its defence of nuance and complexity this chapter completes the move. Yet at the same time, contradictorily perhaps, it hangs on to what I called the 'progressive possibilities' of critical thought by arguing that these more nuanced complex theories constitute an *advance* on those of the past. The reliance on a Foucauldian model as a starting point also serves to place the piece firmly in a distinct theoretical paradigm.

The chapter additionally speculates about what propels people to take up one theoretical position rather than another. By distinguishing between the optimists and the pessimists it suggests – but does not in this instance develop – the possibility that choices are determined by factors outside the parameters of the arguments in question, by preferences determined by psychic and other biographical narratives. In this respect it prefigures the concerns of the Introduction and comments of this book.

The piece also marks a turning point in relation to feminism. Although present here and drawn on in order to illustrate other arguments, feminism has lost its earlier centrality. This reflects a number of professional and personal developments. Teaching in a department in which gender issues were consistently taken seriously by male as well as female colleagues and which included other feminists of long standing[1] meant that I no longer felt solely responsible for ensuring a feminist presence on the syllabus as I had done in previous jobs and could therefore move into areas less obviously focused on the position of women. Although I continued to be a member of the *Feminist Review* editorial collective, my relationship with feminism was attenuated also as a consequence of its diminishing necessity in my personal life. The passage of time had reduced the frustrations and dispersions of child-care. A sense of my own power and good relations with the men in my life – my sons, ex-husband, lover, household members and colleagues – had defused the intense engagement and resoluteness of the earlier period. My earlier sense of marginality was much diminished; I now belonged, even if to marginal groupings. These factors have combined with the general drift towards uncertainty associated with postmodernism as well as with the personal process of becoming more flexible and reflective, of maturation. Together they leave us with the contemporary dilemma which Paul Hoggett has identified in his article 'The culture of uncertainty' but to which he provides no answers:

> How to combine decisiveness with thoughtfulness, a 'visionary consciousness' with a 'questioning consciousness' . . . is the problem . . . how to act decisively, with passion . . . yet preserve the capacity to be proved wrong. (Hoggett, 1989: 35)

Note

1. Specifically Sally Alexander and Catherine Hall whose work has been published widely. For examples, see Terry Lovell (1990).

9

DISCRIMINATING OR DUPED? YOUNG PEOPLE AS CONSUMERS OF ADVERTISING/ART

(with Orson Nava)

This chapter is based on research commissioned by Paul Willis in his capacity as director of the Gulbenkian Enquiry into Arts and Cultural Provision for Young People. It is drawn on, as are similarly commissioned investigations by other authors, in Willis' final report *Common Culture* (1990). The Enquiry was prompted in the first instance by the recognition 'that most young people see the arts as remote and institutional, not part of everyday life. Art is what they are forced to do at school . . . the preserve of art galleries, theatres and concert halls' which they do not attend. The project of the Enquiry was therefore to explore the wide range of cultural forms and symbolic expressions through which young people establish their identities, the ways in which they consume and invest with meaning the practices and spaces that surround them. 'The Enquiry sets out to investigate creativity wherever it is and whatever its forms' (Willis, 1988: 1).

It is in the context of these terms of reference that the following arguments about young people, advertising and art must be understood.

An interesting TV commercial made by the agency Ogilvy and Mather was shown on Channel 4 each Sunday during the spring of 1988. Entitled *Chair*, its object was to promote the agency's own advertising services to potential 'marketing decision makers'. The advert opens with a shot of a modern young man in a stylish flat watching television. At the commercial break he gets up and goes to make a cup of tea. For a moment the camera focuses on the empty chair and the abandoned TV set. Then it cuts to the kitchen but we can still hear the noise of the ads coming from the unwatched television. The young man returns to his chair with his cup of tea just as the commercial break ends. Over the final frame a voiceover informs us that there are 600 commercials on TV every day; 'what's so special about yours?' it enquires of the potential advertisers among us.

As the press release for Ogilvy and Mather states, 'The film confronts the viewer with the question of whether or not people pay attention to commercial breaks.' At the same time it conveys another message. It represents young people as discriminating and hard to reach and suggests that they are likely to ignore all but the most challenging and entertaining commercials. This view of young people is one which is increasingly prevalent among advertisers and their clients and was frequently expressed to us in interview. Articles in trade magazines like *Campaign*, research conducted by advertising agencies like the *McCann-Erickson Youth Study*, advertisements themselves, and a spate of recent conferences organized for marketeers about the difficulties of targeting and persuading contemporary youth are further evidence of this growing preoccupation (Nava, 1988). Within the world of advertising today, concern is regularly expressed about how to reach young people (since they watch less TV than any other age group, even the under-fours) and how to persuade and gratify them, given what is referred to in the trade (and is illustrated in the Ogilvy and Mather ad) as their high level of 'televisual literacy'. Bartle Bogle Hegarty, the agency responsible for the Levi ads, have put it thus: 'Young consumers are sophisticated, video literate and acutely sensitive to being patronised. They pick up clues and covert messages quicker than you would believe.'

This image of young people and advertising is not, however, the one that circulates most frequently. The way in which advertising and consumerism are generally viewed today (although challenged by, for example, Myers, 1986; Nava, 1987) remains deeply influenced by the work of cultural theorists of the 1950s and 1960s such as Vance Packard, who argues in his seminal book *The Hidden Persuaders* (1981, first published in 1957) that people are 'influenced and manipulated [by advertisers] far more than we realize . . . . Large scale efforts are being made, often with impressive success, to channel our . . . habits, our purchasing decisions and our thought processes' (1981: 11). For Herbert Marcuse (1964) one of the most influential thinkers of the Left in this sphere, advertising – as an inherent aspect of consumer capitalism and its pursuit of profit – is capable not only of convincing us to buy, but of creating false needs, of indoctrinating us into social conformity and thus ultimately of suppressing political opposition. More recently, commentators of both the Left and Right who have been preoccupied by what they consider to be a decline in moral standards (see for example the work of Jeremy Seabrook on the one hand and statements issued by Mary Whitehouse on the other) as well as more academic analysts of advertising (Dyer, 1982) have been concerned to establish the effects of a constant diet of television programmes and commercials, particularly on young viewers who are considered to be those most at risk of being corrupted and duped by entreaties to buy.

Given the pervasiveness of these debates, it is not surprising that certain ideas have now become part of received wisdom, a commonsense way of viewing the world. Thus we have a context in which the question of television advertising and youth is likely to conjure up images of under-educated undiscriminating and undisciplined young people who are addicted to TV and who mindlessly imbibe the advertisers' messages along with the materialist values of the consumer society. Characteristic of this view is the notion that there exists a simple cause and effect relationship between advertising and the purchasing of commodities. It is not only assumed that advertisements work but that the young are more likely than any other sector of the population to be taken in by the psychologically informed scheming of the marketeers. Youth are considered to be more vulnerable, more gullible and more inclined to be persuaded to buy totally useless things.

Significantly and interestingly, this is a far more demeaning view of youth than that held by the advertisers themselves. As has already been indicated, the British advertising industry is highly respectful of the critical skills and visual literacy of young people. Indeed, as emerges clearly from our research, no other age group is considered as discriminating, cynical and resistant to the 'hard sell'. Furthermore, no other group is as astute at decoding the complex messages, cross-references and visual jokes of current advertising (except perhaps the industry itself). These critical skills are untutored and seem to arise out of an unprecedented intimacy with the cultural form of the television commercial. No other generation has been so imbued with the meanings produced by quick edits, long shots, zooms, by particular lighting codes and combinations of sound. The young have a unique mastery of the grammar of the commercial; one might say that they have an intuitive grasp of the visual equivalent of the semicolon. This is the case even where, as one bemused advertiser put it, 'they are not very intellectually clever'.

Advertisers work hard to capture this discerning audience and to win its esteem. Indeed many ads appear to utilize the codes that are most likely to appeal to that sector of the population with the most developed analytical skills – that is, the young – regardless of the suitability of the product for this kind of treatment. The British Telecom commercial about the unfortunate Jewish grandson who managed to pass only his pottery and sociology exams, which emerged as the preferred ad in a small-scale survey of young people, is an example of this. In return, young people will watch and rewatch the commercials they consider successful. The tea will wait (or will be made by someone else) while judgement is exercised. Favourite ads will be recorded and viewed again with friends. Phrases will be selected and replayed. Comparisons and connections will be made, messages identified and effectivity assessed. Repetition and familiarity might enhance the rating of some commercials (for example the celebrated Levi Strauss Launderette ad) but others will not survive such close scrutiny. They will be taped over and forgotten.

It is not only 'youth' (fourteen to twenty-four-year-olds) who watch and enjoy TV ads in this way. Research carried out by the Association of Market Survey Organizations indicates that commercials also come high on the list of younger children's preferred television viewing. Favourite ads among those in the six to fourteen-year-old category include Carling's Black Label, Anchor Butter's dancing cows and Mates condoms. They too like advertisements promoting items which they are unlikely to buy.

What emerges quite clearly from this picture is that young people consume commercials independently of the product that is being marketed. Commercials are cultural products in themselves and are consumed for themselves. The success of any particular commercial is, in this respect, completely divorced from its effectivity in promoting sales. Evaluations are made on the basis of criteria which are indistinguishable from those employed in the appreciation of other cultural forms. Our argument therefore is twofold: an analysis of the mode in which the commercial is consumed not only gives us insight into the cultural skills of young people, it also radically interrogates conventional divisions between art and advertising.

The dominant view of 'art' today, despite current debates about postmodernism, is still permeated by nineteenth-century romantic notions of a process abstracted from social relations and untainted by material considerations. The artist in this scenario is an individual possessed of talent and blessed with inspiration. Expressivity and then technique are the privileged categories; modes of consumption are considered largely irrelevant to the creative process. Practitioners and arbiters of such established 'high art' forms have tended to resist the demand for aesthetic recognition and entry to the elite ranks made by others using new techniques and different relations of production. Nevertheless, the range of forms within which 'art' is considered to reside has gradually been extended so that today it encompasses, for example, photography, film, electronic music and more recently video and video scratch.

Advertising however has generally been denied this accolade. Although grudging recognition has been awarded to the occasional outstanding example of 'commercial art', on the whole positive aesthetic evaluations of this field have been unable to compete with the trenchant cultural critiques in which the focus tends to be on how advertisers produce particular meanings which exploit personal insecurities and convince consumers that their identities derive from what they buy (Marcuse, 1964; Williamson, 1978; Dyer, 1982). Artists, critics, and even advertisers themselves, rank advertising extremely low in the hierarchy of cultural forms – if indeed they include them at all. This might be because advertisers – of all cultural practitioners – are the ones least able to deny the cultural and economic context of their work and the significance of audience. Yet the very fact of excluding advertising from the sphere of 'art' forms and identifying it as 'other', as defined predominantly by its material concerns, serves not only to differentiate and cleanse other forms, it also obscures the material determinants which operate across all of them. Studies which examine art and advertising in isolation, or which focus on difference, serve to perpetuate both difference and associated hierarchies.

In contrast, our intention in this chapter is to reveal the interconnections and overlap between commercial and other forms of art, in order to expand our understanding of the ways in which young people exercise critical abilities as audience. The indivisibility of these (apparently) different forms manifests itself at a number of stages. At the level of conceptualization and production, crossovers can be discerned in the utilization of technologies and forms; ideas; and personnel.

Among the technologies and forms which have been requisitioned by the makers of advertisements since the turn of the century are painting, photography, cinema, graphics, animation, pop music, video promos and video scratch. Examples are numerous: Dada and surrealism have been used in cigarette advertising; Michelangelo's drawings have been used by Parker pens. As John Berger pointed out in *Ways of Seeing* (1972), publicity regularly quotes from works of art. Of the popular cultural forms, hip hop and rapping have most recently been in vogue. More critical avant-garde forms like video scratch are also increasingly drawn on, though not always with much understanding. On the whole, however, what is interesting is that these techniques are not only appropriated and 'quoted', they are also developed (this is particularly so for photography, graphics and animation) in the innovative and generously funded climate of advertising today.

At the level of ideas we see that advertisements not only draw specific narratives and images from the other forms, and parody them, they increasingly cross-reference each other. In this sense they constitute the classic postmodernist form (if such a thing exists) wherein boundaries between forms and between their high and popular versions are effaced (Jameson, 1985). Works of art, despite ideologies to the contrary, have always been derivative; in so far as they make use of existing technologies, artistic conventions and archetypal themes, they are collaborative projects. In advertising, however, this process of the appropriation and reworking of ideas and motifs already in the public domain is not only not concealed, it is celebrated. Pastiche is increasingly becoming an integral part of the form.

References are made to different genres of cinema. The Pirelli Tyre ad is a miniature *film noir*, complete with murder plot, *femme fatale* and moody lighting. Carling Black Label has made an ad for its lager which references the cinematic preoccupation with Vietnam yet also appears to be a critique of war films and traditional masculinity: the hero is an intellectual and a refusenik – an inversion of the archetypal Rambo figure. Barclays Bank has made use of the style and images of *Blade Runner* as well as its director, Ridley Scott. The Holsten Pils advertisements are famous for taking quotations from old movies and incorporating them into their own narratives; thus we witness an unlikely encounter in the ladies washroom between Griff Rhys Jones and Marilyn Monroe.

Cross-referencing between ads occurs frequently, particularly where an ad has been successful. In its recent campaign Carling Black Label has made parodic references of this kind its trademark, hence its detailed and witty re-enactment – even the same extras are used – of the famous Levi's Launderette ad, which itself draws on images from 1950s youth movies. In the same vein Carling Black Label references an Old Spice commercial in its ad about a surfer riding a wave into a pub. Another example of an obscure and in this case more laboured reference occurs in a Wrangler ad where the hero puts on a pair of jeans and drives a double-decker bus across a row of parked motorbikes. This is a very coded allusion to Eddie Kidd, star of a 1987 ad for Black Levi 501s, who as a real-life stunt man in the 1970s held the world record for jumping his motorbike across parked double-decker buses.

The fusion of the commercial with other cultural forms is exemplified in an interesting way by a 1988 Independent Broadcasting Authority ruling on an ad for Pepe jeans. This was banned from appearing either immediately before or immediately after a normal programme because stylistically it looked more like a TV drama than a commercial and might delude people about its status. Influences operate in both direction. *Network 7*, for example, a now defunct Channel 4 programme for young people, developed a style of editing and presentation which owed a great deal to television advertising. The employment of cinema and TV actors in commercials also contributes to this merger of forms; not only do such actors draw on theatrical skills and conventions which are then subsumed into the commercial form, they also carry with them their theatrical identities which then work to enhance selected meanings. For example, in the ad which we describe at the beginning of this article the young man is played by Jesse Birdsall, an actor who, over the last ten years, has frequently been cast in the role of generic alienated urban youth and who most recently played one of the lads in *Wish You Were Here*. It is partly because of this performing history that we deduce the ad is referring to ordinary young people, albeit those with aspirations to tasteful interiors. A less subtle example of this process is the frequent use of George Cole, in the persona of Arthur Daley, to advertise a range of products and services.

At the level of behind-the-camera personnel there has in recent years been an escalating rate of crossover between commercials and cinema and TV. For some time now directors have been cutting their teeth on ads and progressing thereafter – where possible – to bigger things, even to Hollywood. Alan Parker, Ridley Scott and Tony Scott are examples of these. More recently, however, the movement has been in the other direction and already established cinema and television directors from a range of political and stylistic backgrounds have been recruited to direct commercials. Thus Ken Russell, director of *Crimes of Passion*, made an ad for Shredded Wheat; Peter Greenaway (*Draughtman's Contract*) and Stephen Frears (*My Beautiful Launderette*) have both directed commercials in the last few years. Ken Loach (*Kes*) made the award-winning ad for *The Guardian* in which the skinhead saves a passer-by from falling scaffolding, and John Amiel (*The Singing Detective*) and Nic Roeg (*Bad*

Timing) made two of the government AIDS warnings. Amiel has described the condensed quintessential dramas currently being made for British advertisers by himself and other established directors as 'little haikus' (Rusbridger, 1988). They exist and are recognized as autonomous creations.

So far we have argued that it is extremely difficult to separate ads conceptually from cultural forms conventionally designated as belonging to the sphere of art because of the consistent pattern of intertextuality and cross-referencing that operates between them. This observation, however, does not address the fundamental objective of the ad which is to sell. As we have seen, what an ad sets out to sell varies enormously, and includes itself, services, generic products, brands, lifestyles, ideas and information. But the fact that it has selling (or persuading) as its central purpose is what above all else is supposed to distinguish it from art forms like song, fiction, film, drama and fine art.

Yet our argument is that even this characteristic does not make it tenable to situate the ad in an analytically distinct sphere. All of the cultural forms referred to above are also in the business of selling. This happens in a range of ways. First of all, and perhaps most familiarly, art objects are themselves constituted as commodities and are bought and sold as investments as well as symbolic markers of wealth. Thus the possession of a Matisse painting denotes the status of its owner in exactly the same way as the possession of a pair of Levis does, through referencing a commonly acknowledged chain of associations about ownership and style. A second way in which marketing considerations enter into questions of art production is that art objects (films for example) must be able to sell themselves in order to be able to justify their existence and the costs initially expended on them.

Then there are more subtle ways in which 'pure' cultural forms are implicated in the processes of advertising and selling. It is not new to point to the fact that fiction, drama and movies are powerful purveyors of ideologies and illusions; one of the central purposes of the discipline of cultural studies has been to identify and unravel these. But what the advertisers call 'lifestyles', and even products, are promoted through these means. Thus *films noirs* for instance have probably been more successful in creating seductive images of smoking than have commercials; and Bertolucci's film, *The Last Emperor*, was likely to have been more influential in encouraging tourism to China (prior to Tiananmen Square) than any campaign designed especially for that purpose. Even quite specific brands are marketed through art forms: Scott Fitzgerald probably did as much to promote Bugattis as the film *Crocodile Dundee* has done to promote Fosters, the Australian beer. Another intriguing example of the way in which specific brands are given publicity through 'art' forms – yet barriers between art and advertising maintained – was an exhibition held at the Institute of Contemporary Arts which consisted wholly of large photographs of advertising hoardings taken by Richard Prince. The paradox here is that overtly 'commercial' photography is never offered space on the walls of galleries like the ICA.

Andy Warhol is one of the most celebrated as well as deliberate and ironic cultural promoters of branded products (see for example his paintings of Brillo pads and Coke bottles). As part of a group of painters in New York during the early 1960s who drew on and reproduced popular imagery, he both challenged the notion of the artist as the possessor of a unique creativity and simultaneously drew attention to the way in which art is a commodity, to be bought and sold like Coca-Cola; hence he became an actor in as well as exponent of what has come to be termed postmodernism. However, despite such cultural interventions and extensive debates about these issues within artistic and literary practice, and despite the obviousness – the banality even – of some of the examples we have cited above, there has been surprisingly little discussion within media studies and cultural theory of the crossovers we have referred to between advertising and other cultural forms. For example if we look at the list of one hundred papers presented at the International Television Studies Conference (ITSC) in London in July 1988 there appears to be one only which addresses the question of merchandising.

Responsibility for the persistent marginalization of advertising as cultural form must in part be attributed to the dominance of a kind of left-humanist-realist perspective – descended from Marcuse and the Frankfurt School – within this intellectual field. This has effectively inhibited any understanding of advertising as other than 'ideological' and inextricably bound up with consumerism, the market and the pursuit of profit under capitalism. In this sense, though perhaps unintentionally, cultural analysts have joined forces with the traditionalist defenders of high cultural forms who have resisted the incorporation of the commercial into the exalted ranks of 'art', who have insisted on keeping advertising in its place.

But the upstart is not acquiescent. Assaults on the historic fortifications of artistic status are escalating and emanate from a number of sectors, not least from young people themselves whose impact on the form will be returned to later. To some extent the criteria used to measure the success or failure of a commercial are negotiated and established within the profession itself. *Campaign*, the weekly of the advertising industry, has its own reviews of the latest commercials which are evaluated for originality, style, humour, technical innovation and, yes, even misogyny. These criteria are indistinguishable from those employed by any newspaper critic to review a movie. In fact, *City Limits* also has an occasional TV commercial review section which operates with these criteria and is listed alongside the other review sections. Prizes awarded to the best ads by the industry itself mobilize distinctions, not between ads and other forms, but between 'good' ads and 'bad' ads. Good ads, the ones that win awards or acclaim, do so on the basis of the 'quality' of the ad as a product in itself, and not on the basis of marketing success (though there may be some covert consideration of what is being advertised). Thus recently several prizes were awarded to a nationally exhibited ad requesting donations towards guide dogs for the blind which apparently raised only a paltry £100. *The Guardian* ad directed by Ken Loach and referred to above also won awards (it was the favourite of advertisers themselves) but has not succeeded in reviving the paper's flagging circulation. Another example of an ad considered successful according to aesthetic and communication criteria but which failed to sell the product was the government's Job Training Scheme series. Only 10 per cent of places offered by the scheme were taken up, and from these there was a 45 per cent drop out.

What we see therefore is that the success or failure of an advertisement is judged on factors extrinsic to its conventionally identified purpose, that is to say, the marketing of a product. Furthermore, advertising is no more homogeneous as a creative form than music, painting, film or drama.

Here we must return to young people. How do youth fit into this analysis of the commercial as (at its best) an increasingly innovative and sophisticated cultural form – as 'art'? What has the relationship of young people been to this redefinition? Is it possible to argue that, as audience, they have contributed to the complexity, elegance and wit of some contemporary television commercials?

In order to unravel and respond to these questions it is necessary to investigate in a little more detail the current state of advertising and marketing theory and practice. What has emerged quite clearly in recent years, concurrently with the refinements in form, is that advertisers no longer have confidence in the old theories about how ads promote sales. This view was frequently confirmed in the interviews we conducted with members of the industry and was reiterated in papers delivered by advertisers at a number of conferences we attended.[1] Beliefs in the power of subliminal messages to penetrate and manipulate the mass psyche no longer have currency. Advertisers are now as aware as other cultural producers that there is no formula or scientific method which can guarantee success. Market research has not come up with the answers. Marketing managers cannot precisely identify the components of a successful campaign; they are unable to anticipate what will spark the public imagination; they do not know exactly who their target audience is, nor how to reach it; and, at a more pedestrian level, they do not even know whether an ad is more effective if placed before or after a particular programme. Some go so far as to insist that advertising is hardly effective at all, that what is required is consistent media coverage in order to shift a product. So what we see is that marketing is a far more haphazard process than the intellectual orthodoxies would have us believe. There are no rules. There is no consensus.

These uncertainties do not mean though that the classic objectives of the industry have been abandoned. Advertisers still aim to increase sales for their clients, and to do so they need to take into account the culture and preferences of young people who constitute a significant proportion of the market both in terms of their own disposable income and their influence on friends and family. They must be recruited, their cynicism must be overcome. Yet in the absence of the confident and clear guidelines of earlier times, how is this to be achieved?

Although the industry continues to be enormously productive, the undermining of old convictions and the growing anxiety about public (youth) cynicism combine to reveal a picture of the advertising process itself in a state of crisis. Indeed the paradox is that the industry's productivity appears to be both a symptom and a cause of its malaise. More numerous and more subtle and sophisticated advertisements have generated more discriminating audiences. As we have already argued, at the forefront of these are the young themselves, whose scepticism and powers of analysis are, in this respect, a great deal more developed than those of older generations. It is through the exercise of these refined critical skills and through the consumption of the ad rather than the product that the young have contributed to the spiralling crisis.

Given the current climate of uncertainty and the lack of clarity about what might be an appropriate response to the crisis, the solution of the marketeers has been to turn to the creative departments within their agencies, to hand over responsibility to individuals largely trained in art schools, who rely not on research and surveys, for which they have little respect, but on imagination, inventiveness and intuition.[2]

Alternatively they have hired film-makers from outside the industry with already established 'artistic' credibility. There is no doubt that the experimental forms produced in this way have had unprecedented success in recruiting and retaining viewers. Above all they have been able to satisfy the gourmet appetites of the discerning young. What emerges quite clearly from this account is that young people, in their capacity as active consumers, have, as Willis (1988) suggests, 'shaped the contours of the commercial culture' which they inhabit. Unlike the young man in the Ogilvy and Mather commercial described at the beginning of this chapter, they do watch the ads. But they do not necessarily buy.

In this chapter we have developed an argument about young people and their relation to contemporary advertising. In order to do this we have used a very undifferentiated model of youth, we have not investigated – or even postulated – distinctions based on class, race or gender because our argument does not require these refinements. Not all youth – and certainly not only youth – read advertisements in the ways in which we (and the advertisers themselves) have argued, though sufficient numbers do to justify our thesis. Our central preoccupation here has been with the consumption of advertising and the skills brought to bear in this process. This has included examining not only transformations in the production of advertisements but also the ways in which historically advertising has been defined. Our argument has been that although ads have in the past been primarily concerned to promote sales, they increasingly offer moments of intellectual stimulation, entertainment and pleasure – of 'art'. To focus on this phenomenon is not to exonerate advertisers and their clients from responsibility in the formation and perpetuation of consumer capitalism. Nor is it to deny totally the influence of advertising in purchasing decisions. Our intention has been to bypass these debates. Instead we recognize the relative autonomy of the ad as product and view it as no more or less inherently implicated in the economic organization of life than any other cultural form. (Advertisements can after all also promote progressive products and causes, like Nicaraguan coffee and the Greater London Council: Myers, 1986.) More importantly, given the terms of reference of the Gulbenkian Enquiry, we have emphasized in this chapter the very considerable though untutored skills that young people bring to bear in their appreciation of advertisements and that they exercise individually and collectively, not in museums and public galleries, but in millions of front rooms throughout the country – and indeed the world.

The critical question arising from this is whether or not the possession of such decoding skills by young people, and the revolution in the advertising process itself, can be interpreted as progressive. Debates of this kind have always surrounded new stages in the dissemination of knowledge. Reading the written word was considered a contentious activity in the nineteenth century: some people thought it would serve to discipline and pacify the population while others feared (or hoped) it would prove subversive. Earlier in this century Walter Benjamin (1973, originally published in 1936) claimed that the new technology of film would help to develop in spectators a more acute and critical perception. Film as cultural form was not only more popular and democratic, it was potentially revolutionary. Arguing against this position, Adorno and Horkheimer (1973), condemned the culture industry for what they alleged was its taming both of critical art and the minds of the people. More recently Fredric Jameson (1985) has asked similar questions about the advent of 'postmodernism'. To what extent can postmodern forms be considered oppositional or progressive? Is there a way in which they can resist and contest the logic of consumer capitalism? Our answer must be that the forms alone cannot be subversive, but that the critical tools as well as the pleasures they have generated, and from which they are in any case inseparable, may indeed subvert and fragment existing networks of power-knowledge.

Notes

1. See for example papers given by Neil Fazakerly, Creative Director at Davidson Pearce, at the Institute of Contemporary Arts 'Talking Ideas' event, July 1988; Winston Fletcher, Chairman of Delaney Fletcher Delaney, at the *Marxism Today* 'New Times' conference, October 1989; and Richard Phillips, Creative Director at J. Walter Thompson at the Forum Communications 'New Wave Young: Targeting the Youth Market' conference, March 1988.

2. See note 1.

COMMENT

Discriminating or Duped? Young People as Consumers of Advertising/Art

(with Orson Nava)

In the summer of 1987 my son Zadoc Nava and a friend, Andrew Lambert, both aged twenty-three and recent graduates from film school, decided to make a commercial for Nicaraguan coffee. They, my other two sons, Orson Nava (then aged twenty) and Jake Nava (seventeen) and I spent many evenings discussing advertising theory, developing a script appropriate to a UK audience and considering means of funding such a project. During these discussions I was struck by how sophisticated and subtle was their grasp of the production of advertising meanings. This confirmed my experience of watching television with them and their friends when I would frequently be oblivious to a wide range of complex textual references which they would identify, appreciate and patiently explain.

About the same time I received a circular in my department at the polytechnic from Paul Willis soliciting research for the Gulbenkian Enquiry into Young People and the Arts. In the context of our discussions about advertising, my sons and I submitted a two-part proposal: the first was to write a theoretical piece on the consumption of commercials by young people; the second was to be a linked piece of cultural practice, namely the Nicaraguan coffee commercial, which would illustrate the use of cinematic conventions, intertextuality and so on referred to in Part I. Perhaps predictably, the Gulbenkian Enquiry commissioned Part I only. The coffee commercial was finally funded from other sources and after completion was shown in arts cinemas around the country.[1] Meanwhile Orson Nava and I, in another example of local intellectual work, under-took to do the research and write up what became 'Discriminating or Duped?'

Our research consisted of looking at ads, scrutinizing *Campaign*, inter-viewing agencies and attending a conference about young people organized by and for advertisers (Nava, 1988). Orson – although disillu-sioned with formal education at the time – had read widely, knew the cultural debates and was highly skilled at decoding commercials. Together we worked through each stage of the argument. The 'vivid examples' requested by Willis were supplied by Orson. I did most of the writing. The process that we adopted worked well. The argument was agreed upon and reviewed each writing day. Problems were discussed and resolved as they arose and the piece was painlessly completed for the deadline.

The central argument clearly engages with and develops questions already raised in Chapter 8 in its 'refutation of the notion that the media and advertising have the power to manipulate in a coherent and unfractured fashion and . . . the notion of mass man and woman as duped and passive recipients of conspiratorial messages'. Our intention was also to 'write against' the common view expressed by Raymond Williams in the 1960s and still widespread today that 'the pretty clever television advertisement' did not belong in the category of 'good' or significant culture (Williams, 1980: 364). This has changed somewhat with the current popularity of postmodernist debate and the interrogation of the ways in which 'art' forms are categorized and consumed. Yet nevertheless, the demonizing of advertising remains commonplace, particularly among feminists and on the Left, and arguments such as ours which appear to exonerate them are still suspiciously received. Michael Schudson's book (1986) *Advertising, The Uneasy Persuasion: Its Dubious Impact on American Society*, which undermines many of the conventional assumptions about the industry and its operations, has not yet been published or widely read in Britain. The copy we ordered from the United States did not arrive until after we had completed and sent off our report to Gulbenkian.

'Discriminating or Duped?' certainly fitted well with Paul Willis' concept of 'grounded aesthetics' and the idea that young people invest with meaning the practices that surround them. The Gulbenkian research team drew on the main premiss of our research to devise questions about favourite ads for their ethnographic studies of young people (Willis, 1990). Sections of our original report were subsequently reproduced by Willis in *Common Culture* (1990) though without being acknowledged according to the conventions of academic publishing. As might be expected, this has led to some confusion about authorship.

Note

1. This was the commercial we had in mind when we referred in Chapter 9 to the progressive possibilities of advertising. It subsequently won a bronze medal in the TV and Cinema Advertising Competition at the 1988 International Film and TV Festival of New York.

10

CONSUMERISM RECONSIDERED: BUYING AND POWER

Consumerism has become a powerful and evocative symbol of contemporary capitalism and the modern Western world. Indeed, in the climate of 1991, faced by the crisis of the environment and the radical transformations in Eastern Europe, it is perhaps the most resonant symbol of all. Highly visible, its imagery permeates the physical and cultural territories it occupies. Modern identities and imaginations are knotted inextricably to it. This much is clear. Yet intellectually and morally it has not been easy to make sense of, and troubling questions have been raised both for the Left and the Right. Within the social sciences and cultural studies it has been a recurring concern, particularly since the consolidation of the consumer society in the aftermath of the Second World War, and investigations of it have spanned a range of disciplines and theoretical debates. It will not come as a surprise to hear that these accounts offer no consistent explanations or responses. Some authors have condemned consumerism, others have welcomed it. Less predictable perhaps, is the conclusion that the different arguments are not easily categorized politically. In fact theories about consumerism (they are of course not unique in this respect) appear to owe as much to the general cultural climate of their formation, to their intellectual genealogy and to personal disposition, as they do to a consistently worked out political critique.

My project in this chapter is to trace the history of these different theorizations in order first of all to draw attention to the influence of the political and intellectual contexts from which they emerged, and secondly, to show how they in turn have shaped and placed limits on the way in which consumerism has subsequently been thought. More specifically I want to show how, during the 1950s and 1960s, both Marxists and conservative critics expressed their condemnation of mass consumption in similar elitist terms, and how, partly in reaction, this produced during the 1970s and 1980s a very different body of work in which the consumer and consumption are defended and even celebrated. I shall go on to argue that these very distinct perspectives have in combination prevented us from recognizing the potential *power* of consumerism – and here I am talking about power in a quite orthodox pre-Foucauldian sense – a power which has been brought into focus latterly by the acceleration of Green activism, by South African boycotts and other instances of consumer sanction and support. Finally I shall propose that consumer politics is able to mobilize and enfranchise a very broad spectrum of constituents, and moreover that it is productive of a kind of utopian collectivism lacking in other contemporary politics.

To arrive at this point in the theoretical narrative it will be necessary to traverse what may be fairly familiar terrain. But this will be more than the routine recitation of what has already been thought and said, because it is only through mapping out the debate and its historical and textual context that it becomes possible to identify the theoretical and political implications of certain routes.

Masses and manipulation

It is worth starting in classic vein, with a few lines on Marx, who set the parameters of subsequent debate by centring his analysis on production. Within this framework, consumption and markets were relatively neglected and the twentieth-century integration of the producers of commodities into capitalist society as consumers was not anticipated. For Marxists and socialists since Marx, political consciousness and political organization have been concentrated at the point of production, around labour. The potential of activism at the point of consumption has barely been addressed. Instead it is Marx's less developed ideas about the relation of commodity fetishism to false consciousness that have proved most influential in this intellectual field and have laid the groundwork for twentieth-century thought not only about consumption, but also about 'mass culture' and 'mass society' more generally.

From the 1930s onwards some of the most significant contributions to this general area were made by the group of cultural theorists known as the Frankfurt School, and one of the best known of these is the essay by Adorno and Horkheimer on the culture industry (1973). Although written in 1944 during the authors' exile to the United States, and containing detailed references to specific American cultural forms, its roots are firmly embedded in the interwar period of Europe, especially, as Swingewood (1977) has pointed out, 'in the failure of proletarian revolutions . . . during the 1920s and 1930s, the totalitarian nature of Stalinism' and the rise of Fascism. Hence their despair and contempt for what they see as the stupidity and malleability of mass society. They are deeply pessimistic not only about the power of the working class to resist control and indoctrination but also about the nature and quality of the capitalist culture industry itself, and their essay is a relentless invective against this. Products of the culture industry, like cinema, radio and magazines, are distinguished from 'art' and are condemned repeatedly for their uniformity, falseness, vileness, barbaric meaninglessness and much more. Although Adorno and Horkheimer offer more nuanced versions of their thesis elsewhere (Held, 1980) this is probably their most influential piece and is significant both for its critique of the culture industry as deliberately anti-enlightenment and for its expression of the authors' profoundly elitist attitude to popular culture and to the consumer.

Their elitism was not unusual during this period, nor were they alone in referencing this model of the easily manipulated subject. Their

European formation and experiences are likely to have influenced various aspects of their theorization, not just their perception of the working class, and are probably implicated in their anti-Americanism and their intellectual and cultural snobbery. European critiques of American democracy and its impact on culture were of course not new; they date back to de Tocqueville, who was among the first to publish his trepidation about this question. From the 1930s onwards, a nostalgic defence of high cultural forms and a contempt for mass culture and mass consumption becomes a recurring theme in cultural criticism of both the Left and the Right; it appears in the work of Adorno and Horkheimer as well as, for example, in that of the conservative English critic F. R. Leavis, though expressed in very different language. America, as the country where these cultural transformations are most clearly taking place, poses the greatest threat in this respect and becomes itself a kind of metaphor for all that is disturbing about modernity and democracy.

This process is accelerated in the postwar period. Dick Hebdige (1988) in his analysis of its specific British manifestation has called it 'the spectre of Americanization'. He draws attention to the way in which a number of significant authors of the 1940s and 1950s from quite different political perspectives (he singles out Evelyn Waugh, George Orwell and Richard Hoggart in particular) use similar imagery to express their anxiety about the advent of a vulgar and materialistic American-inspired consumer culture. He then goes on to explore aspects of this anti-Americanism among official arbiters of taste within the institutions of design and broadcasting. The pervasiveness of these sentiments during this period are attributed in part to the GI presence in Britain during and immediately after war, and to the public mythologies this generated about American affluence and style.

The mythologies must also be set in the context of wartime and postwar austerity. As Frank Mort (1988) has argued, 'austerity' consisted of more than just the inevitable wartime constraints; it was part of a socialist ideology, articulated by the Labour Party, in which Fabianism blended with Evangelicalism to form a moral as well as economic rejection of consumerism. Walvin (1978) has pointed out that the immediate postwar period saw a boom in popular leisure activities despite austerity measures, and that mass consumption for the working class was increasingly seen by them as an entitlement after the deprivation of the war and postwar years. Richard Hoggart (1957), twenty years earlier, was certainly not willing to see the picture in this light. Influenced by the socialist culture described by Mort, he saw the mass consumption that emerged with 1950s affluence as a deeply destructive force. It represented an erosion of the authentic elements in working-class life. Like Adorno and Horkheimer he considered it largely a consequence of American influence (though unlike them he barely touched on capitalism as a force) and he deplored its hedonism, materialism, 'corrupt brightness', 'moral evasiveness' and 'shiny barbarism'. Like Leavis and others to the Right of him, he feared a 'levelling down' of cultural standards. His view of the ordinary person and of the effect the reviled new culture would have on him or her is, however, harder to place; on the one hand he bemoans the passivity and corruptibility of the people; on the other, though less often, he refers to working-class cynicism and what he calls the 'I'm not buying that' stance. Perhaps it is familiarity with his subjects that prevents him from altogether suppressing the notion of working-class agency.

This can be compared with Adorno and Horkheimer's far more sealed-off version in which the amorphous acquiescent masses appear to possess no resources that can enable them to escape the repressive and manipulating powers of capitalist consumer culture. They are almost as vulnerable as Orwell's satirized proles in *Nineteen Eighty-Four*, which was published at about the same time. Herbert Marcuse, also a member of the Frankfurt School in exile but a more significant figure in American intellectual history because of his influential contributions to political thought and the radical student movement during the 1960s, emerges from the same camp. He too has a deeply pessimistic view of the ability of the masses to resist the encroachment of consumer culture.

In *One-Dimensional Man* (1964) he argues that liberal consumer societies control their populations by indoctrinating them with 'false needs' (analogous to false consciousness). People are manipulated through the media and advertising into believing that their identities will be enhanced by useless possessions. In a much-quoted passage which encapsulates his position, he writes: 'People recognize themselves in their commodities; they find their soul in their automobile, hi-fi set, split-level home . . . social control is anchored in the new needs which (the consumer society) has produced' (Marcuse, 1964: 24).

Thus the desiring and buying of things creates social conformity and political acquiescence. It militates against radical social change. In similar vein, Betty Friedan, author of *The Feminine Mystique* (first published in 1963), a seminal text for the early women's liberation movement, reports on an interview with an executive of an 'institute for motivational manipulation' whom she is outraged by, but clearly believes:

> Properly manipulated ('if you are not afraid of the word,' he said), American housewives can be given the sense of identity, purpose, creativity, the self-realization, even the sexual joy they lack – by the buying of things . . . I suddenly saw American women as *victims* of . . . [their] power at the point of purchase. (Friedan, 1965: 128; original emphasis)

We see that Marcuse and Friedan operate with a similar set of assumptions about ordinary men and women, whom they perceive as victims of conspiratorially constructed and deliberately wielded capitalist powers of manipulation.

With hindsight this seems like a rather crude theoretical perspective, but as I argued in Chapter 8, the position of these two influential authors must be understood in the context of the political and cultural climate in the United States during the previous decade. The 1950s saw an unprecedented growth of the consumer society, a term which signifies not just affluence and the expansion of production and markets, but also the increasing penetration of the meanings and images associated with consumption into the culture of everyday life. This was the moment of the consuming housewife – whose 'problem with no name' is the object of Friedan's study – locked into femininity, motherhood, shopping and the suburban idyll. During this conservative period marked by the Cold War, 'consensus' and conformity, the free choice of goods came to symbolize the 'freedom' of the Free World (Ewen, 1976). This period also saw a general shift to the Right among US intellectuals, many of whom expressed support for American affluence, the 'end of ideology' and the political status quo (Ross, 1987; Brookeman, 1984). J. K. Galbraith was among the exceptions here; a liberal critic of capitalism, he also distinguished himself from Marxist economists by criticizing their exclusive focus on production, an important point in the context of this argument, to which I will return. Along with the Marxists, however, and many to the right of him, he believed that advertising could create demand – in Marcuse's terms 'false needs' – and that desires could be 'shaped by the discreet manipulations of the persuaders' (Galbraith, 1958).

We see here the influence of Vance Packard, whose book *The Hidden Persuaders* (1981) enjoyed both popular and academic success during the 1950s. He argued that advertisers, drawing on the specialized knowledge of 'motivational analysts' and using methods like 'psychoseduction' and 'subliminal communication', were able to 'manipulate' people into making particular purchasing decisions. Packard's thesis slotted into widely held anxieties about conspiracies, brainwashing and thought control which were boosted by right-wing alarm about communist influence during the Korean war. This reached its cultural apogee in the film *The Manchurian Candidate* (1962) in which the Soviet professor in charge of 'conditioning' the American hero declares portentously that his victim's brain 'has not only been washed, as they say, it has been thoroughly dry cleaned'. Despite the fact that there has been no serious substantiating evidence for the existence of 'brainwashing' or even of the 'manipulation' described by Packard and picked up by some of the other theorists I have referred to (indeed it is estimated that as many as 90 per cent of new products fail despite advertising: Schudson, 1981; see also Sinclair, 1987) its association with the unknown and unconscious elements of the mind seems to have given it a continuing if uneasy credibility both at popular and more academic levels, on the Left and well as on the Right.

There are a number of pertinent features for my argument which emerge from this picture of the cultural theorists of the 1950s and 1960s. The first of these is a lack of respect for the mentality of ordinary people, exemplified by the view that they are easily duped by advertisers and politically pacified by the buying of useless objects. Their pursuit of commodities and their enjoyment of disdained cultural forms is cited as evidence of their irrationality and gullibility. The idea that certain sectors of the population – women, children and the less educated – are particularly vulnerable to the deleterious effects of cultural forms is an assumption running through Packard's book and repeated elsewhere. Stuart Ewen (1976) has drawn attention to the way in which one of the recurring comic figures in American television dramas during the 1950s was the wife who grossly overspent on a useless item of personal adornment like a hat. It is interesting in general to compare cultural representations and theorizations of the (female) consumer with those of the (male) producer. The activity of the consumer ('labour' would be considered an inappropriate term here) is likely to be constructed as impulsive and trivial, as lacking agency, whereas the work of the producer, even if 'alienated', tends to be 'hard', 'real', dignified, a source of solidarity and a focus around which to organize politically. This is partly a consequence of the peculiar privileging of production within the economic sphere to which I referred earlier, but in the light of the fact that women control 80 per cent of buying (Scott, 1976), it must also be interpreted as part of a wider misogynistic view of women's reason and capabilities. Indeed the ridiculing of women shoppers may be a way of negotiating the anxiety aroused by their economic power in this sphere.

Another characteristic of these texts is the assumption that a distinction can be made between 'true' and 'false' needs. The common position here is not that desires and longings (of the masses in particular) are denied, but that they are considered less authentic and 'real' if they are gratified by material objects and escapist TV rather than, say, political or 'creative' activities. There is a failure to recognize that all desires are constructed and interpreted through culture, that none exist independently of it, and that a hierarchy of authenticity and moral correctness is quite impossible to establish (for a further discussion of this see Kellner, 1983). In addition almost all the theories I have been discussing are tainted in some measure by a distaste for 'vulgar' display and 'low' culture; there is a blindness to the subtle – and not so subtle – meanings that shopping, commodities and popular cultural forms are capable of offering. Finally, many of these analyses also contain an entrenched belief in the monolithic and determining nature of capitalism and hence in the power of state institutions and the culture industries. Combined into a general approach, these elements have created a commonsense way of looking at consumerism, a dominant intellectual paradigm, which has continued to shape thinking in a range of related fields from media studies to feminism, despite the advent of alternative analyses which are critical of these perspectives.

Thus more recent work in the area which continues to operate at least in part with similar assumptions includes Haug's *Critique of Commodity Aesthetics* (first published 1971, reissued 1986) which 'contains distinct echoes of F. R. Leavis' (Frith, 1986); Judith Williamson's *Decoding Advertisements* (1978) which although innovative in its semiological analysis of ads, hangs on to a notion of production as a much more 'real' aspect of people's identity than consumption; Gillian Dyer's *Advertising as Communication* (1982) which condemns advertising for manipulating attitudes and distorting the quality of life, and, like Galbraith, refers to 'basic' needs (though the particularly virulent critique of Dyer's book by Myers, 1986, strikes me as unjustified); and *All Consuming Images* (1988) the latest book by Stuart Ewen, US theorist of consumer culture for whom 'conspiracy' and 'manipulation' remain important concepts. Jeremy Seabrook also fits into this camp. A popular author in the tradition of Hoggart, he has written often and polemically over the last decade about the way in which capitalism and the materialism of the consumer society have corrupted the young and the working class. He describes the process as one of 'mutilation' in which children are 'carried off in the fleshy arms of private consumption . . . to be systematically shaped to the products which it will be their duty to want, to compete for and to consume' (1978: 98). Within media studies as well as among politicians and pressure groups like that of Mary Whitehouse, the continuing debate about 'effects' (of sex and violence in particular) addresses many of the same theoretical questions.

Certain strands within feminism must also be included here. The idea of 'positive images', a widely pursued cultural strategy of feminists, apart from containing rather simple notions of what is positive, also reproduces the belief that images persuade in an unproblematic fashion. More important in its consequences is the very topical debate about pornography. Those feminists who argue for censorship and the suppression of certain kinds of image base their demands on the assumption that images work in specific and predictable ways to produce specific forms of behaviour, and that there are no mediating factors, like context, desire and knowledge, that determine our interpretations and affect our actions. In this version of the argument it is men who are perceived as the cultural dopes, as particularly vulnerable victims of indoctrination, because it is presumed (in an odd *non-sequitur* fashion) that if they see pictures of sexualized bodies they will be persuaded to go out and commit violent acts against women.

There are very definite echoes in this particular debate of several of the elements I outlined earlier. Apart from the belief that people (men) can be easily manipulated, there is also an elitist evaluation of the quality of representation in which some sexualized bodies are aesthetically and morally more acceptable than others. One could go on. But this is not the point of the chapter. What I want to draw attention to are some of the general conventions in the theorization of consumerism, which also extend beyond consumerism.

Pleasure and resistance

Despite its pervasiveness, the general approach outlined above has not been the only way of understanding these issues. Over the last twelve years or so a growing number of authors have insisted on rereading and reinterpreting the component elements of consumerism and have produced work in which the buying of things has been explored within a quite different framework. Among the forerunners here was Ellen Willis who, in a little-known piece, wrote a succinct defence of consumerism in which she stressed the labour, the rationality and the pleasures involved, and criticized authors such as Marcuse for their elitism and sexism (Willis, 1970). At about the same time Enzensberger (1970) criticized Marcuse's notion of false needs. But it was not really until the late 1970s that work structured by this new critical perspective began to emerge in quantity, along with the discipline of cultural studies of which it forms an integral part.

The pertinent studies here have taken as their subject matter aspects of popular culture like youth styles and fashion, popular TV and cinema, romantic fiction and women's magazines, advertising and shopping (examples include Hall and Jefferson, 1976; Hebdige, 1979, 1988; Morley, 1980; McRobbie, 1989; Wilson, 1985; Steedman, 1986; Mort, 1988; Mercer, 1987; Carter, 1984; Radway, 1987; Winship, 1987; Nava and Nava, 1990 and Chapter 9). There are of course significant differences between these contributions, differences of emphasis and level of analysis, but what this body of work has in common is a reassessment and revalorization of popular cultural forms and popular experience, of the meanings consumption produces. Formed in part out of a reaction against the earlier body of work, it constitutes a kind of intellectual and political break, part of a wider loss of confidence in the primacy of the economic and the correspondence between class and class consciousness. This is despite a general allegiance to the Left among these authors. Extremely significant here has been the influence of Stuart Hall who, as director of the Centre for Contemporary Cultural Studies and more recently as a member of the *Marxism Today* editorial board, has played a major part in setting the critical agenda. Of particular relevance to this chapter has been his insistence over the last twelve years that we understand how it is that Thatcherism has managed so effectively to harness popular desires and discontents (Hall, 1988b). These questions have found a renewed importance over the recent period with the political developments which have taken place in Eastern Europe and the centrality to these of consumer imagery.

Thatcherism is one feature of the context in which the cultural studies approach has developed. Another has been feminism. Over the last decade feminism has been transformed from a narrow movement to an extensive presence – recognizable but not always identified by name – which has permeated cultural production, from *Eastenders* and *Cosmopolitan* to the curricula of academe. The feminist concern in the work I have been describing has been to undermine earlier perceptions of women as cultural victims and to examine what is rewarding, rational and indeed sometimes liberating about popular culture. This ties in with the cultural studies emphasis on experience, an important component in emerging audience studies. Radical literary theory has also contributed to the general climate in which this approach has developed by asserting that literary value exists not in any absolute sense, but as a construction of the discipline of literary criticism (Eagleton, 1983) and the high culture/low culture divide has been challenged both within this perspective and from a number of other directions (see, for example, Jameson, 1979). Semiotics and psychoanalysis have also been influential: semiotics through its emphasis on the sign and the symbolic nature of commodities; psychoanalysis in its attention to the unconscious processes in psychic life and the contradictory nature of identity.

More specifically, David Morley has done important work on TV and audience in which he stresses the diverse ways in which messages are read; identity, cultural and political background and viewing context all contribute to the range of possible meanings that any particular text can produce (Morley, 1980, 1986). Feminist work on romantic fiction and TV soaps has explored the progressive elements in these popular forms and has also insisted on acknowledging the complex ways in which the texts are understood, as well as the ambiguous pleasures that they offer (Modleski, 1982; Radway, 1987; Radford, 1986). Erica Carter, in her study of consumer culture in postwar Germany, has explored the symbolic meanings of nylon stockings and how wearing them to work could operate as a form of protest and confrontation in a dreary and routinized existence: 'Consumerism not only offers, but also continually fulfils its promise of everyday solutions . . . to problems whose origins may lie elsewhere' (Carter, 1984: 213). So it can indeed provide women with the 'sense of identity, purpose and creativity' claimed by Friedan's advertising executive, and should not for this reason be condemned. This question is also addressed by Carolyn Steedman (1986), who understands her mother's desire for commodities in postwar Britain as a form of defiance, a refusal to remain marginalized in class terms:

> From a Lancashire mill town and a working-class twenties childhood she came away wanting: fine clothes, glamour, money; to be what she wasn't. However that longing was produced in her distant childhood, what she actually wanted were real . . . entities, things that she materially lacked, things that a culture and a social system withheld from her. (Steedman, 1986: 6)

My own research (with Orson Nava) into the way young people watch TV commercials is another example of this general approach (see Chapter 9). The argument here is that young people are not easily duped, that they consume advertisements independently of the product that is being marketed, and in the process bring to bear sophisticated critical skills; the advertisers respond to this appreciation by frequently directing their ads at young people – as the most literate sector of their audience – regardless of what is being sold. Frank Mort (1988) and Angela McRobbie (1989) have similarly focused on the agency of the consumer in their respective studies and the way in which young people, far from simply waiting for the latest fashions to appear, play an active part through the creation of their own street styles in what is manufactured and marketed.

Dick Hebdige's work (1979, 1988) has had a seminal influence on the development of this general perspective in (among other things) its attention to the symbolic meanings of style and to the way in which the image constitutes not only an integral aspect of contemporary identity but also a form of power and resistance: 'commodities can be symbolically repossessed in everyday life and endowed with implicitly oppositional meanings' (1979: 16). Kobena Mercer has explored similar questions in relation to black hairstyles, which he has argued should be seen as 'aesthetic "solutions" to a range of "problems" created by ideologies of race and racism' (1987: 34). Poststructuralist and postmodernist analyses which stress the overwhelming significance of the sign have of course been very influential here, particularly Baudrillard's (1988) work on consumption and the political economy of the sign in which he argues for a notion of the social 'as nothing other than the play of signs which have no referent in "reality" but only derive their meanings from themselves and each other' (O'Shea, 1989) (but note also the similarities between Baudrillard and the Frankfurt School in their view of the masses). Much of the work that falls into this second intellectual paradigm, however, has been quite historically and experientially rooted and hence is not postmodernist in the sense referred to above.

Much of it has also drawn quite heavily on psychoanalysis. There have been different influences here, all fairly diffuse, but in a cumulative way all emphasizing the complexity of culture and our interaction with it. Lacan's work has been important, particularly his stress on the subject as fragmented and incoherent. We are simultaneously both rational and irrational; we can both consume and reject what we are consuming; desire permeates everything but is by definition never fulfilled. Melanie Klein's emphasis on the relationship between the child and mother has also been influential; Gillian Skirrow, for example, has drawn on Klein's insights about the child's fascination with the internal working of the mother's body in order to explore the particular appeal of video games to boys (Skirrow, 1986). Another application of psychoanalytic theory to consumerism, this time from the object relations school, is offered by Robert Young (1989) who celebrates the pleasures and comforts of sound systems and computers as transitional objects comparable to the teddy bear.

What all these texts have in common is a legitimizing of the consumer and of the commodities and cultural forms that are *actively* consumed by him or her. Also in common they stress the *materiality* of the symbolic.

Explorations of power are confined to this level, to the symbolic and discursive. In this intellectual paradigm the proximity of consumption to production, and hence to the economic, remains unaddressed.

Consumerism and power

It is paradoxical that the orientation of this second paradigm towards fantasy, identity, meaning and protest, although productive in uncovering the agency of the consumer, has in its flight from the economic, succeeded in obscuring the radical potential of consumption almost as much as the earlier paradigm in which the consumer was so denigrated. What I want to do now is to retain the insights about the popular and imaginative appeal of consumption and combine them with an exploration of the possibilities of political activism at the point of consumption.

As I have already pointed out, traditional Marxists and socialists have tended to ignore this general area both theoretically and politically. Their concentration has been uniquely centred on *production* as the motor and therefore also the Achilles heel of capitalism. The 'new movements', like feminism and gay and black organizations, have tended to focus either on changing consciousness through cultural interventions, or on demanding a greater share of state resources. Although politically all these groups are likely to have been involved in the boycott of South African goods (for example), within the conceptual framework that I am examining the potential of activism at the point of consumption has largely been neglected. It is ironic that among the first to point the way at the theoretical level to these possibilities have been liberal economists like Galbraith, through their emphasis on the importance of the consumption process within capitalism. The progressive implications of this intellectual avenue are considerable. Galbraith argued in *Economics and the Public Purse* (accessibly summarized by himself for the less knowledgeable in *Ms* magazine in 1974) that women's labour in the management and administration of consumption was as integral to the continuing existence of capitalism as the labour involved in production, but that in neoclassical economics its value was concealed. Here is a point that can yield a considerable amount for feminists (see, for example, Weinbaum and Bridges, 1979) but it is not one to be pursued right now. What is useful for the argument that I am developing here is the emphasis on the economic significance of the consumer, and hence by implication, on her potential power.

There is, however, no consideration of this potential in the standard consumer literature. What is referred to as 'consumerism' particularly in the United States, is a movement which had its political heyday there during the 1960s (Nader, 1971; Cameron Mitchell, 1986) when it was bracketed with communism and other dangerous 'isms' by some of the giant corporations. It now exists throughout the Western world (see, for example, the Consumers Association and *Which?* magazine in this country) albeit in more moderate form and continues as before in its task of disseminating information and increasing regulative legislation through the exercise of pressure on government agencies. Its object has consistently been to protect and enlighten the consumer by monitoring the quality of prices and goods, encoding and publicizing consumer rights, and so forth. In political terms the movement has engaged activists, but only in pursuit of the goals identified above. There appears to have been no extrinsic political purpose, no exercise of a more general political power.

Consumer co-operatives from the time of Sidney and Beatrice Webb onwards have also focused predominantly on securing low prices and good quality for their members, although they have done this not only by increasing restrictive legislation and consumer rights, but also by developing their own manufacturing and retailing bases. This has sometimes included the establishment of self-help networks. However, as with the consumer rights movements, objectives have normally been restricted to the protective; there has been no attempt to wield political power over a wider range of issues.

Consumer protection must be distinguished from consumer boycotts, which have specific political goals that do not necessarily operate to the material advantage of the consumer. Boycotts date back to at least the eighteenth century and have historically been employed as a political tactic where other forms of struggle are blocked or seem inappropriate. A notable example has been Cesar Chavez who, inspired by Gandhi and frustrated by corrupt and racist American trade union practices, successfully mobilized (during the 1960s and 1970s) what eventually became an international boycott of Californian grapes and other farm produce in order to improve the working conditions of Mexican-American labourers. As he put it, 'The boycott is not just grapes and lettuce, essentially it's about people's concern for people' (Levy, 1975: 256). Product boycotts are a more common form of protest in the United States than in Britain and have increased in recent years (Savan, 1989). Economic sanctions against South Africa and boycotts against firms with interests there, like Barclays Bank, have also proved successful. Consumer boycotts have become one of the most effective weapons available to the black population in South Africa. Disenfranchised in terms of the conventional democratic processes, consumer boycotts enable them nevertheless to wield a measure of direct and instantaneous power. A recent example reported in *The Guardian* (Ormond, 1990) involved a white shop owner who entered the political arena on behalf of the Conservative Party and whose business, as a consequence of the ensuing boycott by blacks, dropped by an extraordinary 90 per cent within two days.

Until recently this form of political activism has involved relatively small numbers of people. However, during the last year or so we have seen an extraordinary growth in a consumer practice that encompasses not only boycotts but also selective buying (the buying of products which conform to certain criteria). This has undoubtedly been stimulated by the global environmental crisis, and fuelled by government inaction. Concern about these issues and the conviction that consumer activism can be an effective form of protest has resulted, according to *The Times* (30 June 1989), in an estimated 18 million Green shoppers in Britain. According to *The Daily Telegraph*, 50 per cent of shoppers operate product boycotts of one kind or another (*The Ethical Consumer* 3, 1989) and to date *The Green Consumer Guide* (Elkington and Hailes, 1989) has been on the *The Sunday Times* bestseller list for almost a year and has sold 300,000 copies. Green consumerism has clearly captured the popular imagination to an unprecedented degree. This is because it offers ordinary people access to a new and very immediate democratic process: 'voting' about the environment can take place on a daily basis. People are not only *not* duped, they are able through their shopping to register political support or opposition. Furthermore they are able to exercise some control over production itself, over what gets produced and the political conditions in which production takes place.

This is facilitated through the type of information researched and disseminated by magazines like *The Ethical Consumer* (first issue published in March 1989, as yet with a small circulation) whose objectives are 'to promote the use of consumer power' and to expand the democratic process. Another example is *New Consumer*, 'the magazine for the creative consumer', which was launched in August 1989. These magazines include both analytical articles and reviews of products and services. Instead of assessing items in terms of value for money (as *Which?* does) the criteria used are whether or not manufacturing companies have involvements in South Africa or other 'oppressive regimes'; whether they recognize trade unions, have decent work conditions and responsible marketing practices; whether they are involved in the manufacture of armaments or nuclear power; and finally what their record is on women's issues, animal testing, land rights and the environment. Articles in back issues of *The Ethical Consumer* include an evaluation of the politics of Green consumerism (their position here is that the Green focus on particular items detracts attention from the overall profile of producer companies) and a review of the US magazine *National Boycott News* in which all organized boycotts are reported. At a more general level the argument is that consumer activism occurs where normal democratic processes are inadequate and where there are 'widespread feelings of powerlessness'. It is clear from reading *The Ethical Consumer* and *New Consumer* (as well as the less analytical *Green Consumer Guide*) that the consumerism advocated by bodies of this kind is neither liberal nor individualistic. On the contrary, it is radical, collectivist, internationalist and visionary; implicitly socialist in its analysis of capitalism, it differs in the importance it attributes to the point of consumption.

In addition, one of the great strengths of this new consumer activism is its appeal to groups who historically have been marginalized from both the production process and the politics of the workplace and government, namely women and the young. Yet they are central to the process of consumption. I have already referred to women's importance in this sphere: it is not only that they have expertise and confidence here, and that they wield 80 per cent of purchasing power; it is also that they are uniquely placed in relation to environmental issues – to food contamination, health care, pollution and, more grandly, the future of the planet – in their continuing capacity as bearers of responsibility for nurturing and for the details of everyday life. This combination has constructed them as a constituency pre-eminently suited to the new consumer activism. And indeed women's magazines regularly run articles about these questions. The Body Shop, which comes out clean on every one of *The Ethical Consumer* criteria, has been one of the most successful chains of stores of recent years. There are many examples which confirm women as political *subjects* in this process, as active, knowledgeable and progressive.

The young constitute another group for whom consumer activism is particularly appealing. As large numbers of celebrated individuals from the music and entertainment industry have become involved in popularizing environmental politics, its sandals-and-renunciation image has given way to something which is much more exciting and fashionable. Ark, the campaigning organization and production company, is an example of this. Environmental consumerism is also urgent and worth while. Perhaps part of its success lies in its appeal to a kind of youthful apocalyptic pessimism as well as, simultaneously, to fantasies of omnipotence and reparation. Utopian and collectivist, it offers something to identify with, to belong to. It is also effective. Although the young may not have as large an income as older members of the population, they – like women – have a disproportionate influence on marketing decisions, as is well known among advertisers. Although relatively powerless in orthodox political terms – many of them are not even eighteen – they too are enfranchised in the new democracy of the market place.

However, the political Left appears to have been blind to the potential of this kind of politics and has excluded it from its repertoire of popular activism (despite the emphasis in certain sectors on the political importance of consumerism's appeal: Hall and Jacques, 1989). There are various reasons for this. First of all, at a general level, the formative traditions of Marxism, trade unionism and the Labour Party seem to have rendered the Left incapable of imagining political struggle outside the workplace, the local state or Parliament. This is ironic, because in its extreme and 'terrorist' forms, consumer activism is far more effective and much easier than striking and picketing. An example which highlights the vulnerability of the point of consumption (as well as the greater take-up of consumer politics in the United States, perhaps because of their weaker labour history) is the case of the cyanide painted on two Chilean grapes which resulted in the loss of $240 million and 20,000 jobs (Jenkins, 1989). This apart, where the Left has looked specifically at consumerism (see, for example, Gyford, 1989) it has tended to be in terms of the collectivity versus the individual; the liberal and defensive consumer rights movement has not been distinguished analytically from the mass exercise of consumer power. Yet another factor which may well have inhibited the serious attention of the Left to consumer politics is the degree of crossover between the Green movement and the alternative health movement. Criticisms of individualism, essentialism and mysticism which have been levelled against the health movement (Coward, 1989) are likely to have spilled over on to consumer activism. Then of course there is the continuing saga of moralistic distaste – with resonances of the Hoggart/Marcuse/Seabrook paradigm – for too much emphasis on acquisition and the buying of things and for what is seen as the licensing of consumer hedonism by, for example, *Marxism Today*. Finally, on the political Left as elsewhere, shopping continues to be trivialized through its (unconscious?) association with women's work and the feminine.

Theorists of consumption and the consumer society have also been at fault here. They too have failed to consider these questions (see, for example, Featherstone, 1990). But as I argued earlier in this chapter, cultural theory cannot be easily disentangled from its wider context, and some of the political points listed in the previous paragraph have also deflected a more academic scrutiny of these issues. Yet current world developments have made this a particularly urgent matter: we are confronted not only by the crisis of the environment, but also by the frailty of socialism in Eastern Europe and the apparent expansion of capitalism into a global system. In this climate it has become all the more imperative to investigate consumerism: to look at how historically it has linked up with other forms of politics; to tease out its contradictions and limits; to examine more closely the proposition that its theoretical marginality owes something to misogyny; to explore its relation to identity and desire; and of course also to develop a sharper understanding of its economic operations and its potential power. It may well be the case that late twentieth-century Western consumerism contains within it far more revolutionary seeds than we have hitherto anticipated. It has already generated new grassroots constituencies – constituencies of the market place – and has enfranchised modern citizens in new ways, making possible a new and quite different economic, political, personal and creative participation in society. The full scale of its power has yet to be imagined.

COMMENT

Consumerism Reconsidered: Buying and Power

'Consumerism Reconsidered' was prompted by my reflections on the engagement of my son Jake in the politics of Green consumerism. He was involved in a project to recruit young people globally into environmental politics and consumer boycotts by tapping into memories of Band Aid and the stylishness of advertisers rather than the more dreary conventions of party politics and the ashcloth imagery of the old New Left. In the event, the project did not do all that well. Nevertheless, for me it raised important questions about the failure of the Left to imagine the potential of new kinds of politics and a different kind of enfranchisement for the less organized sectors of the population. This chapter additionally, but far more tangentially, raises questions about consumerism and the decline of communism, as might be expected given the moment of authorship, just after the cataclysmic changes in Eastern Europe of the winter of 1989–90.

Alongside these specific questions, 'Consumerism Reconsidered' continues to struggle with the notion of the manipulated subject and the importance of historical context, both political and intellectual, for cultural theorization. One of the other recurring themes of the book – divisions within feminism – is here touched on by reflecting on the connections between debates within consumerism and media studies about subjectivity and the power of the image, and those within feminism about pornography. The identification of shopping with femininity, cultural anxieties about this, and the complex history of the associated theoretical marginalization of consumerism, is an area into which I am currently doing research. Interestingly, it is taking me back to a position in which gender and its symbolic meanings are centre-staged. It seems to me that without recognizing the fears generated by women's consumption of mass culture – and here I include cinema-going, consuming magazines and independent urban travel as well as the experience of shopping in department stores – we will not be able to make sense of the idiosyncratic and contradictory ways in which these phenomena have been represented to us (Nava, forthcoming).

The final section of 'Consumerism Reconsidered' also takes us back to one of the key questions of the earlier chapters, to a moment prior to uncertainty (could this be a feature of the 1990s?) in that it explores the impact of the way we understand social life – of theory – on the way we act politically. In this respect then, despite its greater familiarity with the discourse of postmodernism, this final chapter returns us to fundamental political questions inflected by humanist ideas of progress, utopianism and agency, about how to change the world. Or the planet, as we say these days.

BIBLIOGRAPHY

Aaker, D. and Day, G. (eds) (1971) *Consumerism*. London: Free Press Macmillan.

Addams, J. (1910) *The Spirit of Youth and the City Streets*. New York: Macmillan.

Adorno, Theodor and Horkheimer, Max (1973) *Dialectics of Enlightenment*. London: Allen Lane.

Alexander, Sally (1976) 'Women's work in nineteenth-century London: a study of the years 1820–50', in Mitchell and Oakley (1976).

Allen, Hilary (1982) 'Political lesbianism and feminism – space for a sexual politics?', *m/f*, 7.

Althusser, Louis (1971) 'Ideology and ideological state apparatuses', in *Lenin and Philosophy and Other Essays*. London: New Left Books.

Anderson, Perry (1969) 'Components of the national culture', in A. Cockburn and R. Blackburn (eds), *Student Power*. Harmondsworth: Penguin.

Appignanesi, Lisa (ed.) (1989) *Postmodernism: ICA Documents*. London: Free Association Books.

Bachelli, Ann *et al.* (1970) 'Women's liberation', in *Black Dwarf*, 5 September.

Banks, J. A. and Banks, O. (1965) *Feminism and Family Planning in Victorian England*. Liverpool: Liverpool University Press.

Banks, O. (1981) *Faces of Feminism*. Oxford: Martin Robertson.

Barnett, A. (1986) 'Ideas in search of a home', *The Guardian*, 17 November.

Barrett, Michèle (1980) *Women's Oppression Today*. London: Verso.

Barrett, Michèle and McIntosh, M. (1982) *The Anti-Social Family*. London: Verso.

Barthes, Roland (1977) *Image Music Text*. London: Fontana.

Baudrillard, Jean (1988) 'Critique of the political economy of the sign', in Poster (1988).

Bauman, Zygmunt (1983) 'Industrialism, consumerism and power', *Theory, Culture & Society*, 1 (3).

Bauman, Zygmunt (1988) 'Is there a postmodern sociology?', in *Theory, Culture & Society*, 5 (2–3).

Beechey, Veronica (1979) 'On patriarchy', *Feminist Review*, 3.

Bender, Lauretta and Blau, Abraham (1937) 'The reaction of children to sexual relations with adults', *American Journal of Orthopsychiatry*, 7.

Benjamin, Walter (1973) 'The work of art in the age of mechanical reproduction', in *Illuminations*. London: Fontana. (Originally published in 1936.)

Bennett, F., Heys, R. and Coward, R. (1980) 'The limits to financial and legal independence', in *Politics and Power*, 1. London: Routledge & Kegan Paul.

Bennett, F., Campbell, B. and Coward, R. (1981) 'Feminists – the degenerates of the social?', in *Politics and Power*, 3. London: Routledge & Kegan Paul.

Benston, M. (1969) 'The political economy of women's liberation', *Monthly Review*, September.

Berger, John (1972) *Ways of Seeing*. Harmondsworth: Penguin.

Bernstein, B. (1977) *Class, Codes and Control, Vol. 3: Towards a Theory of Educational Transmissions*. London: Routledge & Kegan Paul.

Bhaba, Homi (1990) 'The third space', in Rutherford (1990b).

Blanch, M. (1979) 'Imperialism, nationalism and organised youth', in Clark *et al.* (1979).

Blom, P. and Smith, R. (eds) (1986) *The Future of Consumerism*. Lexington.

Bone, A. (1983) *Girls and Girls-only Schools*. Manchester: Equal Opportunities Commission.

Bowlby, John (1953) *Child Care and the Growth of Love*. Harmondsworth: Penguin.

Brannen, Julia and Wilson, Gail (eds) (1987) *Give and Take in Families*. London: Unwin Hyman.

Brennan, Teresa (ed.) (1989) *Between Feminism and Psychoanalysis*. London: Routledge.

Brookeman, Christopher (1984) *American Culture and Society since the 1930s*. London: Macmillan.

Burman, S. (ed.) (1979) *Fit Work for Women*. London: Croom Helm.

Burnett, J. (1977) *Useful Toil*. Harmondsworth: Penguin.

Califia, Pat (1981) 'Man/boy love and the lesbian/gay movement', in Tsang (1981).

Camden Area Youth Committee Report (Camden Report) (1982) *'Out of Sight' A Report on how the ILEA Youth Service in the Camden Area is Meeting the Needs of Girls and Young Women*. Camden: CAYC.

Cameron Mitchell, Robert (1986) 'Consumerism and environmentalism in the 1980s', in Blom and Smith (1986).

Campbell, Beatrix (1980) 'Feminist sexual politics', in *Feminist Review*, 5.

Campbell, Beatrix (1987) 'The skeleton in the family's cupboard', *New Statesman*, 31 July.

Carter, Erica (1984) 'Alice in consumer wonderland', in McRobbie and Nava (1984).

Cartledge, S. and Ryan, J. (1983) *Sex and Love*. London: Women's Press.

Chapman, R. and Rutherford, J. (eds) (1988) *Male Order: Unwrapping Masculinity*. London: Lawrence & Wishart.

Chodorow, N. (1978) *The Reproduction of Mothering*. Berkeley: University of California Press.

Clark, J., Critcher, C. and Johnson, R. (eds) (1979) *Working-Class Culture*. London: Hutchinson.

Clarke, Wendy (1983) 'Home thoughts from not so far away: a personal look at the family', in Segal (1983c).

Cockburn, Cynthia (1988) 'Masculinity, the Left and feminism', in Chapman and Rutherford (1988).

Cohen, Philip (1982) 'Schooling for the dole', *New Socialist*, 3.

Cohen, Stanley (1972) *Folk Devils and Moral Panics*. London: MacGibbon & Kee.

Connolly, Clara (1990) 'Splintered sisterhood: anti-racism in a young women's project', *Feminist Review*, 36.

Connor, Steven (1989) *Postmodernist Culture*. Oxford: Blackwell.

Cooper, David (1971) *The Death of the Family*. London: Allen Lane.

Coote, A. and Campbell, B. (1982) *Sweet Freedom: The Struggle for Women's Liberation*. London: Picador.

Corrigan, Paul (1979) *Schooling the Smash Street Kids*. London: Macmillan.

Coward, Rosalind (1989) *The Whole Truth*. London: Faber & Faber.

Coward, Rosalind and Women Against Violence Against Women (WAVAW) (1982) 'What is pornography? Two opposing feminist viewpoints', *Spare Rib*, 119.

Cowie, C. and Lees, S. (1981) 'Slags or drags', *Feminist Review*, 9.

Creed, Barbara (1987) 'From here to modernity: feminism and postmodernism', *Screen*, 28 (2).

Crockford, S. and Fromer, N. (1972) 'When is a house not home?', in Wandor (1972).

David, M. (1980) *The State, the Family and Education*. London: Routledge & Kegan Paul.

Davidoff, L., L'Esperance, J. and Newby, H. (1976) 'Landscape with figures', in Mitchell and Oakley (1976).

Davies, B. (1981) 'Social education and political education: in search of integration', *Schooling and Culture*, 9.

Davin, Anna (1978) 'Imperialism and motherhood', *History Workshop Journal*, 5.

Deem, R. (ed.) (1980) *Schooling for Women's Work*. London: Routledge & Kegan Paul.

Delamont, S. (1978a) 'The contradictions of ladies' education', in Delamont and Duffin (1978).

Delamont, S. (1978b) 'The domestic ideology and women's education', in Delamont and Duffin (1978).

Delamont, S. and Duffin, L. (eds) (1978) *The Nineteenth-Century Woman*. London: Croom Helm.

Delmar, R. (1972) 'What is feminism?', in Wandor (1972).

Delphy, Christine (1977) *The Main Enemy*. London: Women's Research and Resource Centre (WRRC).

Delphy, Christine (1981) 'Women in stratification studies', in Roberts (1981).

Delphy, Christine and Leonard, Diana (1980) 'The family as an economic system', paper given at 1980 University of Kent SSRC Conference: Sexual Deviations: Patterns and Processes.

Donald, James (1989) 'Schooling, popular culture, government, ideology and beyond', PhD, Open University, Milton Keynes.

Donzelot, J. (1979) *The Policing of Families*. London: Hutchinson.

Douglas, Mary (1966) *Purity and Danger*. London: Routledge & Kegan Paul.

Duffin, L. (1978) 'Prisoners of progress: women and evolution', in Delamont and Duffin (1978).

Dunbar, R. (1970) 'Female revolution as the basis for social revolution', in Morgan (1970).

Dworkin, Andrea (1981) *Pornography: Men Possessing Women*. London: Women's Press.

Dyer, Gillian (1982) *Advertising as Communication*. London: Methuen.

Dyer, Richard (1990) 'Straight acting', *Marxism Today*, August.

Dyhouse, Carol (1981) *Girls Growing Up in Late Victorian and Edwardian England*. London: Routledge & Kegan Paul.

Eagleton, Terry (1983) *Literary Theory*. Oxford: Oxford University Press.

Edholm, F., Harris, O. and Young, K. (1977) 'Conceptualizing Women', *Critique of Anthropology*, 9 and 10.

Ehrenreich, B. and English, D. (1979) *For Her Own Good: 150 Years of the Experts' Advice to Women*. London: Pluto.

Eisenstein, Z. (ed.) (1979) *Capitalist Patriarchy and the Case for Socialist Feminism*. New York: Monthly Review Press.

Elkington, John and Hailes, Julia (1989) *The Green Consumer Guide*. London: Gollancz.

Enzensberger, Hans Magnus (1970) 'Constituents of a theory of the media', *New Left Review*, 64.

Ewen, Stuart (1976) *Captains of Consciousness*. New York: McGraw-Hill.

Ewen, Stuart (1988) *All Consuming Images*. New York: Basic Books.

Ewen, Stuart and Ewen, Elizabeth (1982) *Channels of Desire: Mass Images and the Making of American Consciousness*. New York: McGraw-Hill.

Featherstone, Mike (1988) 'In pursuit of the postmodern', *Theory, Culture & Society*, 5 (2–3).

Featherstone, Mike (1990) 'Perspectives on consumer culture', *Sociology*, 1.

Feminist Anthology Collective (1981) *No Turning Back*. London: Women's Press.

Fernbach, D. (1980) 'Ten years of gay liberation', *Politics and Power*, 2. London: Routledge & Kegan Paul.

Finn, D., Grant, N. and Johnson, R. (1977) 'Social democracy, education and the crisis', *Working Papers in Cultural Studies*, No. 10. Centre for Contemporary Cultural Studies, University of Birmingham.

Firestone, S. (1970) *The Dialectic of Sex*. New York: Morrow.

Fitzpatrick, Michael and Milligan, Don (1987) *The Truth about the AIDS Panic*. London: Junius.

Foster, Hal (1985) *Postmodern Culture*. London: Pluto Press.

Foucault, Michel (1979) *The History of Sexuality*, Vol. 1. London: Allen Lane.

Foucault, Michel (1980) *Power/Knowledge*. Brighton: Harvester Press.

Fraser, Nancy and Nicholson, Linda (1988) 'Social criticism without philosophy', *Theory, Culture & Society*, 5 (2–3).

Freud, Sigmund (1986) 'An autobiographical study', in *The Pelican Freud Library*, Vol. 15. Harmondsworth: Penguin.

Friedan, Betty (1965) *The Feminine Mystique*. Harmondsworth: Penguin.

Frith, Simon (1981) 'Youth in the eighties: a dispossessed generation', *Marxism Today*, 25 (11).

Frith, Simon (1986) 'Beyond the avarice of dreams', *New Statesman*, 4 July.

Galbraith, J. K. (1958) *The Affluent Society*. Boston: Houghton Mifflin.

Galbraith, J. K. (1974) 'How the economy hangs on her apron strings', *Ms*, May.

Garner, Lesley (1987) 'Overboard on child abuse', *The Daily Telegraph*, 1 July.

Garnsey, E. (1978) 'Women's work and theories of class stratification', *Sociology*, 12 (2).

Gay Left Collective (1981) 'Happy families? Paedophilia examined', in Tsang (1981).

Gay, Peter (1988) *Freud: A Life of Our Time*. London: Dent.

Gillis, J. R. (1974) *Youth and History*. London: Academic Press.

Girlsline, A Newsletter for Girls and Young Women, Spring 1981.

Goldthorpe, J. H. (1980) *Social Mobility and Class Structure in Modern Britain*. Oxford: Oxford University Press.

Gordon, Linda (1977) *Women's Body, Women's Right*. Harmondsworth: Penguin.

Gordon, Linda and Dubois, Ellen (1983) 'Seeking ecstasy on the battlefield: danger and pleasure in nineteenth-century feminist sexual thought', *Feminist Review*, 13.

Grace, Gerald (1978) *Teachers, Ideology and Control*. London: Routledge & Kegan Paul.

Grace, Gerald (ed.) (1984) *Education and the City*. London: Routledge & Kegan Paul.

Griffiths, D. and Saraga, E. (1979) 'Sex differences and cognitive ability: a sterile field of enquiry', in Hartnett *et al.* (1979).

Gyford, John (1989) 'There's more to life than shopping', in *Chartist*, 127.

Hall, Catherine (1979) 'The early formation of Victorian domestic ideology', in Burman (1979).

Hall, Stuart (1987) 'Minimal selves', in *Identity*. London: ICA Documents.

Hall, Stuart (1988a) 'Brave new world', *Marxism Today*, October.

Hall, Stuart (1988b) *The Hard Road to Renewal: Thatcherism and the Crisis of the Left*. London: Verso.

Hall, Stuart (1990) 'Cultural identity and diaspora', in Rutherford (1990b).

Hall, Stuart and Jacques, Martin (eds) (1989) *New Times*. London: Lawrence & Wishart.

Hall, Stuart and Jefferson, T. (eds) (1976) *Resistance through Rituals: Youth Subcultures in Post-War Britain*. London: Hutchinson.

Hall, Stuart, Critcher, C., Jefferson, T., Clarke, C. and Roberts, B. (1978) *Policing the Crisis: Mugging, the State, and Law and Order*. London: Macmillan.

Halsey, A. H., Heath, A. F. and Ridge, J. M. (1980) *Origins and Destinations: Family, Class and Education in Modern Britain*. Oxford: Clarendon Press.

Hamblin, A. and Bowen, R. (1981) 'Sexual abuse of children', *Spare Rib*, 106.

Hanmer, J. (1977) 'Community action, women's aid and the women's liberation movement', in Mayo (1977).

Hansen, S. and Jensen, J. (1971) *The Little Red Schoolbook*. London: Stage 1.

Hartmann, Heidi (1979) 'Capitalism, patriarchy and job segregation by sex', in Z. Eisenstein (ed.), *Capitalist Patriarchy and the Case for Socialist Feminism*. New York: Monthly Review Press.

Hartmann, Heidi (1981) *The Unhappy Marriage of Marxism and Feminism*. London: Pluto Press.

Hartmann, M. and Banner, L. (1974) *Clio's Consciousness Raised*. New York: Harper & Row.

Hartnett, O., Boden, G. and Fuller, M. (1979) *Sex-role Stereotyping*. London: Tavistock.

Harvey, David (1989) *The Condition of Postmodernity*. Oxford: Blackwell.

Haug, Wolfgang (1986) *Critique of Commodity Aesthetics*. Cambridge: Polity.

Heath, A. (1981) *Social Mobility*. London: Fontana.

Hebdige, Dick (1979) *Subculture: The Meaning of Style*. London: Methuen.

Hebdige, Dick (1981) 'Towards a cartography of taste 1935–62', *Block*, 4.

Hebdige, Dick (1982) 'Hiding in the light', *Ten-8*, 9 (1).

Hebdige, Dick (1985) 'Some sons and their fathers', *Ten-8*, 17.

Hebdige, Dick (1988) *Hiding in the Light*. London: Routledge.

Held, David (1980) *Introduction to Critical Theory*. London: Hutchinson.

Henriques, J., Hollway, W., Urwin, C., Venn, C. and Walkerdine, C. (1984) *Changing the Subject*. London: Methuen.

Himmelweit, Susan (1983) 'Production rules OK? Waged work and the family', in Segal (1983c).

Hindess, Barry (1978) 'Classes and politics in Marxist theory', in G. Littlejohn *et al.* (eds), *Power and the State*. London: Croom Helm.

Hirst, Paul (1981) 'The genesis of the social', in *Politics and Power*, 3. London: Routledge & Kegan Paul.

HMSO (1960) *The Youth Service in England and Wales* (The Albermarle Report). London: HMSO.

HMSO (1969) *Youth and Community Work in the Seventies*. London: HMSO.

HMSO (1982) *Experience and Participation: Report of the Review Group on the Youth Service in England* (The Thompson Report). London: HMSO.

Hodges, J. (1981) 'Children and parents: who chooses?', in *Politics and Power*, 3. London: Routledge & Kegan Paul.

Hodges, J. and Hussain, A. (1979) 'Review article: Jacques Donzelot', *Ideology and Consciousness*, 5.

Hoggart, Richard (1957) *The Uses of Literacy*. Harmondsworth: Penguin.

Hoggett, Paul (1989) 'The culture of uncertainty', in Richards (1989).

Hollis, P. (1979) *Women in Public: The Women's Movement 1850–1900*. London: Allen & Unwin.

Hudson, A. (1983) 'The welfare state and adolescent femininity', *Youth and Policy*, 2 (1).

Inner London Education Authority (1981) *Youth Service Provision for Girls*. London: ILEA.

Jackson, Stevi (1978) *On the Social Construction of Female Sexuality*. London: Women's Research and Resource Centre (WRRC).

Jameson, Fredric (1979) 'Reification and utopia in mass culture', *Social Text*, 1.

Jameson, Fredric (1985) 'Postmodernism and consumer society', in Foster (1985).

Jenkins, Simon (1989) 'Handing victory to a serfdom of fear', *Observer*, June.

Jephcott, P. (1954) *Some Young People*. London: Allen & Unwin.

Kaplan, Cora (1983) 'Speaking/writing/feminism', in Wandor (1983).

Kellner, Douglas (1983) 'Critical theory, commodities and the consumer society', *Theory, Culture & Society*, 1 (3).

Kellner, Douglas (1988) 'Postmodernism as social theory', *Theory, Culture & Society*, 5 (2–3).

Kelly, Liz (1988) 'What's in a name? Defining child sexual abuse', *Feminist Review*, 28.

Kuhn, A. and Wolpe, A. (eds) (1978) *Feminism and Materialism*. London: Routledge & Kegan Paul.

Land, Hilary (1976) 'Women: supporters or supported?', in Leonard Barker and Allen (1976).

Land, H. (1980) 'The family wage', *Feminist Review*, 6.

Land, H. (1981) *Parity Begins at Home*. London: EOC/SSRC.

Lawson, J. and Silver, H. (1973) *A Social History of Education in England*. London: Methuen.

Leonard, Diana (1980) *Sex and Generation*. London: Tavistock.

Leonard Barker, Diana and Allen, Sheila (eds) (1976) *Sexual Divisions in Society*. London: Tavistock.

Levy, Jacques (1975) *Cesar Chavez*. New York: Norton.

Lovell, Terry (ed.) (1990) *British Feminist Thought*. Oxford: Blackwell.

Lyotard, Jean-François (1984) *The Postmodern Condition*. Minneapolis: University of Minnesota Press.

MacCabe, Colin (ed.) (1986) *High Theory/Low Culture*. Manchester: Manchester University Press.

Malcolm, Janet (1984) *In the Freud Archives*. London: Jonathan Cape.

Malpass, P. (1982) 'Octavia Hill', *New Society*, 4 (November).

Marcuse, H. (1964) *One-Dimensional Man*. Boston: Beacon Press.

Marks, P. (1976) 'Femininity in the classroom: an account of changing attitudes', in Mitchell and Oakley (1976).

Masson, Jeffrey (1984) *Freud: The Assault on Truth: Freud's Suppression of the Seduction Theory*. London: Faber.

Mayhew, H. (1968) *London Labour and the London Poor*. New York: Dover.

Mayo, M. (1977) *Women in the Community*. London: Routledge & Kegan Paul.

McCann, P. (1977) *Popular Education and Socialization in the Nineteenth Century*. London: Methuen.

McDonough, R. and Harrison, R. (1978) 'Patriarchy and relations of production', in Kuhn and Wolpe (1978).

McIntosh, Mary (1977) 'Reproduction and patriarchy', *Capital and Class*, 2.

McIntosh, Mary (1978) 'The state and the oppression of women', in Kuhn and Wolpe (1978).

McMahon, Marian (1991) 'Nursing histories', *Feminist Review*, 38.

McRobbie, Angela (1978) 'Working-class girls and the culture of femininity', in Women's Studies Group (1978).

McRobbie, Angela (1980) 'Settling accounts with subcultures: a feminist critique', *Screen Education*, 34.

McRobbie, Angela (1982) 'The politics of feminist research: between talk, text and action', *Feminist Review*, 12.

McRobbie, Angela (1989) 'Second-hand dresses and the role of the ragmarket', in A. McRobbie (ed.), *Zoot Suits and Second-Hand Dresses*. London: Macmillan.

McRobbie, Angela (1991) 'Teenage mothers: a new social state?', in *Feminism and Youth Culture: From Jackie to Just Seventeen*. London: Macmillan.

McRobbie, Angela and Nava, Mica (eds) (1984) *Gender and Generation*. London: Macmillan.

McWilliams-Tullberg, R. (1980) 'Women and degrees at Cambridge University, 1862–1897', in Vicinus (1980).

Mercer, Kobena (1987) 'Black hair style politics', *New Formations*, 3.

Mercer, Kobena (1990) 'Welcome to the jungle: identity and diversity in postmodern politics', in Rutherford (1990b).

Mercer, Kobena and Julien, Isaac (1988) 'Race, sexual politics and black masculinity', in Chapman and Rutherford (1988).

Middleton, David and Edwards, Derek (eds) (1990) *Collective Remembering*. London: Sage.

Mill, J. S. (1869) *On The Subjection of Women*. Oxford: Oxford University Press.

Millett, Kate and Blasius, M. (1981) 'Sexual revolution and the liberation of children', in Tsang (1981).

Minh-ha, Trinh T. (1990) 'Woman native other', *Feminist Review*, 36.

Minsky, Rosalind (1990) 'The problem of the unconscious in modern feminist theory', *Feminist Review*, 36.

Mitchell, Juliet (1971) *Women's Estate*. Harmondsworth: Penguin.

Mitchell, Juliet (1975) *Psychoanalysis and Feminism*. Harmondsworth: Penguin.

Mitchell, Juliet and Oakley, Ann (eds) (1976) *The Rights and Wrongs of Women*. Harmondsworth: Penguin.

Mitchell, Juliet and Rose, Jacqueline (eds) (1982) *Jacques Lacan & The Ecole Freudienne: Feminine Sexuality*. London: Macmillan.

Modleski, Tania (1982) *Loving with a Vengeance*. London: Methuen.

Moi, Toril (1990) 'Feminism and postmodernism', in Lovell (1990).

Moody, R. (1980) *Indecent Assault*. London: Word is Out/Peace News.

Moody, R. (1981) 'Man/boy love and the Left', in Tsang (1981).

Moore, Suzanne (1986) 'Permitted pleasures', *Women's Review*, 10.

Morgan, Robin (ed.) (1970) *Sisterhood is Powerful*. New York: Vintage.

Morley, David (1980) *The 'Nationwide' Audience*. London: British Film Institute.

Morley, David (1986) *Family Television*. London: Comedia.

Morris, Meaghan (1988) *The Pirate's Fiancée*. London: Verso.

Mort, Frank (1986) 'Image change: high street style and the new man', *New Socialist*, 43 (November).

Mort, Frank (1988) 'Boys own? Masculinity, style and popular culture', in Chapman and Rutherford (1988).

Mount, Ferdinand (1987) 'Children need justice not moral panic', *The Daily Telegraph*, 3 July.

Mulvey, Laura (1989) *Visual and Other Pleasures*. London: Macmillan.

Myers, Kathy (1986) *Understains: The Sense and Seduction of Advertising*. London: Comedia.

Nader, Ralph (1971) 'The great American gyp', in Aaker and Day (1971).

Nava, Mica (1972) 'The family: a critique of certain features', in Wandor (1972).

Nava, Mica (1980) 'Gender and education', *Feminist Review*, 5.

Nava, Mica (1981) ' "Girls aren't really a problem": so if "youth" is not a unitary category, what are the implications for youth work?' *Schooling and Culture*, 9.

Nava, Mica (1984) 'The urban, the domestic and education for girls', in Grace (1984).

Nava, Mica (1987) 'Consumerism and its contradictions', *Cultural Studies*, 1/2.

Nava, Mica (1988) 'Targeting the young: what do the marketeers think?' unpublished paper for the Gulbenkian Enquiry into Young People and the Arts.

Nava, Mica (forthcoming) 'Shopping around: women, modernity and consumerism', in Nava and O'Shea (forthcoming).

Nava, Mica and Nava, Orson (1990) 'Discriminating or duped? young people as consumers of advertising art', *Magazine of Cultural Studies* (MOCS), 1.

Nava, Mica and O'Shea, Alan (eds) (forthcoming) *The British Experience of Modernity*, London: Routledge.

Nicholson, Linda (ed.) (1990) *Feminism/Postmodernism*. London: Routledge.

Northern Women's Education Study Group (1972) 'Sex-role learning: a study of infant readers', in Wandor (1972).

Oakley, Ann (1972) *Sex, Gender and Society*, London: Temple Smith.

Oakley, Ann (1976) *Housewife*. Harmondsworth: Penguin.

Oakley, Ann (1981) 'Interviewing women', in Roberts (1981).

Oren, L. (1974) 'The welfare of women in labouring families 1850–1950', in Hartmann and Banner (1974).

Ormond, Roger (1990) 'Great white hope', *The Guardian*, 2 February.

O'Shea, Alan (1989, unpublished paper) 'Popular culture: theories and histories', Department of Cultural Studies, Polytechnic of East London.

O'Sullivan, S. (1982) 'Passionate beginnings', *Feminist Review*, 11.

Owens, Craig (1985) 'The discourse of others: feminists and postmodernism', in Foster (1985).

Packard, Vance (1981) *The Hidden Persuaders*. Harmondsworth: Penguin. (Originally published in 1957.)

Palmer, Alix (1987) '30,000 children at risk in Britain today', *Star*, 31 July.

Parmar, Pratibha (1989) 'Other kinds of dreams', *Feminist Review*, 31.

Pearson, G. (1983) *Hooligan: A History of Respectable Fears*. London: Macmillan.

Peterson, A. D. C. (1971) *A Hundred Years of Education*. London: Duckworth.

Phillips, Anne (1981) 'Marxism and feminism', in Feminist Anthology Collective (1981).

Piercy, Marge (1978) *Woman on the Edge of Time*. London: Women's Press.

Pizzey, E. (1974) *Scream Quietly or the Neighbours Will Hear*. Harmondsworth: Penguin.

Poster, Mark (ed.) (1988) *Jean Baudrillard*. Cambridge: Polity.

Presland, E. (1981) 'Whose power? Whose consent?' in Tsang (1981).

Pykett, Lyn (1990) 'Class(room) wars', *Women*, 1 (1).

Radford, Jean (ed.) (1986) *The Progress of Romance*. London: Routledge.

Radford, Jill (1982) 'Marriage licence or licence to kill?', *Feminist Review*, 11.

Radway, Janice (1987) *Reading the Romance*. London: Verso.

Rantzen, Esther (1987) 'Listen to the children's cry', *The Sunday Times*, 5 July.

Richards, B. (ed.) (1989) *Crisis of the Self*. London: Free Association Books.

Riley, Denise (1988) *'Am I That Name?' Feminism and the Category of 'Women' in History*. London: Macmillan.

Rivière, Joan (1986) 'Womanliness as masquerade', in V. Burgin, J. Donald and C. Kaplan (eds) *Formations of Fantasy*. London: Methuen.

Roberts, Helen (ed.) (1981) *Doing Feminist Research*. London: Routledge & Kegan Paul.

Robins, D. and Cohen, P. (1978) *Knuckle Sandwich*. Harmondsworth: Penguin.

Root, J. (1986) *Open the Box: About Television*. London: Comedia.

Rose, Jacqueline (1986) *Sexuality in the Field of Vision*. London: Verso.

Rose, N. (1979) 'The psychological complex: mental measurement and social administration', *Ideology and Consciousness*, 5.

Ross, Andrew (1987) 'Containing culture in the cold war', *Cultural Studies*, 3.

Rowbotham, S. (1972) 'Women's liberation and the new politics', in Wandor (1972).

Rowbotham, Sheila, Segal, Lynne and Wainwright, Hilary (1979) *Beyond the Fragments*. London: Merlin Press.

Rubin, Gayle (1981) 'Sexual politics, the new right and the sexual fringe', in Tsang (1981).

Rubinstein, D. (1977) 'Socialization and the London School Board 1870–1904: aims, methods and public opinion', in McCann (1977).

Rusbridger, Alan (1988) 'Ad men discover a fatal attraction', *The Guardian*, 3 March.

Ruskin, J. (1902) 'Of queens' gardens', in *Sesame and Lilies*. New York: Homewood.

Russell, Diana (1984) *Sexual Exploitation: Rape, Child Sexual Abuse and Workplace Harassment*. Beverly Hills: Sage.

Rutherford, Jonathan (1987) 'The sins of the fathers', *London Daily News*, 26 June.

Rutherford, Jonathan (1990a) 'A place called home: identity and the cultural politics of difference', in Rutherford (1990b).

Rutherford, Jonathan (ed.) (1990b) *Identity: Community, Culture, Difference*. London: Lawrence & Wishart.

Savan, Leslie (1989) 'The rising tide of boycotts', *Utne Reader*, 35.

Schools Council *Sex Role Differentiation* (Newsletter 3).

Schudson, Michael (1981) 'Criticising the critics of advertising', *Media, Culture & Society*, 3 (3).

Schudson, Michael (1986) *Advertising, The Uneasy Persuasion: Its Dubious Impact on American Society*. New York: Basic Books.

Scott, Ann (1988) 'Feminism and the seductiveness of the "real event"', *Feminist Review*, 28.

Scott, Roger (1987) 'How the children were taken away', *Daily Mail*, 13 July.

Scott, Rosemary (1976) *The Female Consumer*. London: Associated Business Programmes.

Seabrook, Jeremy (1978) *What Went Wrong?* London: Gollancz.

Segal, Lynne (1983a) 'Sensual uncertainty, or why the clitoris is not enough', in Cartledge and Ryan (1983).

Segal, Lynne (1983b) '"Smash the family?" Recalling the 1960s', in Segal (1983c).

Segal, Lynne (ed.) (1983c) *What Is To Be Done About the Family?* Harmondsworth: Penguin.

Segal, Lynne (1987) *Is the Future Female?* London: Virago.

Segal, Lynne (1988) 'Look back in anger: men in the 50s', in Chapman and Rutherford (1988).

Segal, Lynne (1990) *Slow Motion: Changing Masculinities, Changing Men*. London: Virago.

Sennett, R. (1977) *The Fall of Public Man*. Cambridge: Cambridge University Press.

Sharpe, S. (1972) 'The role of the nuclear family in the oppression of women', in Wandor (1972).

Shaw, J. (1980) 'Education and the individual: schooling for girls, or mixed schooling – a mixed blessing?', in Deem (1980).

Shears, Richard (1987) 'The making of Doctor Marietta Higgs, crusader', *Daily Mail*, 26 June.

Shrew (1970) The Journal of the Women's Liberation Workshop, January.

Silver, P. and Silver, H. (1974) *The Education of the Poor*. London: Routledge & Kegan Paul.

Simon, Brian (1974) *Education and the Labour Movement 1870–1920*. London: Lawrence & Wishart.

Sinclair, John (1987) *Images Incorporated*. London: Croom Helm.

Skirrow, Gillian (1986) 'Hellivision: an analysis of video games', in MacCabe (1986).

Smart, C. and Smart, B. (1978) *Women, Sexuality and Social Control*. London: Routledge & Kegan Paul.

Smith, M. and Taylor, T. (1983) 'The problem of men: sexism and the male trainer', *Working with Girls Newsletter*, 14.

Spare Rib (1981) 'Sex Under Sixteen', *Spare Rib*, 108.

Spender, D. (1982) *Women of Ideas*. London: Routledge & Kegan Paul.

Spock, B. (1963) *Baby and Child Care*. London: New English Library.

Stedman Jones, G. (1976) *Outcast London*. Harmondsworth: Penguin.

Steedman, Carolyn (1986) *Landscape for a Good Woman*. London: Virago.

Stuart, Andrea (1990) 'Feminism: dead or alive?', in Rutherford (1990b).

Summers, Anne (1979) 'A home from home: women's philanthropic work in the nineteenth century', in Burman (1979).

Swingewood, Alan (1977) *The Myth of Mass Culture*. London: Macmillan.

Tabrizian, Mitra (1987) 'The blues', *Ten-8*, 25.

Tabrizian, Mitra (1990) *Correct Distance*. Manchester: Corner House.

Tang Nain, Gemma (1991) 'Black women, sexism and racism: black or antiracist feminism?', *Feminist Review*, 37.

Tanner, Leslie (ed.) (1970) *Voices from Women's Liberation*. New York: Mentor.

Thompson, Ann and Wilcox, Helen (eds) (1989) *Teaching Women*. Manchester: Manchester University Press.

Thompson, P. (1975) 'The war with adults', *Oral History*, 3 (2).

Toner, Michael (1987) 'Should a father be afraid to kiss his daughter good-night?', *Sunday Express*, 28 June.

Tsang, Daniel (ed.) (1981) *The Age Taboo: Gay Male Sexuality, Power and Consent*. London: Gay Men's Press.

Vicinus, M. (ed.) (1980) *A Widening Sphere: Changing Roles of Victorian Women*. London: Methuen.

Wakeman, Alan (1975) *What Exactly Is Heterosexuality?* London: Gay Sweatshop.

Walkerdine, Valerie (1981) 'Sex, power and pedagogics', *Screen Education*, 38.

Walkowitz, J. (1980) *Prostitution and Victorian Society*. Cambridge: Cambridge University Press.

Walvin, James (1978) *Leisure and Society*. London: Longman.

Walvin, James (1982) *A Child's World*. Harmondsworth: Penguin.

Wandor, Michelene (ed.) (1972) *The Body Politic*. London: Stage 1.

Wandor, Michelene (ed.) (1980) *Strike While the Iron is Hot*. London: Journeyman Press.

Wandor, Michelene (ed.) (1983) *On Gender and Writing*. London: Pandora.

Watney, Simon (1987) *Policing Desire*. London: Methuen.

Webster, Paula (1981) 'Pornography and pleasure', *Heresies*, 12.

Weeks, Jeffrey (1981) *Sex, Politics and Society: The Regulation of Sexuality since 1800*. London: Longman.

Weeks, Jeffrey (1985) *Sexuality and its Discontents*. London: Routledge.

Weinbaum, Batya and Bridges, Amy (1979) 'Monopoly capital and the structure of consumption', in Eisenstein (1979).

Weir, Angela (1977) 'Battered women: some perspectives and problems', in Mayo (1977).

Weir, Stuart (1987) 'What if the state kidnaps your child?', *London Daily News*, 23 July.

Whitehead, A. (1981) '"I'm hungry mum": the politics of domestic budgeting', in Young et al. (1981).

Whiting, Pat (1972) 'Female sexuality: its political implications', in Wandor (1972).

Widdowson, Frances (1980) *Going up into the Next Class: Women and Elementary Teacher Training 1840–1914*. London: Women's Research and Resource Centre (WRRC).

Williams, J., Twort, H. and Bachelli, A. (1972) 'Women in the family', in Wandor (1972).

Williams, Raymond (1975) *The Country and the City*. Harmondsworth: Penguin.

Williams, Raymond (1979) *Politics and Letters*. London: New Left Books.

Williams, Raymond (1980) *The Long Revolution*. Harmondsworth: Penguin.

Williamson, Judith (1978) *Decoding Advertisements*. London: Marion Boyars.

Williamson, Judith (1986) 'The problems of being popular', *New Socialist*, 41 (September).

Willis, Ellen (1970) ' "Consumerism" and women', in Tanner (1970).

Willis, Paul (1977) *Learning to Labour: How Working Class Kids get Working Class Jobs*. London: Saxon House.

Willis, Paul (1988) Unpublished 'Position paper' for the Gulbenkian Enquiry into Arts and Cultural Provision for Young People.

Willis, Paul (1990) *Common Culture*. Milton Keynes: Open University Press.

Wilmott, P. (1966) *Adolescent Boys of East London*. London: Routledge & Kegan Paul.

Wilson, Deirdre (1978) 'Sexual codes and conduct: a study of teenage girls', in Smart and Smart (1978).

Wilson, Elizabeth (1977) *Woman and the Welfare State*. London: Tavistock.

Wilson, Elizabeth (1980) 'Beyond the ghetto', *Feminist Review*, 4.

Wilson, Elizabeth (1983a) *What Is To Be Done About Violence Against Women?* Harmondsworth: Penguin.

Wilson, Elizabeth (1983b) 'The context of "Between Pleasure and Danger": the Barnard conference on sexuality', *Feminist Review*, 13.

Wilson, Elizabeth (1985) *Adorned in Dreams*. London: Virago.

Wilson, Elizabeth (1990) 'Deviant dress', *Feminist Review*, 35.

Wilson, Elizabeth (1991) *The Sphinx in the City*. London: Virago.

Winship, Janice (1981) *Woman Becomes an 'Individual': Femininity and Consumption in Women's Magazines 1954–69*. Occasional Paper 65, Centre for Contemporary Cultural Studies, University of Birmingham.

Winship, Janice (1985) ' "A girl needs to get street-wise": magazines for the 1980s', *Feminist Review*, 21.

Winship, Janice (1987) *Inside Women's Magazines*. London: Pandora.

Wolf, Naomi (1990) *The Beauty Myth*. London: Chatto & Windus.

Wolff, Janet (1985) 'The invisible *flâneuse*: women and the literature of modernity', *Theory, Culture & Society*, 2 (3).

Women's Studies Group (eds) (1978) *Women Take Issue*. London: Hutchinson.

Women's Theatre Group (1980) 'My mother says I never should', in Wandor (1980).

Wood, Julian (1984) 'Groping towards sexism: boys' sex talk', in McRobbie and Nava (1984).

Wood, N. (1982) 'Prostitution and feminism in nineteenth-century Britain', *m/f*, 7.

Wortis, R. (1972) 'Child-rearing and women's liberation', in Wandor (1972).

Young, K., Wolkowitz, C. and McCullagh, R. (eds) (1981) *Of Marriage and the Market*. London: CSE Books.

Young, Robert (1989) 'Transitional phenomena: production and consumption', in Richards (1989).

INDEX